BLAME

BLAME

DEATH, DISABILITY, AND THE SEARCH FOR JUSTICE FOR GUY MITCHELL

DUSTIN GALER

Published by ECW Press
665 Gerrard Street East
Toronto, Ontario, Canada M4M 1Y2
416-694-3348 / info@ecwpress.com

Editor for the Press: Jen Albert
Cover design: Jess Albert

LIBRARY AND ARCHIVES CANADA CATALOGUING IN PUBLICATION

Title: Blame : death, disability, and the search for justice for Guy Mitchell / Dustin Galer.

Names: Galer, Dustin, 1983- author

Identifiers: Canadiana (print) 20260119245 | Canadiana (ebook) 20260119296

ISBN 978-1-77041-847-9 (softcover)
ISBN 978-1-77852-562-9 (PDF)
ISBN 978-1-77852-561-2 (ePub)

Subjects: LCSH: Mitchell, Guy, 1974-2012. | LCSH: Developmentally disabled—Ontario—Ancaster—Biography. | LCGFT: Biographies.

Classification: LCC HV1570.5.C32 A5345 2026 | DDC 305.9/085092—dc23

This book is funded in part by the Government of Canada. *Ce livre est financé en partie par le gouvernement du Canada.* We acknowledge the support of the Canada Council for the Arts. *Nous remercions le Conseil des arts du Canada de son soutien.* We would like to acknowledge the funding support of the Ontario Arts Council (OAC) and the Government of Ontario for their support. We also acknowledge the support of the Government of Ontario through the Ontario Book Publishing Tax Credit, and through Ontario Creates.

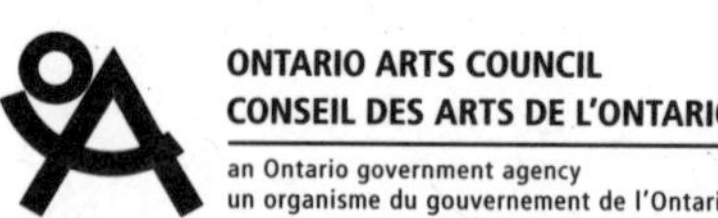

PRINTED AND BOUND IN CANADA

PRINTING: MARQUIS 5 4 3 2 1

For Manav Saini

∞

CONTENTS

PROLOGUE

Flashes of blue and red lit up the darkening country sky, emergency vehicles crowding this normally desolate stretch of road in a sleepy rural community. Towering evergreens cast colourful shadows on the grassy field with a small pitch-black hole at its centre.

"9-1-1. Police, fire, ambulance?" answered the dispatcher.

"Um, ambulance, please."

"Stay on the line."

Not much earlier, the slight thirty-eight-year-old man with a ginger goatee grabbed his jacket from a corridor of overstuffed cubbies, dozens of scattered shoes and debris, and bounded out the door towards the long driveway that insulated the house from the road. It was a cool evening in early spring, gravel crunching under his sneakers as he shuffled in a unique gait towards his destination. He inhaled deeply, clearing his lungs of the eyewatering stench that stained his clothes.

"What is your emergency?"

"Um, I have somebody who fell in a well."

An emotionally intelligent yet intellectually disabled man known for his energy and sociability, he delighted in helping others. Focused on his mission, he rounded the corner and passed an abandoned camper trailer and creaky old barn, now desolate, the starving horses long since departed. The area opened to a grassy field dotted with sinkholes where a house once stood.

"Is that person inside the residence right now?"

"No, they're in the well!"

He veered off the driveway and stumbled into the long grass, his shaky double vision only sometimes corrected by glasses that were often misplaced or being repaired. In front of him, a small rectangular opening in the ground led to an underground cistern normally used to water the animals and garden. A flimsy plywood cover occasionally sat precariously on top, the definition of an accident waiting to happen.

"And when you looked in, you just called in, and you couldn't get his attention?"

"I couldn't get any response from him. I tried to pull him out on my own so I could do CPR and couldn't get him out."

"Okay, how deep is it?" asked the dispatcher.

"It's a cistern. It's very deep, and he's floating at the top."

Bracing himself against the concrete lip of the opening, the man likely grabbed a bucket and leaned far into the hole, the waterline just beyond reach. He had lived here in relative harmony with his host family for much of his life. Now, the filthy house had no running water and no heat.

"Okay. All right, listen. I'm going to get some extra assistance, okay? So, you tried to pull him out, and you could not?"

"I couldn't lift him out on my own, no."

"Okay. Just stay on the line with me for one moment, okay? Don't hang up. Are you there by yourself?"

"Yes," the caller answered after a brief pause.

Only the man and his carer know what truly happened that night. It seemed like the kind of freak accident that could have happened to anyone. But within hours, questions began to form about what was really going on. Upon entering the residence, police, social workers, and family were shocked. Blame seemed unequivocal at first, until it wasn't. In a packed courtroom three years later, the public would learn the truth about who was responsible for what happened to Guy Mitchell.

1.

WE SPEAK FOR THE DEAD TO PROTECT THE LIVING

It was a hot and sticky July morning when people began filtering into the courthouse. Past the enormous royal coat of arms intricately carved in limestone, through bronze gilded marble hallways with chandeliers hung from impossibly high ceilings, a small crowd filed into a nondescript courtroom. In this formulaic arrangement of podiums and seating, justice would be rendered in one form or another. "Steel Town" was the city of Hamilton's usual moniker owing to its prodigious steel manufacturing output. A hub of smoggy industrial activity for much of its history, it earned other nicknames, such as "Toronto's Brooklyn" and the "Ambitious City," among less flattering ones, such as "the armpit of Ontario." That "absolutely awful small steel town outside Toronto" concluded actress Kathleen Turner, holding her nose after one summer film shoot. Beyond these catch-all projections, the city's working-class heritage bred its way into the character of its people — gritty, down-to-earth, hardworking, straight-talking.

To Diane, Hamilton was simply home, the setting of her greatest joy and deepest sorrow. She clutched her purse past the gauntlet of media cameras and microphones outside the courtroom and took her seat in one of the pews, the harsh fluorescent light illuminating the hardship and grief written in her slumped shoulders and sombre expression. Born and raised in the city, Diane never expected to find herself sitting here now under these terrible circumstances.

Diane thought of her visit two months earlier to the church she used to attend as a kid. The small Victorian red-brick building backed onto a farmer's field in the frontier between suburban outskirts and wide-open expanses of the countryside. Diane came here each Mother's Day, crossing a field of freshly cut spring grass dotted with half-forgotten headstones to rest a laurel of flowers at her son's grave. *Guy Thomas Mitchell 1974–2012* was chiselled in granite, an entire life condensed into a short horizontal dash. She stood in silent reflection, the hum of traffic whizzing by as memories of her son percolated in her mind. Cradling his tiny slippery body in her arms after a painful and traumatic birth. Dressing him in adorable outfits for pictures with Santa. Squeals of delight as she placed another expertly frosted birthday cake in front of him. Those mornings she ended up on the floor in tears when he refused to get dressed for school. His image in the rear-view mirror as he was ushered into another family's home.

"Oyez! Oyez! Oyez!" cried the bailiff. The traditional announcement that a court of law was now in session snapped Diane out of her daydream. Like everyone else, she was here to find out what really happened to her son and, maybe, to help save someone else from the same fate.

"Ladies and gentlemen, we are summoned here this day to inquire into and determine for our sovereign lady, the Queen, the identity of the deceased, when, where, how, and by what means the deceased came to his death," proclaimed the bailiff.

A jury of five citizens had been randomly plucked from the city's population to learn how and why one of the most vulnerable members of their community quite literally fell through the cracks to his death. The jurors were ordinary people with little experience or understanding of the developmental services sector, but over the course of the proceedings, they would learn what life was really like for adults with developmental disabilities, their families, and the people who dedicate their lives to supporting them.

"We speak for the dead to protect the living," goes the motto of the coroner. Also known as a medical examiner in some jurisdictions, the coroner descended from a quasi-judicial figure stretching back to tenth-century England in the reign of King Richard the Lionheart.

While a coroner may never have stood with the Sheriff of Nottingham against the likes of the rascally Robin Hood and Maid Marian, early iterations of the role played an important part in civil administration, something that has continued up to the present. Sudden or unexplained deaths come across their desks, such as when a death occurs while a person is in custody, at a construction site, or at a psychiatric facility, or when a child dies as the result of a criminal act by their custodian. An inquest may also be held at the discretion of the coroner if they determine there is enough information from a death investigation to support one, and it is desirable for the public to have an open and full hearing of the circumstances of a death. The jury must answer five questions regarding the death: who (identity of the deceased), when (date of death), where (location of death), how (medical cause of death), and by what means (natural, accident, homicide, suicide, undetermined). The goal is not to ascribe criminal or civil responsibility but to provide a list of recommendations to prevent future deaths in similar situations.[1]

Of the millions of deaths that occur each year around the world, only a tiny fraction is ever investigated by a coroner, and only a small number of those investigations lead to inquests. Any inquest, then, is a highly extraordinary act of public recognition that a person's death holds a meaningful lesson for the rest of us, a unique opportunity to reflect on what happened so that it doesn't happen again. Inquests strike at the very heart of public trust in our institutions, offering assurances of accountability when something has gone wrong and hope that we may move forward with a greater understanding of why someone died, including a road map to a better future. Whether an inquest is successful or not depends largely on the quality of the jury's recommendations, which are entirely nonbinding, and the degree to which the court of public opinion forces those responsible for the death to be accountable for their actions and policies. Even then, the ability and desirability to enact change often take resources, which are not always readily or willingly provided.

Entering the courtroom from a hidden chamber, the presiding coroner, Dr. Jack Stanborough, strode confidently to the judge's bench at the front of the room. A quick-witted man with a grave expression, sporting a crop of wild curly hair, snub nose, and penetrating gaze, he took his job extremely seriously.[2] He survived leukemia as a child when such a diagnosis was a virtual death sentence, an ordeal that sparked his fascination with the power of doctors. "The work we do is a tool for change," he once told an interviewer. "My experience with the medical profession when I was six convinced me that was what I wanted to do."[3] He became a family physician, then an emergency doctor before making the jump to medical examiner. For Dr. Stanborough, the coroner's office was a place to effect real change, and he was determined to use this power to the fullest.

The outspoken Dr. Stanborough wasn't certain at first whether there should be an inquest in this case. In the days following Guy's death, he indicated his reluctance to the local newspaper. "An inquest is done when there may be added value to public safety," he told the *Hamilton Spectator*. "My first impression would be, no, this is a unique and tragic one-off scenario. I always hate stepping on the investigating coroner's toes; I never make a decision until all the reports are in."[4] A few months later, with the police investigation ongoing, Dr. Stanborough was still on the fence. But when he learned more about the case and the extent of the systemic failures that contributed to Guy's death, he was finally convinced this was a case that warranted public dissection.

Little did he know it would also be his last. "In May of 2016, I was terminated without cause, with a nice package, and told not to rock the boat anymore," he griped, adding he believed he was sacked for being too critical of government agencies.[5]

Assisting the coroner with the prosecution of the inquest was Crown Attorney Karen Shea. It was her duty to direct the case for the coroner's office, call witnesses, and open examinations much as she would do when prosecuting criminal cases. Shrouded in a long black solicitor's gown with white collar neck tabs despite the heat, she had the tone and appearance of a friendly soccer mom with a mane of wavy blonde hair and intense blue eyes that widened when she spoke. Shea knew how to command attention, always one or two beats ahead, gently but directly guiding the conversation to where she wanted it to go. When she became animated, her voice exuded confidence and effortlessly commanded the attention of everyone in the room, her incisive delivery cutting through any ambient noise until she was satisfied her point was heard. First called to the bar in 1993, Shea's bread and butter was in prosecuting prominent murder cases, including the 2008 trial of Johnson Aziga, the first person in the world to be convicted of murder for nondisclosure of his HIV status.[6]

Next to Shea sat Jeffrey Manishen, an attorney representing the service agency that supported Guy. A prominent local lawyer, Manishen was a veteran litigator who worked as an assistant Crown attorney in the 1970s before becoming a criminal defence attorney in 1985 with one of the largest law firms in the area. He had an enviable track record and won multiple awards in criminal defence. Eloquent and sharp-witted, Manishen had the appearance of a seasoned attorney, his grey curly hair framing a pale face creased by decades of long nights poring over case briefs. He deposed witnesses with the flair of any cinematic trial lawyer, practically shouting his examinations if it served his point, perhaps channelling dramatic skills he learned when acting in and producing a lawyer-performed version of *12 Angry Men* for local theatre.

Dr. Stanborough used simple and easy-to-understand language to explain the reason why everyone had assembled on July 6, 2015. "This inquest is examining the death of a thirty-eight-year-old man. But that's not the salient issue. The salient issue is that we have people in society who are vulnerable because of physical issues or psychological reasons, emotional reasons, cognitive ability, or a combination thereof. So, society wants to protect and save and help these people. We allocate resources to government and organizations to make sure people are safe, so they don't die unexpectedly and they live in an environment that is safe and protective and provides for their activities of daily living. We care about these people. We do that by allocating funds and resources, and having organizations created to provide oversight to vulnerable people."

Despite inquests being fact-finding missions with no resulting criminal or civil liability, some courtroom exchanges that would take place in the coming days would resemble those of a trial. This was especially so as discussion of the investigation revealed increasingly shocking details and infuriating evidence of a lack of accountability. Other attorneys representing the government, Guy's family, and associated agencies also sat at the table, cross-examining dozens of witnesses, everyone here to play their part in piecing together what happened to Guy. But before any examination could take place, the jury first needed to get to know Guy, and who better to explain than his own mother.

2.

THE MOTHER

"Do you swear to tell the whole truth and nothing but the truth, so help you, God?" asked the bailiff.

"Yes, I do," Diane affirmed. Her voice quivered as she took her seat in the witness stand. She was a short, apprehensive, grey-haired woman who spoke hesitantly, anxiously adjusting her glasses as if uncomfortable in situations where she was the centre of attention. It had been three years since her son died, and sitting here now in front of an audience of people filled her with mixed emotions. She was grateful for the potential of some good to come out of all this, but speaking of him now was also like tearing a bandage from a festering wound.

"Good morning," Crown Attorney Shea greeted Diane. "Can you tell us about Guy? What was he like growing up? What were his difficulties?"

"Well, he had to be watched all the time," Diane started. "He had occasional outbursts when he wouldn't do what he needed to and could be hard to handle at times."

"Oh, babies develop at different times, Mrs. Mitchell," said the pediatrician. "Nothing to worry about."[7] The chubby-cheeked infant with a shock of red hair looked as precious as any Gerber baby — the standard of adorableness for generations. But Diane knew something was wrong.

The clues came slowly. It had been a hard delivery. She lost too much blood and needed transfusions. Eventually, the doctor used forceps, leaving indents on the baby's head. Looking back, Diane felt this was the possible cause of her son's developmental challenges, despite what the doctors said. Mother and baby remained in hospital for nearly a week afterwards, the newborn swaddled in a white blanket, his tiny pink fist pressed against his cheek as she fed him from a bottle. "He was very passive and quiet in the hospital and wouldn't eat," Diane recalled. "He wouldn't breastfeed. The nurses said, 'I wish he had the feisty temperament to go with that red hair!'"[8] At home, he would sleep all the time. It seemed Diane was always waiting for her son to wake up.

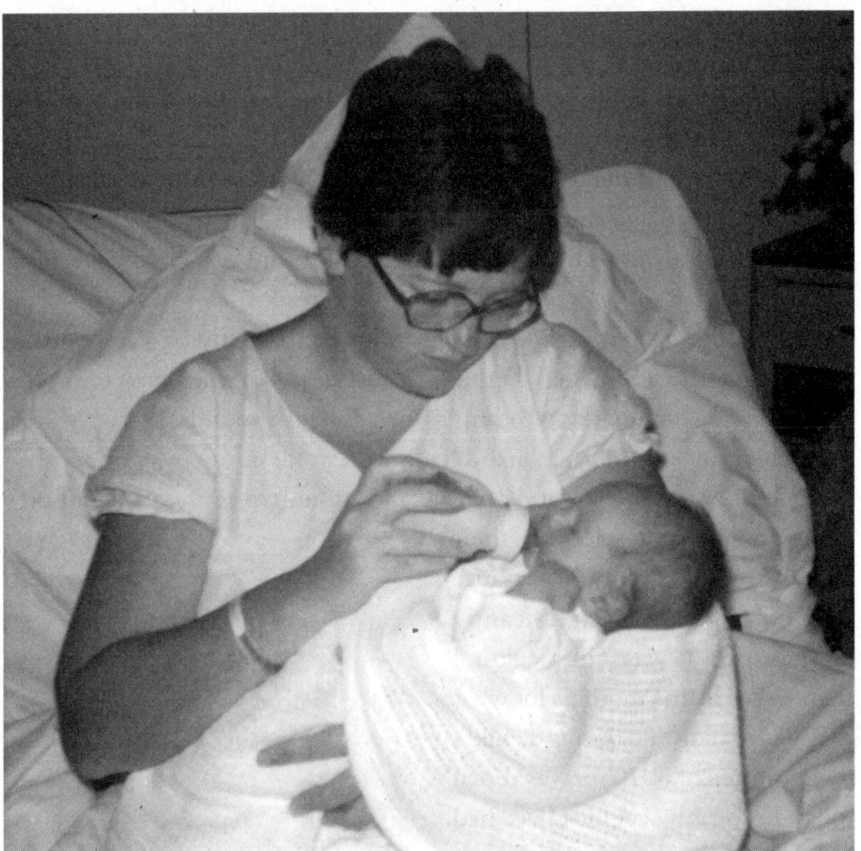

Diane Paton and her son, Guy Thomas Mitchell, as an infant.

Since his birth, Diane recorded each detail of Guy's development in a blue keepsake scrapbook, a ritual cherished by many 1970s-era mothers. Born at a small community hospital on September 4, 1973, Guy weighed six pounds fifteen ounces. Twenty inches long, he had blue eyes and red hair; Diane has a lock still preserved in a small paper envelope. His first words were "Da Da." He loved bananas and was only slightly underweight as he grew. He rolled over at seven months, sat up at ten months, crawled at eleven months, and walked at eighteen.

These weren't significant delays, but there were other things too. By the time he began to crawl, Guy was always bumping into things, an indication something was wrong with his depth perception or coordination. It wasn't clear if he could hear all that well either since others would sometimes have to shout to grab his attention, something that affected the development of his speech. Diane found herself comparing Guy to his cousin who was five months older than him, and she was increasingly certain his development lagged behind, but she was not sure what to do about it. She mentioned her concerns to a public health nurse, her family doctor, and her husband, Jim, but no one would listen to her. "First-time mothers always think the worst," they all told her. "They overreact when there's nothing wrong." Many of the responses to Diane's pleas for help came in the form of unsolicited parenting advice. "Try putting fewer obstacles in his way." "Perhaps he just needs to learn how to listen." "Spend more time reading to him so he can learn sounds."

Generations of mothers like Diane were told, in one way or another, their child's developmental delays were their fault, a consequence of prenatal actions or choices as their child grew. And though pediatric science had evolved significantly by the 1970s, it was still a cultural tradition to blame mothers for what they did or didn't do during a child's development.[9] "If he was born today, I probably wouldn't have had to go through a lot of what I went through," Diane later said.

When Guy started walking, he became hyperactive, flying from one activity to the next. He had to have eyes on him all the time because he never seemed to settle.

Once, Diane went to the washroom for a few minutes and returned to find the window open and Guy throwing pots out of it. He was a constant blur of activity. He'd plop down in his blue- and yellow-patterned jumpsuit, madly pulling Tupperware and cereal out onto the kitchen floor and tearing into boxes of Quaker oatmeal. He was obsessed with paper of any kind and would joyously tear through magazines for hours. At Christmas, he could barely sit still long enough to take a picture with the shopping mall Santa, unable to contain his excitement and curiosity about the jolly old man in the red suit as the exasperated elves tried to take a snapshot.

Later, more troubling signs emerged. Guy didn't seem sensitive to cold or heat. In winter, he always needed reminders to wear a hat and mittens, and wouldn't think twice about plunging his bare hands into a bank of snow. One time, Diane walked into the kitchen to find Guy's hand on the hot stove. She quickly snatched his arm away to reveal a throbbing palm, though he never made a sound. That's when Diane realized he had an unusually high tolerance for pain. "Is this normal?" she thought. She constantly worried about him seriously injuring himself and wondered if he might grow out of some behaviours on his own or whether he just needed more of her love and guidance. Surrounded by others who disbelieved her when she raised concerns, she gave more and more of herself to her child, hoping and praying it was all just a phase.

When he was two years old, Diane took Guy to get his eyes and ears checked at the local children's hospital. He should have started talking in two- or three-word phrases, but that wasn't happening, and he was always so restless. In the hospital waiting room, Diane flipped through a magazine as Guy busied himself with toys, fiddling with the wooden bead maze ubiquitous to doctors' offices that always seems to capture the attention of children just long enough to make the wait bearable. Exhausted

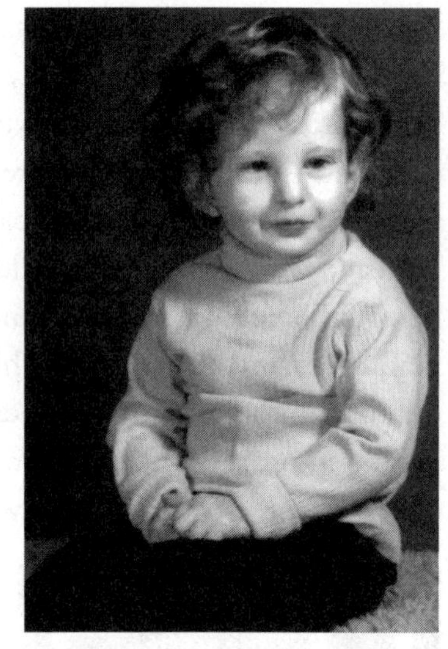

and anxious, Diane wondered what the specialist might find and if it would give her any answers to grasp onto in the daily struggle to understand her son.

"What do you notice right away about his eyes?" the pediatrician asked Diane. "First, he sees something with one eye and then with the other. Not at the same time."[10]

"Oh, he's going to get glasses and he'll be fine," Diane thought.

Fitted with a pair of thick black plastic-rimmed glasses framed by his head of curly red hair, Guy could not have been more adorable. But he hated wearing his glasses, and they would often go missing, left on the floor and stepped on, or thrown out the window along with the rest of the pots and pans. Eventually, Diane got him a pair of glasses fitted with a headband, cheap insurance against his inevitable attempts to free himself from the dizziness and shaky double vision he experienced.

The specialist referred Diane to an audiologist to check his hearing. Child-friendly hearing tests involve more interaction compared to the tests commonly known to adults, which typically require the individual to wear earphones while enclosed in a large Soviet-style metal tank. Screening tests look at a child's behavioural responses to certain sounds, which progress to playful games where a toddler is asked to touch or move a toy when they hear a pitch through specially fitted earphones. The child might also be trained to look at a sound source and rewarded when they correctly respond to an intermittent sound.[11] The results of these tests showed Guy had nearly 60 percent hearing loss in one ear and 40 percent in the other.

More testing followed with a range of other specialists with regular follow-up appointments that had Diane returning to the hospital on a regular basis for months. There were tests for speech language pathology, tests of his gross and fine motor skills, tests of his cognitive skills, tests of his social skills, and evaluations of his activities of daily living.[12]

The battery of testing was confusing and aggravating for Guy, and mentally and psychologically exhausting for Diane, especially since she had little support for the endeavour at home. Jim still thought there was nothing wrong with Guy and encouraged Diane to give their son more guidance as if an endless well of patient parenting could solve whatever deficits he might have.

Guy already started attending a local nursery school, but the team of doctors now felt he should attend a special program so they could have more time to make a full determination of his needs. Jim resisted this, along with any suggestion Guy wasn't "normal." Jim seemed convinced all these tests were just to find something that wasn't there; that his boy might be a little different from other toddlers, but he was still too young to determine what, if anything, might be wrong with him. Eventually, the doctors were able to convince Jim that the special nursery school was all part of the assessment process and was therefore essential if they were going to be able to give their recommendations about what to do next.

When the tests were finally complete after a year or so, the team of pediatricians called Diane and Jim into the hospital. They crowded around a conference table in a small meeting room with the team of doctors to listen to the results of the assessment. "Mr. and Mrs. Mitchell, we regret to inform you that your son is mentally retarded," one of the doctors stated matter-of-factly. At the time, "mental retardation" was a broad clinical term that didn't necessarily correspond to a definitive diagnosis or plan of treatment. "He will need to take special education classes and will never live independently as he grows older. There are some programs he can attend, but he will likely never hold a job and will be dependent on you for the rest of your life."

Diane held Guy close on her knee, nodding along with the results of the diagnosis, her long-standing suspicions finally confirmed. The answer filled her with a cocktail of emotions: relief from the acknowledgement of the situation, sadness over the loss of what might have been, guilt from the belief it may somehow have been her fault, anger at the lack of support she experienced, and hopefulness for what was to come next. But Jim crossed his arms and remained stone-faced. "There's nothing wrong with him," he declared frostily, furrowing his brow. "My son is not retarded. He's young, maybe he'll grow out of it. He just needs to be around other normal kids and that'll help straighten him out. Just tell us what to do and we can fix this." The doctors informed the Mitchells there was nothing to be done to "fix" Guy, no course of treatment or plan other than special education classes that could help him develop to his potential. But not long after the meeting, Jim pulled Guy out of the special nursery school and returned him to the regular school. "He'll be fine," Jim reassured Diane. "He's just a little behind the other kids but he'll catch up. You'll see."

ooooo

Diane and Jim met in the mid-1960s. They were both members of a bowling league. They dated for three or four years and married in 1969. At first, the Mitchells lived in an apartment before purchasing a three-bedroom bungalow with a sprawling front lawn and private backyard on the edge of suburban sprawl, acres of farmland right at their doorstep. It was the kind of neighbourhood that conjured images of idyllic childhoods spent biking and playing up and down the streets, far removed from the blast furnaces and clattering rail yards where Jim spent his days as a steelworker.

Guy and his father, Jim, at Wasaga Beach in 1974.

It could have been that vision of a normal, happy future for his young family that prevented Jim from accepting what the doctors were telling him about his son. Born in 1941, Jim was an only child with few family members beyond his parents and aunt and uncle. A short, stocky man with a large head and hands calloused from working long hours at the steel mill, he beamed with pride at his son's first birthday. At the beach on summer weekends, the Mitchells would pack a picnic lunch and soak up the sun. Cradling Guy in his arms, Jim would kneel in the

An infant Guy and his parents, Jim and Diane, in 1973.

warm, wet sand on the shore, gently dipping his tiny feet in the water. A kind man and loving father, Jim also proved quite stubborn and his enduring refusal to recognize his son's special needs increasingly grated against Diane's desire to ensure their son got the kind of support and schooling he needed. Theirs was a relatively happy marriage, but their fundamental differences on what to do about their son eventually escalated to raised voices and slammed doors.

In this, Diane and Jim played out a scenario common to many parents of special needs children. Like many traditional marriages, Jim spent most of his days at work, following hundreds of other men in the daily commute down the escarpment to the steel mills and leaving Diane to carry out the bulk of the child-rearing and domestic duties. Diane therefore was far more involved in raising Guy than Jim and had an arguably higher emotional investment in the outcome. Having spent more time raising him and as the person who took him to most of his doctor's appointments, Diane simply knew Guy better than anyone else. The mother-cub relationship Diane shared with Guy transformed her into a fierce protector of what she believed was best for her son. This protective drive may have seemed out of character for the normally calm and reserved woman, but the bond between mother and son was no match for one man's stubborn attitude. As this new dynamic filtered through their marriage, Diane and Jim became increasingly emotionally distant from each other.

Things finally came to a head in 1978 when Guy approached his fifth birthday, and it was time to decide where he would attend kindergarten that September. Jim wanted Guy to attend a regular school and be with the "normal" kids. Diane thought Guy would benefit from closer attention in a special needs school. Jim put his foot down, but Diane wouldn't budge. It would become the defining moment of their marriage. To be clear, no child is ever responsible for the dissolution of a marriage as relationship success flows primarily from underlying factors, behaviours, and choices made between two adults. Doctors used to justify institutionalizing disabled children by citing the strain they put on a marriage, and perhaps some continue to make these claims. However, recent studies indicate that the increase in divorce rates when a child with disabilities is involved is only marginal.[13]

The tug-of-war didn't last long, and Jim left his family before Guy turned six years old. They sold the house, and Diane moved in with her parents, Hannah and Harold Jackson. The Jacksons' house was not that far away, situated on the border of farm country, where Diane and her older sister, Carol, grew up. Diane had memories of attending the one-room schoolhouse that once served the area. There were far fewer people in the neighbourhood back then, but it eventually grew as the farmland around them unfolded into cookie-cutter suburbs. At home, the children would help their father with the sprawling vegetable gardens he maintained, filling the one-acre plot with as much productive land as possible. They reaped the benefits of their hard work as the gardens usually yielded an abundant harvest, and they would transport the surplus to the farmer's market to sell to vendors.

Diane's father always dreamed of having a home he could call his own, a place where he could raise his family and find some stability in his life. Harold's early years in England were marked by tragedy when his mother died during childbirth, and he was forced to immigrate to Canada at fifteen. As a young man in a new country, Harold worked odd jobs to make ends meet. He worked on boats and farms until he met Hannah, who lived near Woodstock, Ontario. The couple were both working at a farm estate, Harold on the land and Hannah in the house as a domestic servant. They fell in love and in 1948 got married back in England in the West Riding of Yorkshire village of Staincross, east of Manchester. After the nuptials, the couple returned to settle in Hamilton, where they hoped to start a family and build a comfortable life for themselves.

In the 1940s, Hamilton was a city where working-class dreams were made. Known as the "Ambitious City," it was a place where people like Harold could find a good job, carve out a decent living, and raise their families in peace and prosperity. Harold was fortunate to find work at the Otis Elevator factory, located in the heart of the industrial sector, where he was able to earn a good wage, thanks in part to the relatively high rates of unionization. For Harold, his new home in Hamilton was a dream come true.

Hannah Jackson was an affectionate and devoted grandmother who cherished Guy. After bath time, she would wrap him in a giant towel, her tender hugs making Guy squeal with delight. She embodied the essence of a 1970s-era grandmother, sporting her iconic wing-tipped cat eyeglasses and curly red locks, continually whipping up delicious treats and hearty homemade meals that would often include fresh vegetables from their garden. Despite Hannah's best efforts to keep Guy occupied with crafts and toys, he was too much like his Grandpa Harold, who loved to be outdoors. Both Harold and Guy wore the same style of black-rimmed glasses and would spend countless hours working together in the garden, a stooped figure and his miniature clone. Guy would follow Harold's every move, hoeing up plants, weeding between the rows, and sprinkling water where it was needed. Eventually, they would harvest the fruits of their labour. Harold loved spending time with his grandson and would give him small tasks to make him feel like he was contributing to their gardening efforts. It was one of the earliest demonstrations of Guy's inclination to be of service to others, a trait that would stay with him throughout his life. For Hannah, Harold, and Guy, time spent together in the garden was a source of joy and fulfillment. It was a way for them to connect with one another and the natural world around them.

Grandma and Grandpa Jackson with Guy at the dinner table.

It took Diane several months to land on her feet after Jim left. Guy's constant needs meant she couldn't commit to a full-time job. Hannah's health was declining, and Harold was already in his eighties, so expecting full-time care from them was unreasonable. Diane investigated after-school programs, but none would take him. She got a part-time job at a real estate office, and though Jim would remain an important part of Guy's life, Diane was effectively a single working-class mother learning how to parent a child with special needs on her own. After a period of searching, Diane finally found a house to rent. The move to a new home was both exciting and overwhelming for Guy, who had never experienced adapting to a new home, since his grandparents' home was already familiar to him. As Diane unlocked the door to their new place, Guy burst through the threshold, running in every direction as he explored his new surroundings. He darted from the living room to the dining room to the kitchen and back again, until Diane called out to him to calm down.

"Slow down, Guy. What are you doing?" Diane pleaded.

As Guy came to a stop, he realized that he didn't know where the bathroom was. "Where the heck is the toilet?" he exclaimed.

For Guy, the smallest changes in his routine and environment could feel overwhelming. Diane gently guided him down the hallway, taking lots of time to help him get comfortable in their new home. One night, Diane sat him on a laundry basket next to the sink in the bathroom to wash his hands and prepare for bed. However, the following night, the laundry basket was missing, and Guy appeared confused. "Who moved the sink?" he blurted out. Diane had to be extremely patient with him, taking the time to help him adjust to his new home.

In 1982, Diane secured a spot for Guy at Glenwood, a special day school for children with special needs. Glenwood was originally a two-room brick schoolhouse in the rural setting of West Flamborough. These grounds had seen generations of schoolchildren dating back to 1845 with a log schoolhouse that was later replaced in 1865 by a stone building, and finally a brick building built in 1955. Enrolment dwindled, and the school shut down in 1973. This presented an opportunity to repurpose the facility into a day school that catered to students with special needs.[14] Glenwood provided education until age twenty-one with a smaller staff-to-student ratio than regular public schools and was unique in the region for its specialized learning environment.

Glenwood's rural location may have been predominantly about finding whatever space was available to educate special needs students. In the 1970s, few community services existed for people with developmental disabilities. But the location also conformed to prevailing public attitudes about the location of community services for people with developmental disabilities. In the 1960s and 1970s, some community members grew concerned about the proliferation of group homes and special education schools, worried their proximity might impact property values, quality of life, and public safety. Such fears were drawn from long-standing prejudices that depicted disabled people as the root of various social problems that plagued society, fears that ultimately led to the needless incarceration of generations of people in residential hospitals. The long dislocation of people with developmental disabilities from community life bred ignorance about them that resurged when residential institutions were shut down and they moved closer to communities. To avoid potential conflict with such NIMBY (not-in-my-backyard) community opposition, many group homes and schools were forced to outlying areas and neighbourhoods.

As time passed, Glenwood relocated to a suburban area; teachers still reminisce about an immensely interactive place that provided ample opportunity for teachers, students, and their families to develop close relationships with one another.

More recently, there has been a debate on whether to segregate children with special needs in separate schools or to integrate them into regular public schools. There are strong arguments in favour of integration. Some parents saw special day schools as an extension of the institutional model, given how they separated children from the opportunity to learn and socialize in mainstream public schools. Those parents wanted their children to be educated in regular public schools, either fully integrated with educational assistants or in special needs classrooms within a regular public school. This approach promotes inclusion and helps to break down barriers between children with and without disabilities. Children with special needs can learn alongside their peers, and their classmates may learn valuable lessons about empathy, understanding, and diversity. Integration can also help to build confidence and self-esteem in children with special needs and give them access to a wider range of educational opportunities. Additionally, integrating children with special needs into regular public schools may help to prepare them for adult life, as they will have to learn to navigate and interact with people from different backgrounds and abilities, a crucial life skill that becomes essential as they grow into adults. Advocates for separate schools argue that students may benefit from more individualized attention and assistance from teachers and staff who possess specialized training in addressing their specific requirements.

Diane believed Guy's development depended on the extra support and attention that is typically only available in specialized settings like Glenwood. When Guy was at a regular public school, he would often return with cuts on his head or hands, a worrying pattern that led Diane to believe he wasn't being watched closely enough. At Glenwood, class sizes were much smaller, and the teacher had aides and volunteers able to spend hours of one-on-one time with each student, something next to impossible in a regular classroom or even many special education classes. There were other advantages to separate schools that might have factored into Diane's decision. Often these schools have more resources and equipment available to assist with learning and development. Some parents also feel that their child may be less likely to face bullying or discrimination. The decision to place children with special needs in separate schools or integrate them into regular public schools is ideally based on the individual needs of the child and their family. The goal should be to provide children with the best possible education and support to help them reach their full potential, which may look different depending on the individuals, their family dynamics, and locally available options.

At Glenwood, Guy thrived. His teachers agreed he was a sweet, delightful, and lovable young man. His academic skills might have been limited, but he had an excellent memory and was quite the social butterfly. Once he was introduced to someone, their name was forever locked in his mind. Frank Ernest, a dedicated volunteer in numerous developmental services programs, was always impressed with Guy's extraordinary memory. Guy would only encounter Frank's wife once a year at an annual barbecue, yet he never failed to greet her with a cheerful "Hi, Joyce!" before quickly moving on to something else that piqued his interest. This incredible recall left a lasting impression on those he interacted with throughout his day. He would quickly pick up on people's routines and remark on any changes. He would ask people about their evening or weekend plans and follow up with questions about how it went the next time he saw them. His positive attitude and inquisitiveness were something most people would aspire to.

Guy's favourite greeting was the high-five. And not just any high-five. Those who knew him were forewarned to expect one whenever he walked into a room. The strength of the hit was like a barometer of how well he liked a person. A light tap was usually not enough. With the right person, he would leap into the air like a basketball player gaining height to gather enough driving force to deliver the kind of contact necessary to make the hapless recipient truly understand how excited he was to see them. He would wait for the reaction, content only with responses such as, "Whoa, that was a good one!" or an (only slightly feigned) exaggerated nursing of one's hand. In each case, the response would always bring a satisfied grin to his face.

Guy's all-time favourite activity was his "papers." He loved handling papers and would obsessively hoard any kind he could get his hands on. It isn't clear when exactly he discovered how much joy paper gave him, but when stacks of papers began piling up around the house, Diane bought him a briefcase. It became the eternal accessory that he would dutifully tote wherever he went. One time, Guy was given some money to take home, but it disappeared along the way, the bills ripped into satisfyingly tiny pieces of confetti. A dedicated "papyrophiliac," Guy savoured the texture and sound of paper and would quietly while away the hours handling, folding, crumpling, and writing. It seemed to be one of the few things that could hold his attention long enough to have him sit still. Sometimes he said he was doing business stuff. Another time he would say he was a banker. He would line up several pens and scribble wavy lines representing sentences, sometimes writing left to right or right to left. As Guy was unable to read or write, the meaning of his

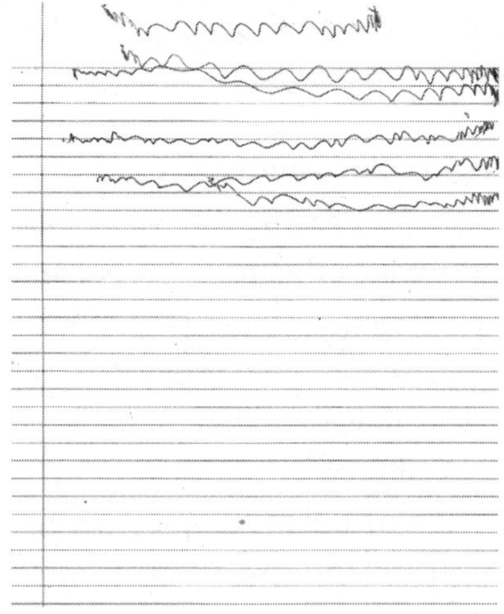

A sample of Guy's writing. He always enjoyed working on his papers.

scribbles was not always apparent. However, over time he was able to develop a signature, represented by a few slashes for "G-U-Y," which he could use to sign certain documents. If someone tried diverting his attention or took his papers away when he wasn't done with them, he would stomp his feet and pound his fists on the table. To others, Guy's preoccupation with papers may have seemed like an obsession, but, to him, his papers always made perfect sense and they brought him boundless joy.

ooooo

As Guy approached his teen years in the mid-1980s, his high energy level and intractability became increasingly hard for Diane to handle on her own, and the years of constant vigilance over him began to wear on her. If Guy didn't want to do something or became fixated on an activity (like his beloved papers), it became increasingly difficult to redirect him. The impending arrival of the bus or scheduled appointments meant nothing to him, and efforts to move him along usually resulted in a meltdown. Mornings were always the hardest, an endlessly repetitious and exhausting struggle to get him ready and out the door each day.

"Guy, please just put this on. You like school, remember?" Diane sighed heavily, trying to wrestle the squirming boy into a pair of brown slacks.

"Noooo!!"

"Come on, Guy, we're already late!" she called after him as he slipped away, streaking down the hallway, pounding his adolescent fists against the walls.

Diane slumped to the floor in tears. He had been like this all week. She felt the anxiety well up inside her, a wave of emotion bred from a decade of such mornings. Clutching the telephone, she dialled the principal, Ms. Margaret McRoberts. "I'm so sorry, but Guy won't get dressed, and I . . . I don't know what to do!" she stammered, unleashing a flood of tears.

"Diane, it's okay. This happens. I'll be right over," McRoberts reassured her. The veteran educator spoke in a soft English accent with the confidence of decades of experience handling similar calls from exasperated parents. Despite her petite stature, she possessed a serene yet authoritative demeanour; an elegant woman with 1950s-style blonde pincurls and low-heeled pumps that click-clacked down linoleum hallways, a classic soundtrack familiar to generations of schoolchildren.

It wasn't long before Guy was dressed and off to school with his principal. It wasn't the first time McRoberts had intervened to help Diane with Guy and it wouldn't be the last. Standing next to him years later at his graduation ceremony, she spoke fondly of his progress. "Guy has been with us since he was about knee high to a grasshopper. Sometimes when he was small, we had great difficulty getting him to school. So much so that one day I went to his house, plucked him out from in front of the television set, and brought him here in his pyjamas."

For Diane, McRoberts's intervention that morning was both a relief and dreaded confirmation that something needed to change. "Well, that was really hard for me," she remembered. "I knew I needed help, but I didn't know how."[15] Diane knew she wanted to continue to play an active part in her son's life, but she felt she couldn't do it alone anymore. She worried she wasn't providing Guy with the guidance he needed to grow to his fullest potential and that the daily struggle was even doing him harm.

McRoberts reached out to the board of education, who sent a social worker. The worker arrived early one morning to observe Guy's routine. Afterwards, Diane and the social worker sat together to discuss her options. There was no way Diane would have considered placing him in an institution. She read articles and saw news programs about what conditions were really like behind closed doors: overcrowded, understaffed, crumbling buildings that seemed more geared towards warehousing people than supporting their development. Besides, most residential hospitals were not accepting new intakes since they were in the long process of winding down. Most of the few group homes in the area already had long wait-lists, so that was also out of the question. And there were few to no resources at the time to support families who endeavoured to keep their children at home.

"Have you heard of the Extend-A-Family program?" the social worker asked. "They match a host family with a handicapped person and take that person here and there for a day to give the parent a break." Diane thought it was an interesting arrangement that could eventually work up to an overnight stay for respite. The worker matched Guy with a young couple with a small boy around four years old. They wanted to sensitize their son to people with disabilities, so they came and spent a day with Guy. The next day, she got a call from the social worker. The family had no further interest. They wanted a child who used a wheelchair and felt Guy needed too much supervision. Guy was never matched with another family from the program.[16]

Another option was home sharing, a program that had just been introduced in 1985 as an alternative to group homes where individuals are paired with families willing to provide housing and daily support. Similar to foster care, home sharing provided the opportunity for individuals with developmental disabilities to live with host families who received a stipend to invite them into their home and assume responsibility over their daily care. Foster children and those whose families still maintained guardianship could mature into adulthood with the assurance that their host families would provide a secure and nurturing home to aid them. An ideal host family was described in program literature as one capable of providing a safe and secure family home setting, promoting a high quality of life, and supporting individuals towards the goal of community inclusion. The program was contracted out to local service agencies tasked with administering the matching process and ongoing monitoring of the placement.

Diane had never heard of this before and agreed it might be worth looking into. The social worker explained she could help Diane find a suitable home where Guy would live with a family who would be able to manage his behaviours and offer daily assistance. Diane would be encouraged to take an active part in her son's life, unlike an earlier era dominated by an institutional system of residential hospitals that provided total care for children and adults with developmental disabilities. She insisted she would want to see him each week, take him to medical appointments, and make important decisions about his care. Diane recognized the limitations of raising Guy at home on her own, but the last thing she wanted was for him to think she was abandoning him.

Not everyone is cut out to be a home provider. According to an observer who worked in the developmental services sector, the screening process for applicants was insufficient, leading to a high rate of unsuccessful matches. "I could easily name five individuals who were unsuccessful in their home-sharing arrangements. It seems like some families think that it's as easy as getting a puppy — a fun and cute addition to their household. But in reality, it's not that simple." New home providers may come to the realization too late that they cannot simply take a weekend trip or attend an event without considering the needs of the individual they are sharing their home with. "Only one family that I know of has been successful, and that's because they fully integrated the person they were home sharing with into their family." These home providers treated the individual like their own child, taking them to weddings and other events. "But this is not the norm," the observer noted. "Many people are attracted to the financial benefits of home sharing, but they don't fully comprehend the restrictions it places on their lives." While it may seem like a nice concept in theory, the truth is that most people are ill-equipped to handle the responsibilities and limitations that come with such a lifestyle.

Diane was introduced to a couple who took in Guy for a few days to assess his needs and ensure he was a good fit for the program. Host families in this program received a small stipend, but they were expected to have other income and otherwise be financially stable. Soon after Diane agreed to consider home sharing, the social worker called to say they found a match, and Diane could take Guy to meet the family at their home. She picked him up from school and drove him to the family's home, which was in a nice suburban neighbourhood with a park across the street. The couple had a boy about half Guy's age and fostered another young girl who lived with a disability. The house was nice, and the couple seemed friendly, but Diane worried about the level of supervision they were able to provide for Guy. She got her answer when she returned at eight o'clock. "Oh, they had a great time," the woman said.

"The three of them went to the park and played while we watched from the window." Diane was taken aback. She thought she had been clear that Guy needed to be watched closely, so he wouldn't wander off into a dangerous situation. "If Guy could go across the street and play at a park without proper supervision, why would he need to go live with them?" she thought to herself.[17] Diane thanked the couple for their time and called the social worker to say she didn't think they would be a good fit.

A few weeks later, Diane got a call from the social worker about another match. This one seemed more promising. The mother was an educational assistant at a special needs school and therefore had the greater level of understanding and experience Diane was looking for in a home provider. Diane picked up Guy from school and drove him to the family's home. The woman greeted them eagerly while the husband hung back, soon revealing that he did not share his wife's enthusiasm for the idea of inviting Guy into their home. The three-bedroom home was nice, but already full with their own two young children. Their boy made it known he was unhappy about the prospect of having to share a room with Guy. Diane also learned Guy would be their first home sharer and they were still in the process of figuring out how it would all work out. Diane concluded this also wasn't the right home for him. "I just thought it would be a little much for Guy to be their first client," she later remarked.

More weeks passed, and Diane began to think that perhaps she wouldn't ever find a family that could provide Guy with the kind of home she envisioned for him. After all, it wasn't as if there were a line around the block of potential home providers willing to and capable of opening their homes and lives to a boy who needed an extraordinary level of guidance and supervision. One morning, just as Diane was beginning to forget about the whole thing, there was a knock on her door. She wasn't expecting any visitors, and she opened it to find a man dressed in a suit. "A Jehovah's Witness or door-to-door salesman," she thought before the man introduced himself. "Hello, my name is Bill Santor, and I'd like to talk to you about your son. My wife is a special needs teacher, and we'd like to help."

3.

THE FOSTER MOTHER

People come to the sleepy village of Jerseyville to enjoy the fresh, clean air as much as the peace and serenity of the countryside. It's a rural bedroom community outside the suburban town of Ancaster, far removed from the busy streets of Hamilton. People here have a desire for space and a respect for privacy that goes hand in hand with a strong commitment to neighbourliness. This culture of supportive reciprocity is bred from the necessities of rural living, whether it's keeping an eye on someone's house or lending a piece of equipment. A farming community settled by United Empire Loyalists in the late 1770s fleeing New Jersey during the Revolutionary War, the Jersey Settlement became known as Jerseyville in 1852 when the opening of a local post office demanded a new name.[18] Once an important railway stop, its relocated train station provided the backdrop for iconic scenes from television dramas *Anne of Green Gables* and *Road to Avonlea*, nostalgic fiction for a simpler time that never really existed.

Just outside the village sat the Santor property, a twenty-five-acre tract of land with an old farmhouse close to the road, a one-and-a-half-storey wood-framed structure with an angled roofline, light-coloured clapboard siding, and a steep exterior staircase that led to the small room that made up the upper storey. Even with the addition of a newer kitchen, the house was quite small, its three bedrooms, living room, and dining room all crammed together. Next to the house stood a rusted, neglected pump that drew water from an old well, the advent of modern plumbing rendering it obsolete. Most rural properties in the area had a well that tapped into the underground aquifer, but the water here was sulphurous and many had fresh water trucked in. A pit had been dug and a 3,000-gallon cistern was installed, a water tank that required regular deliveries of fresh water. The opening had been fitted with a heavy concrete lid that would freeze shut in winter, so it was replaced with two wooden lids. Behind the house sat an old barn with corroded metal siding and a crumbling rubblestone foundation that had seen better days. Once a working farm, the horse stalls in the lower section now housed a couple of ponies for leisure riding while the upper haylofts were increasingly used for storage to free up space in the crowded home. In the acres beyond, the narrow stretch of property opened out into fields and woodlands stretching all the way to a highway.

For Bill and Karen Santor, it was their dream property. In 1982, the couple bought the land with its unlimited potential to raise their children and foster children in a private sanctuary. When Diane first visited, she was surprised so many people could live in such a tiny space together. Besides Bill and Karen, their four biological kids, and Karen's mother, Guy was to share a bedroom with the eldest son, William, but would eventually end up in the basement when even more foster children were invited into the small home.[19] There were plans to build a much larger house farther back from the road, but the project moved slowly as Bill planned and did most of the work himself as funds allowed.

Despite the overcrowded living conditions, Diane thought the Santors were a good fit as the host family for Guy. In contrast with the other families, Karen seemed confident, and she had the experience and family support to back her up. Karen worked at Glenwood, where Guy attended school, and students often took field trips to the Santor property to learn about farm life and to see the animals. Bill showed Diane several letters of recommendation from other parents who placed children in their home. "I thought, at least he's close in Jerseyville." Diane's options for where to place her son were quickly dwindling. "He could have been anywhere. But at least he's close to home. He'll still go to the same school, and I can see him regularly."[20]

To Diane, Karen's role as the main caregiver was just as important as the family who supported her. Bill Santor was a music teacher with four children from his first marriage. He was a short, stocky man with thinning grey hair, thick glasses, and a serious expression. His previous marriage dissolved in the late 1960s or early 1970s, and he moved in with Karen, a recent high school graduate who played in the girls' school marching band, which he conducted. Despite the nearly twenty-year age difference, Karen was a young woman who carried herself with the intelligence and maturity of someone beyond her actual years. Tall with long dark hair, a melodious singing voice, and bold personality, she matched Bill in both wit and self-confidence. Eventually, they married and had a son and three girls together.

By all accounts, Karen was an exceptional person. She studied early childhood education at the local community college and quickly developed a passion for helping children with disabilities by becoming a special needs teacher. In June 1981, the Santors invited their first foster child into their home, a ten-year-old girl named Cindy who wore a helmet and required round-the-clock attention. There were more foster children, some with disabilities and others who just needed a good home. The duration of a child's stay in the Santor home could range from months to years depending on their individual needs and situation, and it wasn't long before Karen developed a reputation as someone to whom child-welfare authorities could turn when they needed someone to take on the heavy responsibilities of caring for children with complex medical conditions or developmental disabilities. In fact, there were so many children coming and going in the Santor residence that Karen and Bill's children saw their home as a revolving door for those in need. It's unclear whether it was Karen's plan from the very beginning to be a foster mom to so many children, but her experiences with the developmental services system convinced her she needed to do everything she could to help vulnerable children in need.

Karen's first-hand experience as a special needs teacher and foster parent quickly snowballed into volunteer work as an advocate. A widespread community living movement was already transforming the lives of children and adults with disabilities as resources shifted away from large institutions such as residential hospitals. The Santors did their part by working with parents of children with developmental disabilities to establish the North Wentworth Association for the Mentally Retarded, a service agency later renamed Choices. It all began, as it often did, with a meeting of concerned parents who wanted more local services for their rural community. Local associations like this one formed the backbone of the community living movement that sought to plug gaps caused by the government policy of deinstitutionalization. Most communities were not equipped to handle the magnitude of resources needed to allow children and adults with developmental disabilities to thrive, so local associations like the one started by the Santors stepped in to provide essential day-program and group-home services, which were overseen by a volunteer board of directors. In the beginning, such organizations received little to no government funding, instead partnering with voluntary service clubs such as Rotary, Kiwanis, and Civitan to help fund their programs.

The immense challenge of establishing such an organization on a bootstrap budget invited the talents of people like the Santors. One of their contemporaries described them as being type A leaders. "Both Bill and Karen have very strong personalities. They know what they believe and are prepared to advocate for their beliefs. They are able to do so with humour most of the time and usually come across as even-tempered. However, they can be very assertive if crossed."[21] Karen embraced this assessment, describing herself as "intimidating" with "a low tolerance for incompetence," a "capable," "driven," "supermom."[22] Once, after being informed that someone at Choices had submitted a formal complaint about the cleanliness of her home, Karen immediately drove down to the building, stormed into the room where the complainant was working, and began berating them in front of clients. The conflict spilled out into the parking lot before she finally got in her car and left.

Bill similarly described himself as "Type A, perfectionist, concise, innovative, and creative with numbers." When asked how others would describe him, he responded, "I don't care."[23] The whole Santor family was expected to help too. "Each natural child is responsible for one of the foster/AC [alternate care] children," Bill wrote. Describing their family as "full, big, and busy," Bill and Karen said they used typical parenting and discipline techniques, including time outs, negotiation (with older kids), consistency, and rewards with positive reinforcement.[24]

ooooo

Sending her twelve-year-old son to live with another family was the most difficult decision of Diane's life. It was an act performed out of pure love and devotion, one that grated against every traditional vision of motherhood. And yet, it also fulfilled every motherly instinct to care for and protect her child. The day she dropped Guy off at the Santors' filled Diane with the same mix of relief and anxiety she experienced that morning when Principal McRoberts came to the rescue. She had to believe that the Santors were in a better position to provide Guy with the support he needed to thrive, so that she could remain hopeful about what the future held for him.

As Diane packed Guy's bags and loaded him into the car, she inventoried her feelings, an overwhelming combination of contradictory impulses that eventually hardened into the resolve that this was what was best for her son. In the twenty-minute drive to the Santors', Diane assured Guy how much fun he was going to have living on a farm and the friends he would make, how brave he was, and how she would see him every weekend. As the driveway carried them towards the farmhouse, Karen emerged to meet them outside, familiar with the charged emotions that accompany moments like these. All the details were already worked out, so Diane hugged and kissed Guy goodbye as Karen guided him towards the house to distract him.

Diane watched through the rear-view mirror as Guy was ushered inside, the finality of the vision causing a fleeting moment of panic. "What am I doing?" she thought. "Did I make the right decision?" It was a painful, surreal moment that also marked a new beginning for Guy and a different chapter in their mother-son relationship. For Diane, there were tears, sleepless nights, and feelings of guilt and regret. But just as they had both moved on after Jim left, Diane was determined they would get through this too. She knew she would always be his mother and would remain an active participant in his life even if she wasn't with him every day or didn't know exactly what he needed to grow to his potential. In the end, Diane concluded that she wasn't letting Guy go, but setting him free.

The transition was hard on them both. "He didn't like it at first. It was a big adjustment, and that was hard for me to watch," Diane later remembered.[25] One can only imagine what might have been running through Guy's mind. Who were all these new people? Why couldn't he see his mother every day? Change was hard for Guy. The disruption in his normal routine and adjustment to a new living environment with its different rules and patterns was scary to him, as it can be for many people regardless of cognitive ability. The process led to some meltdowns and other behavioural responses. Although Guy was usually able to express himself verbally, wetting or soiling himself was an uncontrollable way for him to demonstrate he was stressed or upset about something. After he moved in with the Santors, there were several incidences of him wetting himself, but Karen reassured Diane this was normal, and that Guy would soon adjust.

After a month or so, he did. He would spend the school week at the farm and weekends with Diane or Jim. When he was home, Diane soon noticed Guy would dress himself in the mornings, something he had never done before. "Something must be working," she thought. Guy bonded with all the Santors, but especially their son, William. He remembered when Guy joined their flock because he found it nice to have another boy around who was about the same age and who he could play with instead of his three sisters. The boys would watch TV, especially *Jeopardy*, play games, and do farm chores together. "I remember him carrying arms full of hay. He really liked the goats," William said.[26] Guy's easygoing nature and desire to please others meant he got along with everyone. William's sister Kathryn would say, "Guy, who do you like best. Me or William?" Guy would say Kathryn. Then William would ask him, "Guy, who do you like best. Me or Kathryn?" Guy would say William. For the Santor kids, Guy blended perfectly into their family and soon became just another sibling in their hectic household.

Guy's personality blossomed over time, and he became a sociable and outgoing individual. When he moved his body, his gestures and mannerisms were reminiscent of Mr. Bean, a quirky, sporadic energy that never seemed to settle. Guy tended to stand close to whomever he was conversing with, completely focused on their words and body language. If the person he was speaking with felt uncomfortable with their proximity and took a step back, Guy would shuffle forward with a sense of taut energy that needed to be released, as if connected to the person by an elastic band stretched to its limit. This behaviour showcased Guy's intense interest and enthusiasm for connecting with others, even if it revealed a certain lack of awareness of social boundaries. His impaired hearing and shaky double vision may have encouraged these close encounters, his own attempt to be present with people by filling his field of vision with a single person and craning his neck to hear what they were saying. The effort it took him to hold his attention to their words may have also aided his fantastic memory.

After a time, three more foster boys with intellectual disabilities were added to the already bustling farmhouse. One of the new boys was David. Six years Guy's junior, David was slender with a blonde buzz cut and limited vocabulary. He soon became like Guy's younger brother, tagging along with him to school; they played games and teased each other. They got in trouble together too. Once, Guy snuck out of the house late at night to jump on the trampoline in the backyard. "It's not safe for you to be out there by yourself," Karen scolded. The following night, Guy crept

Guy (right) and his friend and housemate David (left) at the Santor house, both men enjoying the barbecue.

back out to the forbidden trampoline, but this time, he brought David with him. They bounced and laughed, jumping higher and higher, often crashing into each other because of Guy's coordination issues. When Karen heard the familiar squeaking of the trampoline springs, she looked out to see the boys carrying on. This time, all she could do was laugh because he wasn't out there by himself, just as she had instructed. Guy followed the rules.

As Guy settled into his new life with the Santors, Diane managed to secure a full-time job and relished the quality time she could now spend with her son. Instead of the daily struggle of managing meltdowns and constant vigilance, she could devote energy to reconnecting with her son. They would go out for special lunches and to church on Sunday mornings. At Christmas, Easter, and other holidays, Guy would always spend a few days at home with Diane and stepfather Dave, as well as happy hours with his stepsister and stepbrother laughing and tickling their feet. Whenever Guy got his hands on a radio, nearby listeners were treated to a relentless barrage of sound as he frenetically spun the control knob from one end of the frequency spectrum to the other. At home, Guy would always insist on helping with the chores, hauling the trash out to the garbage area he called the "dumpster dumpster."

One of Guy's favourite activities as he got older was bowling. Five or ten pin, he loved the challenge of casting the ball down the alley and celebrating when he got a strike or spare. He joined a bowling league called the Alley Catz that always played on Saturdays. Diane or a helper would pick him up from the Santors' and drive him to the town of Dundas, always making time for a stop at McDonald's for lunch. It was here that Guy truly thrived in his peer group, any visual or gait-related challenges sidelined as he racked up points

Guy and the Alley Catz bowling team win first place in 1999.

on the scoreboard. There were tournaments where there would always be a winner, but Diane helped ensure everyone got a trophy regardless of who won. Lined up next to his friends to take pictures with their newly acquired prizes, Guy was proud of his accomplishment, his trophies still lovingly preserved on a shelf in his room at Diane's apartment.

A major highlight of the year was the couple weeks each summer Guy would spend at the trailer in Honey Harbour, located in the heart of Georgian Bay's cottage country. Each year, they would go the last couple weeks in August around Labour Day, so Diane and Dave could host a birthday celebration for Guy complete with corn roast, hot dogs, and birthday cake. At first it was a small affair, but it eventually grew to fifty people, many of whom treated the annual event as the official end of summer. Guy's excellent memory meant he always knew who was or wasn't there and why. And if someone arrived late, he'd break away and race up to greet them, often before they even managed to emerge from their car. There are countless stories of good times at the cottage. Guy had a voracious appetite despite his rail-thin frame. Diane would make a big breakfast of pancakes and bacon that would disappear almost instantly as she set it down in front of him. Then off he went "trailer hopping" to have second or third breakfasts with all the neighbours. It was often a struggle for Diane to keep Guy with her at their own trailer as he preferred to follow one family or another throughout the day in their close-knit vacation community.

Guy and the whole gang at Guy's annual corn roast and birthday party at Honey Harbour in 2007.

Guy also had excellent comic timing. He had the ability to deliver uproarious and unforeseeable one-liners with the same serious and committed demeanour as any deadpan comedian. Once, he overheard Diane jokingly call Guy's stepfather Dave a twit. The next day, as Guy spotted Dave's truck pulling up, he casually called out, "The twit is home!" One of Guy's favourite neighbours at the trailer park was Rob. Most mornings the two of them would make the trek to the local convenience store to "get the paper," though really it was an excuse to visit the bakery next door. One day, Rob joked to Diane as he and Guy were leaving, "We're going cruising for chicks." As they pulled up to the bakery, Guy looked confused and asked, "Where are the chickens?" Guy delighted being pulled around on the lake. "I went water skiing!" he would tell bewildered friends and staff on his return. "Really? On skis?" they would reply, amazed he could manage that level of hand-eye coordination. "Yeah, but I did it on a tube," he clarified.

One time, Guy and a small group of people were out on the lake in Rob's boat when the motor malfunctioned, and they could only move very slowly in reverse. The mood turned tense as they entered the busy main channel where they were at risk

ABOVE: Guy "water-skiing" (tubing) at Honey Harbour in 2007.

Guy and his friend Rob at Honey Harbour in 2008.

of being struck by other fast-moving boats. Oblivious to the danger, Guy chirped, "Buddy Rob, we're on the boat!" The resulting collective laughter provided a much-needed distraction, helping everyone relax until they reached the shore.

ooooo

Guy once came close to being declared mentally incompetent. In 1988, when he was fifteen years old, his great aunt and uncle left him a large sum of money (over $50,000 in 2023 terms). The money was held in trust until Guy turned eighteen, but, after his eighteenth birthday, Guy's father, Jim, tried to withdraw the money for himself without telling Diane. Their lawyer refused to release the money, so Jim made an application to the court to have Guy declared mentally incompetent. After their divorce, Diane retained sole custody of Guy and remained his guardian until he turned eighteen. This kickstarted a war between Diane and Jim that escalated when Bill and Karen Santor got involved to defend Guy against the application. At one point, Diane, Jim, and Guy each had their own lawyers to represent them in the case. By 1994, the issue was still unresolved, and Diane was out of province when Choices executive director, Hal Bushey, drafted a letter to the court on behalf of Diane and the Santors stating their intention to support Guy in contesting the application. Apparently, even the Office of the Public Trustee was unaware of Jim's application. Guy was prohibited from receiving disability benefits from the government that were needed to pay for his accommodation with the Santors and day-program expenses until the issue was resolved. Eventually, the application failed, and the money was deposited in a joint account that required both Diane and Jim's signatures to make withdrawals, a caveat that led Jim to block most transactions. Jim would come to regret his actions many years later, and Diane could not have known at the time how this unfortunate situation would come to play a key role in later events in Guy's life.

At that time, Guy also needed to be attached to a local service agency if he wanted access to funding for day programs and residential supports, with the agency taking a 5 to 10 percent cut for administration fees. Before the introduction of individualized funding in Ontario during the

1990s, the selection of an agency was critical since all funding to support people with developmental disabilities had to pass through a developmental services organization.

As one advocate, Martha Fox, once put it, "The harsh reality is that there will never be enough dollars to allow for true individualized planning and support unless there is a complete overhaul of how we value the choices individuals want to make and how those choices are both respected and funded." Although Guy never experienced institutional living, he faced his own challenges in his home-share arrangement with the Santors. His funding was funnelled through Choices, leaving him with little control over how it was spent. Ironically, even though he had no experience living in an institution, he still found himself in a situation where his choices were limited by the funding arrangements meant to support him.

Transitioning from Glenwood to Choices was a scary and stressful process that represented a big change in Guy's daily routine. Instead of a school bus picking him up each morning from the Santor farm, a paratransit service called DARTS (Disabled and Aged Regional Transit Service) arrived to take him to Choices. The accessible white buses and vans carried people from all walks of life with drivers providing door-to-door service for people with mobility needs or those who required a greater level of supervision. First introduced in the 1970s, paratransit services like DARTS were often poorly resourced and understaffed, and were plagued with problems, making them unreliable at best and dangerous at worst. Because it was a shared ride service, the driver would often make multiple stops at other addresses before delivering riders to their destinations, and with relatively few buses on the road, many riders like Guy would spend up to an hour on the bus for a drive that would typically take fifteen to twenty minutes. This meant he, and others at the Santor residence, were up early to make it in time to the eight o'clock start of the day program. Consequently, numerous DARTS drivers became acquainted with regular riders like Guy, who would spend a considerable amount of time onboard the buses each week, with any changes to drivers or absences sure to be promptly detected and remarked upon by Guy.

Thankfully, Guy was not on his own during his move to Choices. Several of his peers from Glenwood also transitioned to the adult program, and one of the staff members, Anne, happened to change jobs to join Choices as well, providing Guy with plenty of familiar faces to ease his adjustment. Anne commenced her employment at Glenwood as an educational assistant in the mid-1980s and subsequently worked at Choices during the early 1990s alongside Guy. A university graduate who loved working with children and adults with developmental disabilities, Anne grew up in England with a sister who lived with physical and cognitive disabilities and was therefore familiar with many of the roadblocks towards independent living. Anne got to know Guy well at Glenwood, especially when he participated in "a weekend away," where small groups of children were invited to spend the weekend with a trusted staff member to provide their parents with some respite. "Guy would come at least once or twice a month for the weekend," Anne recalled. "He was absolutely delightful and fun. Always wanted to help. We would go grocery shopping on Friday to pick out what we wanted to make for dinner together. He would get excited and fall over his own feet at times but was always very helpful."[27] At Choices, Anne recalled Guy would participate in chaperoned camping trips up north. "In the winter, we would do cross-country skiing. I can remember him once falling backward on his skis. He was on his back with his feet up in the air, legs and skis crossed over each other. I have no idea how he ended up in that position. I stood there thinking, 'I'll have to take one of your skis off because I can't untangle you!' In summer, there was lots to enjoy, like swimming, crafts, and campfires. It was lots of fun, and he totally enjoyed all those activities."[28]

Prior to new management in the mid-1990s, Anne remembered Choices as a small but vibrant organization that was very engaged and interacted with the local community. "We had a lawn crew of five or six high-functioning clients who went out with lawn mowers and weed whackers to maintain the lawns of customers. They would do crafts, then have a craft sale or bake and then have a bake sale. We had gardens at the back where we raised different vegetables that we'd harvest."[29] Guy was interested in the lawn crew, but there were concerns about his safety around the equipment, so this became more of a long-term goal for him. Eventually, he found his way into the Hut, a storage shed located behind the main building that was like a mini warehouse for shipping and receiving bulk paper products for various social agencies and shelters. Guy thrived in this work environment, a place where he could be helpful to others — something he cherished above all else — and a great training ground for transferable skills he might one day use in a supported work environment. "Guy just loved it," Anne remembered. "When people came, he'd help them carry out things and he got to be known for how helpful he was."[30]

Things began to change at Choices in the mid-1990s when a new CEO was appointed. Direct and plainspoken with dark hair and great bushy eyebrows that framed a droopy expression, the CEO was a seasoned service-club member with experience in the developmental services sector who had very different ideas about how Choices should be run. Suddenly, staff found the management style had become more autocratic, and priorities shifted to growing the organization by attracting ever-larger numbers of people leaving residential hospitals. This change in leadership coincided with the preplanned closure of two large residential hospitals nearby. Usually the people most likely to leave residential care were considered "easier to handle"; they were relatively easy to place in group homes and services in the community. By the late 1990s, those still in residential hospitals often had severe behavioural issues and violent tendencies, due at least partly to the trauma of lifelong institutionalization. These individuals also came with higher funding allotments, in some cases up to $200,000 per year, that service agencies would use to expand their residential and day-program services. Over time, the CEO boasted that the number of staff at the Choices day program and group homes increased over eighteen-fold.

With that exponential growth came higher turnover rates as staff quickly burned out in an increasingly toxic workplace with threats of unionization on the horizon. Anne remembered the rapid transformation of Choices as a kind of regression. "We used to make enough soup to feed fifty people. We'd go to the grocery store the day before, and I could have a whole room of people chopping up vegetables and we'd make this fabulous soup. One day I was called down to the office and was asked why I was doing this and what might be the practical application. 'Well, Dwayne peeled a carrot. He's never done that before in his life,' I said. The sense of achievement each individual got from doing something like that was immense, plus the fact they could eat this the next day and they had succeeded in something that was then shared. But that was no longer allowed. I asked if I could run an exercise or yoga class. 'No, no, we can't do that,' they said. 'You've got to do what each individual wants.' We were incredibly restricted in what we could do because we weren't allowed to do things as a big group. With forty clients and seven staff, figure it out. It was this whole new philosophy of individualized plans. And that's great, and people should get to do what they want, but let's also be realistic."[31]

This shift away from group activities towards managing difficult behaviours also had an impact on clients. "So, you take somebody like Guy Mitchell who's a very gentle soul, and suddenly he's in with individuals who are extremely violent," Anne remembered. "In the two years I was there, we went from a nice easy day program where we could do fun things that were entertaining and educational for the clients to an incredibly restricted environment. In many instances, you'd have three staff with one client because they are having an outburst. People such as Guy and many others would be sitting on the sidelines because staff were attending to the individuals with behavioural issues."[32]

ooooo

The Santors led much of this change from their positions on the board of directors at Choices. Privately, they planned to foster even more children and adults at home if only Bill could finish constructing the now decades-long project of building their larger house at the back of the property. Bill envisioned it as a sustainable building with geothermal in-floor heating and solar electricity with five bedrooms, four bathrooms, and a total of twenty-two rooms. The house was as much a testament to Bill's ingenuity as Karen's dedication as a special-needs teacher and foster mother, the ultimate representation of her family's unwavering commitment to help people with developmental disabilities find their place outside the walls of institutions. It was to be a kind of unofficial group home, one Bill and Karen could run without the kind of oversight that would accompany an actual group home. When constructing his expansive new home, Bill originally planned to incorporate a unique heating system that involved using several tons of sand with piping to effectively heat the building.

It was an enormous project that would have proved too great for Bill and Karen, who were both teachers, if not for the substantial income from their work with special-needs children, foster children, and adults with developmental disabilities that brought in between $1250 and $3000 per individual per month. Finding caregivers who are willing to provide specialized care was not easy for agency administrators, so the Santors knew their services would be required long into the future, hence the great size of the home.

Sadly, Karen would have to realize this dream on her own as many of Bill's forward-thinking environmentally friendly plans never came to fruition; he was diagnosed with a brain tumour, which would ultimately claim his life in April 1999 at the age of sixty-seven. It was a terrible shock for the whole family, presumably especially for his youngest teenage daughter, Keri, who appeared to share at least some of her father's traits of intelligence and bold spirit. During his latter years, Bill entered retirement and devoted a significant portion of his time to volunteering, performing household tasks, and taking care of their foster children and adults while Karen was away at work. Bill also assumed the role of the home's grill master and cook, guaranteeing that everyone was well-fed; he prepared mouth-watering dishes using the frequent donations of bread and other food items supplied by Frank, a family friend and long-time member of the Choices board. Bill was remembered fondly by fellow teachers and colleagues at Choices in a write-up for the local newspaper. "He was a one man show," one colleague exclaimed. "I've never known anyone who stuck so close to the principles he believed in," another commented.[33]

As Karen picked up the pieces from this devastating loss, her attention turned first to the long drawn-out project of finishing their new home. Unfortunately, most of the plans for their new house were lost with Bill's passing since he never wrote them down. Instead, Karen hired contractors to finish the job, so they could move in as soon as possible. The solar panels were never installed, nor was an innovative rainwater collection system. The complex in-floor geothermal heating system was scrapped in favour of an oil tank in the garage, and a new cistern twice the size of the existing one was installed to supply running water. Water deliveries were trucked in every three weeks with occasional top-ups of the older cistern at the front of the property, which still provided water for the garden and a couple of ponies that were living in the old barn.

By 2001, the Santors were finally able to move into their new home. Guy and David got the top floor loft, its vaulted ceiling and skylight illuminating their boys-only den. Guy picked one corner and David the other, but the open-concept floor plan meant this was a shared space with little privacy, which may have been appealing to them given their close bond and Guy's sociability. Diane remembered Guy being very excited about the move with the anticipation of years waiting and watching the slow construction of an impressive structure many times the size of the existing house. He loved the shared loft, with plenty of space to spread out and enjoy racing remote-control cars, listen to music, and watch the clouds roll by overhead. Diane got Guy a new bedroom set and shopped for other things he could put up to help make the space his own. A picture of Guy with his mother and stepfather, Dave, hung above his dresser, a constant reminder of their love and affection.

The following years passed in relative tranquility, with one exception. In 2003, Diane took Guy to a medical appointment. "He was always in a rush, and as we entered through a side door with some steps, he unfortunately fell down them." She rushed to his aid, but it was uncertain whether he was conscious or not. Some people nearby called for an ambulance, and he was taken to McMaster Hospital for medical attention. "I went home, had my husband drive me to McMaster, and fortunately he was all right." Afterwards, however, Guy would sometimes go through periods where he would not talk to or engage with others, even if spoken to. He was eventually referred to a neurologist who concluded he may have suffered a concussion, which may have resulted in dizziness, nausea, confusion, memory loss, mood changes, and difficulty sleeping.

Besides this event, Guy continued his work in the Hut, learning new skills and making friends. Life on the farm suited him as there were always chores to do and he would often be the first to volunteer, eagerly throwing on his shoes and jacket to race out the door to help. He would take out the recycling and regularly helped with the yardwork. He leaped on the trampoline with abandon and devoted lengthy hours to his paperwork, scribbling and filing away his documents. He would swiftly gather any stray papers in his vicinity, and promptly shush away anyone who dared to interrupt him. There were bowling tournaments and Special Olympics skiing, his trophy collection bursting from the shelves in his room at Diane's apartment. There were more summer trips to Honey Harbour, more birthday cakes and corn roasts, and Christmas celebrations with the whole family. Over time, Guy grew into an adult with a circle of friends, family, and a purpose in life.

ooooo

Change came swiftly and without notice. In the spring of 2011, Karen started exhibiting signs of an unknown illness. She went to the doctor in late May and was diagnosed with type 2 diabetes. But diabetes didn't seem to explain her increasingly erratic behaviour. She would attempt to flush clothes down the toilet while laughing maniacally. Sometimes her words didn't make sense, and she started sleeping far more than usual. She would miss scheduled visits with social workers and paratransit pickups for Guy and David, something she never did before. Suddenly, the woman who built this intricate informal group home in the countryside, played a crucial role in Choices, and tirelessly engaged in various other community activities, found herself unable to perform the endless caregiving duties required of her. During this time, police were called to the house when a passing motorist encountered one of her adopted children, Jennifer, squatting in the middle of the road. No one was even aware she had left the house. The unravelling of everything Karen had built over her forty-year career came fast and furious.

After Karen started to forget to give medication to the foster kids, the Children's Aid Society quickly took action and removed the children from the Santor home and relocated them to a different home. Although necessary, it was a devastating blow to Karen personally. Following this event, she left the board of the service agency to which she had dedicated thirty years of her life. By June, she was diagnosed with glioblastoma, an aggressive type of brain cancer that would soon land her in palliative care. Karen was unable to withstand the required surgery, so the cancerous tumour grew, spidering out across her brain, causing violent seizures and robbing her of the ability to communicate or even stay awake for periods of time. Her bewildered children did their best to make her comfortable in her final days, but in August 2011 she died at age sixty-one, leaving behind a devastated family and an uncertain future for Guy.

Guy took Karen's death hard. Her funeral was one of the few times anyone can ever remember him crying. She had been like another mother to him for more than twenty-five years and her sudden absence was profoundly confusing and upsetting. Guy had a hard time understanding the finality of death; that a beloved person could simply vanish one day. "When is Karen coming back?" he'd repeatedly ask. "What's taking her so long?" He withdrew from others, retreating to his room. He had meltdowns. He started soiling himself. He had trouble sleeping and would stay up late listening to the radio on low volume for hours, listlessly flipping from one station to the next. Guy was in pain.

It was a traumatic ending for all the Santor children, but particularly for Keri. The grief of losing both parents at a young age must have been extremely difficult. But now, there were new problems on the horizon. In the absence of Karen's hand on the wheel, the Santor home, that hive of activity and sanctuary for so many, quietly descended into chaos. No one would suffer this transition more than Guy.

4.

THE DAUGHTER

Fluorescent lights buzzed overhead as the court reporter tapped incessantly on the keyboard of her computer, the only other sounds in the courtroom being the occasional cough or shuffle of spectators as they shifted in their uncomfortable pews.

"How would you describe Keri at the time of Karen's death?" Crown Attorney Shea asked Diane on the witness stand.

"I often wondered how come she never worked, but she was there helping her mother. I never noticed anything that felt wrong," Diane stammered.

"So, Karen Santor died in August 2011," Shea reminded the jury before turning back to Diane. "At that time, when decisions were being made about where Guy would be living, was there ever a meeting with people at Choices and Keri Santor where you all sat down and talked about what might be best for Guy?"

"No," Diane responded.

"But Keri then took over care of Guy, David, and eleven-year-old Jennifer?"

"Yes. My first thought was that Guy and David would have to find new homes, and that perhaps Guy would remain there for a little while. But Keri wanted to take over and told me that she was given the house by her mother for a year and that she was going to look after them for that year."

"Did you have any concerns about a twenty-six-year-old taking over the care of two adults with developmental disabilities as well as an autistic child?" Shea questioned Diane.

"I wondered if she would be able to handle it, and how she would handle it financially. But at first it seemed with everything that happened in terms of losing her mother, it seemed that it was okay."

ooooo

Born in 1985, Keri studied dance in Toronto and briefly ran a local dance school in the town of Ancaster. An attractive woman with auburn hair, blue eyes, and a coy smile, Keri was highly intelligent, a member of Mensa like her dad, and someone who kept books on quantum physics above her bed. After all the other Santor children left home, Keri remained. It appeared she helped her mother at home with the caregiving duties, but when Karen really needed help, she would call someone else in. Sometimes Keri would disappear to her room for days. Some say she had a drinking problem. For all her talents and positive attributes, including what appeared to be genuine affection for Guy and others in the home, Keri was also extraordinarily bad-tempered and deceptive, often provoking altercations with family, neighbours, helpers, and police. During Karen's sickness, Keri treated her siblings as an unwanted intrusion while they took turns looking after the vulnerable residents of the house and spending time at the hospital. "When I get back from the hospital, I want you gone!" she allegedly barked at her brother one day while their mother lay dying in hospice.

Karen gave her daughter one year to live in the house before it was put up for sale. Decisions needed to be made about where Guy, David, and Jennifer would live, and there seemed to be no expectation on behalf of anyone that Keri would continue providing care to the two men. Karen wanted Keri to apply for guardianship of Jennifer so that she didn't immediately end up back in the foster system, though it appeared there were no instructions about her formally adopting the severely autistic eleven-year-old girl. The world Karen had crafted for herself was not easily transferrable, and the level of responsibility was far beyond the capabilities of most people, let alone a young woman in her mid-twenties with no formal training to care for people with complex needs. Beyond the care of the residents, there was also maintenance of the large house and rural property with its ponies, dogs, cats, and grounds to consider.

Surprisingly, Keri insisted she could handle it all. She agreed to become a guardian for Jennifer and to continue looking after Guy and David, each of whom came with a stipend to cover their expenses. "I consider them my brothers," she told everyone. Technically and legally, it was up to Guy to decide where he wanted to live, and he insisted he didn't want to leave the farm. Karen Santor was never his legal guardian, but rather a support system overseen by their partnership with Choices through the host-family program. Guy was legally free to leave at any time regardless of any diminished capacity he may have had for making safe and informed decisions. When Karen and Bill applied to foster Guy in 1986, the Children's Aid Society (CAS) vetted the home and family. When Guy turned eighteen, he ceased to be a foster child but continued living at the home while he attended Glenwood School. On his twenty-first birthday, he became a client of Choices, at which point, there was another vetting process. It might have just been a formality given the Santors' foundational role at Choices, but Karen and Bill still went through the intake process to officially become his host family and receive a portion of his benefits in exchange for sharing their home with him.

But no one vetted Keri.

At some point in the days following Karen's death, the CEO and director of operations decided Keri would be grandfathered in as the home provider for Guy and David. No screening or onboarding process would take place. Keri grew up with these men and said she wanted to continue what her mother started. She had lived experience, and that was good enough. The shared-living arrangement had been in place for such a long time, it seemed the least disruptive option for Guy and David who otherwise would have been immediately removed from the home and eventually found placements with other families or in a group home. What could be better than allowing Guy to remain in the home he had literally grown up in? Keri was cast as the saviour of the situation, selflessly putting the needs of others before herself while still struggling to process the tragic death of her mother.

The financial stability of the household was not investigated, nor did an inspection of the home take place. If normal procedure were followed, it might have been discovered that Keri's driver's licence was allegedly suspended due to impaired driving charges and unpaid fines. Or that the house was not normally nearly as presentable as it was on inspection days. Or that Keri did not appear to have any income besides the monthly stipends set aside for Guy and David. Or that there had been a recent history of police, CAS, and SPCA (Society for the Prevention of Cruelty to Animals) involvement at the property. These incidents might be seen as isolated occurrences — the removal of the foster children from Karen's care, ten-year-old Jennifer found squatting in the middle of the road, multiple eyewitness statements about the poor condition of the Santor home and property — but, together, they provided powerful insight about the suitability of the home for vulnerable residents. Unfortunately, none of these agencies shared their information with one another or with Choices, either by request or as a matter of policy pertaining to adults with developmental disabilities. The Santors were long considered inscrutable while Karen and Bill were in charge, so it can only have been out of loyalty to them that Keri was given a pass by Choices leadership. She was taken at her word and allowed to simply pick up where her mother left off. It did not appear anyone at Choices knew at the time that Keri had only one year to live in the home as there were no plans made to relocate Guy and David.

Initially, the arrangement with Keri seemed to be working out well. She showed up to meetings about Guy's support plan, asked questions, and sought out training opportunities. She packed adequate lunches with plenty of healthy food to eat. Guy showed up to the Choices day program well-groomed with clean, fresh clothes. Keri dutifully filled out the daily communication books that passed between her and day-program staff, a low-tech way of keeping everyone on his support team up to date on any issues or concerns at home or at Choices. At meetings with the home support worker, Jennifer, Keri reported Guy was withdrawn and sleeping more than usual as he struggled to process the loss of Karen. On the surface at least, it seemed Keri was managing the difficult transition as well as could be expected of her. A generous, selfless volunteer who put the needs of Guy and others before her own.

ooooo

It wasn't long before the cracks in the facade began to show. For Diane, red flags appeared as early as September 2011, just one month after Karen died. Guy rarely missed a day working at the Hut, but that month there were at least two absences. It was very uncommon for Guy to miss the day program, given that his daily routine was an incredibly important part of his overall well-being. DARTS paratransit rides were always scheduled in advance, so picking up and delivering him to Choices ran like clockwork. In one instance, when Guy and David didn't show up one morning, day-program staff got worried when there was no phone call or communication from Keri as to why the men were absent. They called the Santor home, but no one answered. They called Diane next, but she had no idea where Guy was. Diane called Keri and got no answer either, then called Jennifer, the support worker. Five hours later, Jennifer returned her call when she learned Keri took the men to the disability benefit office to get their disability benefit information updated. Keri admitted she never informed anyone at Choices, even though she would have known that to be proper protocol.

Not long afterward, Diane arranged to pick up Guy from the Santor residence to attend a walkathon fundraiser held annually by Choices, an event he always looked forward to. As Diane exited her car and approached the front door, she heard someone yelling in an angry voice just inside. It was Keri screaming at Guy for soiling his pants just as he was about to be picked up. Diane, a calm and patient woman, had never heard anyone talk to her son like this before. If Guy did something wrong or needed redirection, a gentle or firm voice was all that was needed to get him back on track; angrily screaming at him would not do anything other than frighten him.

As Diane opened the door, Keri's tone shifted, her flushed face contorting into regretful exasperation as she strained to explain the commotion and her concern that he would now be late for the walkathon. "That's okay," Diane reassured Guy. "Let's get you cleaned up and a fresh pair of pants." In the car as they drove off, Diane turned to Guy. "You know, Keri can't be yelling at you like that," she told him. Diane knew Guy would often soil himself when he was under stress; it was his way of communicating to others that something was wrong. She knew he was still grieving Karen, her death still fresh in his memory. As a co-founder of Choices, Karen would have normally attended the walkathon with him, and her conspicuous absence from the moment likely compounded the confusion and pain he was experiencing. "I know you miss Karen," Diane reassured him. "It's hard on everybody, but we have to try to do our best." Diane then called Jennifer, the support worker, to advise her about what happened. Two days later, Jennifer reported back that she had no concerns about Keri or the arrangement.

Another time, Diane was returning Guy to the Santor residence and while she stood in the entryway to see him off, David heard her voice and wanted to come see her. As he descended the stairs, Jennifer, the autistic girl who also lived there, rushed up behind David and pushed him down the stairs. "Oh my god, David! Are you okay?" Diane cried out from the bottom of the staircase. David was unharmed, but the incident prompted Diane to consider what if that happened to Guy. Both men were unsteady on their feet and could be seriously injured from a fall like that. Keri was unconcerned about the prospect of such an injury, so Diane called Jennifer to report the incident.

"That could have been Guy," Diane speculated to Jennifer. "What should I do?"

According to Diane, Jennifer allegedly told her the team at Choices also wasn't sure what to do about the situation at the Santor farm, a statement Jennifer later denied under oath. "I would never have said that," she testified. "Tim [Choices manager] called me and said Diane had concerns. I called Diane and asked her what her concerns were. She said she had concerns about the time they were going on the walkathon, and Guy had smeared feces and was banging on the walls, and because she heard Keri yelling and screaming at Guy. She said she was keeping an eye on things and that she had no more concerns. Those were her concerns at the time."

Jennifer testified that she checked up on the situation with Keri and advised Diane everything was fine at the Santor home. According to Diane, Jennifer added a perplexing offer. "We can remove Guy if you want. We can have him placed somewhere else very quickly." The offer to promptly rehouse Guy on Diane's orders contradicted testimony by Choices managers that placements took time to arrange and technically it would take more than Diane's wishes to remove Guy from the home. Guy was never declared mentally incompetent, and according to new regulations, any changes to his living situation required his express consent, and he had already indicated he wished to continue living at the Santor residence. Jennifer also failed to inform Diane there had been an escalating pattern of cancelled home visits and that both Guy and David had started showing up to the day program filthy, soiled, and without proper lunches, details the inquest jury would soon learn from multiple witnesses.

If Diane had been given all the available information at the time, it would likely have influenced her assessment about whether the Santor home remained a safe place for her son under Keri's supervision. It may have also strengthened her existing concerns and confirmed her desire to relocate Guy to another home. Instead, Diane decided it might be better not to disrupt Guy's long-standing living arrangement at the Santor residence, knowing such a time was soon approaching anyway. "He's had so much to deal with since Karen's death, maybe now is not the right time," she told Jennifer.

Other warning signs kept emerging as time wore on. Diane and her husband Dave were snowbirds, following the migration patterns of hundreds of thousands of other Canadians to the tropical warmth of Florida during the cold winter months. That year, however, they decided to cut their usual extended absence short. Diane didn't know exactly what was wrong, but there was something holding her back, a nagging feeling that she needed to stay close to monitor her son. One Saturday in February, Diane picked up Guy and took him to the bowling alley. In between sets, Diane told Guy the news of her upcoming short absence. "Mom and Dave are going to Florida just for a few weeks next month. We won't be gone long this year," she told him.

Guy paused to process this, like a computer buffering to handle a backlog of information. Then suddenly, he had a total meltdown. He picked up a five-pin bowling ball and threw it overhand through the air and stomped his feet. The ball bounced harmlessly down the lanes, but the noise caused everyone to turn to see what happened. Diane was shocked at his reaction. Guy had meltdowns before, but she had no idea why he would respond like that when he knew she went on vacation each year during the winter. Later, she suspected his reaction was him trying to communicate something else. But what? Meltdowns are an explosive, frustrating, uncontrollable experience for individuals who become overwhelmed when they cannot communicate their feelings any other way. Like a pot bubbling over with too many ingredients or too much heat, Guy's meltdowns were usually about much more than just a response to immediate circumstances. Soiling himself, stomping, banging, or, in this instance, throwing a bowling ball, usually indicated something else was bothering him.

At the time, no one at Choices had informed Diane that David had been temporarily removed from the Santor home for respite after a series of events that demonstrated Keri needed a break. On April 10, 2012, David showed up at the day program with a cut on his head. He was shaking and walked stiffly, which caused alarm among staff who called Jennifer to investigate. Besides the cut, he had problems with his foot and a sore wrist, so Choices managers requested he be taken to urgent care where he was examined by doctors. An X-ray revealed nothing significant; his wrist and foot were fine. Keri told Jennifer it was an accident. "He bumped his head on the monkey bars at the Jerseyville playground," she allegedly said. But David contradicted Keri's story, saying he had fallen. The torrent of excuses often carried a hint of plausibility but were rarely, if ever, fully investigated or verified. In this case, neither Jennifer nor anyone else at Choices followed up to figure out why there was a discrepancy. If they had, they might have discovered that Jerseyville Park (the only playground in Jerseyville) did not even have monkey bars. Guy was likely confused and upset that his "little brother" wasn't there and now, with Diane's news, he was going to be left alone with Keri. He didn't know how to express why it was so upsetting for him to be left alone at the Santor house.

While Diane was on the witness stand being questioned by Choices' lawyer Mr. Manishen, a subtle narrative emerged that she could have done more to protect her son from what happened, a suggestion that strengthened over the course of subsequent witness testimony given by Choices staff. Perhaps this was to shift some of the blame off Choices or simply an effort to capture the fullest picture, but such a narrative strayed perilously close to older cultural practices of "mother blaming," insinuations of a mother's culpability when medical authorities do not have ready answers or when institutions fail parents and their children. Whatever the aims or purpose of propagating such a narrative, whether intentionally or subconsciously, Diane's testimony revealed much more about the fault lines within the agency and system of oversight responsible for Guy than it did about her role in his death.

"You were present at a meeting that took place August 31, 2011, just a few weeks after Karen Santor's death?" Mr. Manishen asked Diane. "You heard what was discussed amongst the staff as well as with Guy. Everybody collaborated on what the plan should be?"

"Yes," she responded, clarifying that the meeting was not about changing Guy's living arrangements, but a regularly scheduled discussion that took place quarterly to update his support plan.

The next meeting was in February 2012. "If you had any concerns about Guy's programming, activities, or the Santor home, there would be an opportunity for you to express that?" Mr. Manishen asked.

"Yes."

"Did you have any concerns at that time?"

"No."

"What did you remember raising?"

"I don't remember. We were talking about his programming and what was going to happen."

"At the planning meeting, do you have any recollection of raising any concerns at that time of his care or Keri's home?"

"I don't believe so." Diane expressed her dismay that Guy was removed from his beloved work program at the Hut, but she had no authority to make decisions about what happened at the day program. "What could I do? They're going to do what they're going to do." She shrugged.

Mr. Manishen's voice suddenly rose, and he allegedly pointed his finger in Diane's direction for emphasis. "Jennifer said to you, 'We are concerned about the same issues as you are,'" Mr. Manishen continued. "And Jennifer asked if you'd been thinking about removing Guy from the current placement, and you said you weren't sure. Keri seems to have been reassuring you that things were better." Diane blushed and took a deep breath as she was led back to the regretful moment when she apparently could have acted to remove Guy before things got worse. If only she had acted sooner. If only she knew everything that was going on. If only . . . if only . . .

"That was the conversation where I asked . . . I wanted her take on things. I wanted to know what advice she would have because he had gone through so many changes with Karen dying, and did I want to take him out right then, or . . ." Diane's voice trembled. She paused to collect herself before she pushed through. "And she said they've got the same problem. 'We don't know what to do.'" Her eyes welled with tears as she considered the scenario that placed all the responsibility for monitoring Guy's placement on her shoulders.

"I'm just going from the note I have, and if you need to take a break we can."

"I'm fine," Diane rasped, defiantly wiping away her tears.

Diane was a trusting person by nature. A woman of faith, she felt there were enough checks and balances in place to protect her son and ensure he received the care she was told he was getting despite her reservations about Keri. Some would later suggest a mother's intuition should have enabled her to see the warning signs behind the facade. Maternal instincts aside, she often saw Guy only after he had been freshly groomed, during prescheduled pickups and meetings at the Santor house. And she knew nothing of the struggles Choices staff were having with Keri during the months when things deteriorated, nor the broken internal mechanics of the agency that prevented timely action to address these problems. She certainly knew nothing of an old cistern that lay like a trap hidden in the grass waiting to expose all of this to the world.

With only a few months before the Santor house was to be put up for sale, time was running out for Keri. Choices reassured Diane there was a plan in place, and that it would be a smooth transition for Guy. But how true was this assertion, and who else could shed light on what was going on at the Santor farm?

5.

THE BROTHER

"All rise. This inquest is now resumed. Please be seated," barked the bailiff.

"Are there any matters of business?" Dr. Stanborough asked.

"No, Mr. Coroner," replied Crown Attorney Shea.

"You may call your next witness."

"The next witness is William Santor," Shea announced. A tall, impeccably dressed man, William took the witness stand. He had short dark hair and thick eyebrows and spoke articulately with the cool confidence of a businessman accustomed to high-powered conversations.

"You are the brother of Keri Santor and son of Karen Santor?"

"Yes."

"What was your relationship like with your sister Keri?" asked Shea.

"Acrimonious," he replied. He took time to consider his responses, answering slowly and deliberately in a calm, authoritative tone.

"Was it always that way?"

"We were quite apart in age," William began, explaining that in the mid-1990s he was at the stage of life where he was moving out of the family home when Keri was not yet ten years old. The siblings never developed a close relationship and remained unaffectionate as adults. From a distance, William learned his sister was a skilful liar. "She was a masterful manipulator. You never knew where you stood with her," he said. "You always wondered if she was being truthful with you. It caused a lot of conflict."

ooooo

Karen died in the evening of August 8, 2011, surrounded by her loving family. William was named executor of her estate, a task that would force him and Keri to work together one way or another. Keri was required to maintain the house during her limited term occupancy, but it appeared she was not living up to those responsibilities. When arrears on the mortgage raised the risk of a default on the loan in November, William arranged for the balance to be paid out of the estate. But it seemed nobody was paying the water delivery or oil company. Normally, Karen would hand a cheque to the Waterman deliveryman, Henry, who arrived promptly every three weeks to fill up the tank, but after Karen died, the house racked up arrears of around $2000 in unpaid invoices. Calls and letters to the house went unanswered. Henry delivered water to the property for years and knew how much the residents relied on him, so when invoices stopped being paid, he visited the property on multiple occasions to gain an understanding about whether they still needed him to come by. No one would answer the door on these occasions or respond to the numerous attempts to make contact. There were a few other water delivery companies like the Waterman in the area, so Henry called around to see if the Santors opened an account with another company, but it appeared they had not. Despite thousands of dollars owing to his company, Henry dropped off a final load of water on December 21, 2011. "I didn't want them to go through Christmas with no water," he testified at the inquest. A similar situation presumably unfolded with the oil company that supplied heating oil to the furnace, but that tank also soon ran dry. The only remaining source of heat for the home was a decorative wood fireplace on the main level.

If William was aware of how these financial difficulties played out in relation to the mortgage, it seemed he didn't realize that the only household income at the Santor farm were government disability benefit cheques for Guy and David. Choices provided Keri with stipends meant to cover expenses such as clothing and food for the men, but such stipends were never intended to be the sole income for a home provider. The bulk of Guy's individualized funding passed through the agency, possibly to discourage misuse of such funds by home providers, though with few accounting requirements demanded by Choices, such an argument was hard to substantiate.

At the inquest, William expressed his disappointment at not being given the opportunity to intervene to assist Keri in addressing the financial limitations that contributed to the deterioration of the situation at the Santor farm. "We grew up with Guy. He is family to us. Same with David," William told the jury. "They're family. You look after them. Had we been made aware there were problems, that there was no water, we would have provided." But with poor lines of communication between the siblings that continued to deteriorate, Keri didn't disclose any financial issues she might have been having with the upkeep of the Santor property. Had she revealed an inability (or unwillingness) to keep up with the water and heating bills, it's possible Guy and David would have been removed from the home, taking with them her only source of income.

At one point, the estate lawyer needed important documents to be signed by Keri, but getting in touch with her proved especially difficult. Karen collected a pension from her teaching career, but survivor beneficiary funds for dependent Jennifer would not be released until Keri signed papers that made her Jennifer's legal guardian. Multiple meetings with the lawyer would be scheduled, and Keri would either cancel or simply not show up, leaving those funds frozen in Karen's pension account. Calls, texts, and emails went unanswered, or there was always one excuse or another. Meanwhile, Keri started telling others her siblings were trying to oust her from the family home, an unsubstantiated accusation that presumably explained her lack of cooperation with the estate lawyer. There were critical documents that needed to be signed by Keri to allow Karen's will to pass through probate for insurance purposes, so when she failed to show up to a meeting at the lawyer's office, they agreed to meet her at the farm.

They scheduled the meeting for a Sunday afternoon, the lawyer leading the way in his pickup truck. As they arrived at the property, they discovered the driveway blocked with Karen's old Pontiac minivan. Keri drove the vehicle to the end of the driveway and parked parallel to the roadway to prevent access to the property. Perhaps she felt threatened, or she didn't want her brother and the lawyer to see the state of the house.

Baffled by Keri's actions, the lawyer pulled out the necessary paperwork and got some of the signatures he needed as perplexed drivers drove by. "I'm not signing this," Keri said regarding the paperwork dealing with her becoming a legal guardian for Jennifer. "I want to have my lawyer review this first, so you can forward it to their office." The estate lawyer reminded her that Karen's pension funds would not be released until that paperwork was put through. "I see what you're saying now," the lawyer commented to William later, noting that he smelled alcohol on Keri's breath. "We have an issue. Let's just get this done so we can move forward." After some more time passed, the estate lawyer called William to advise he still hadn't received any signed documentation from Keri regarding the guardianship of Jennifer. The estate lawyer and William called the offices of the lawyer Keri said she retained to represent her. "I know Keri, but I don't represent her in this," the lawyer responded.

William was torn up about what to do next and he implored his other two sisters to help him find a solution. "What do we do? How do we handle this?" They considered making a joint application for guardianship of Jennifer, but it wasn't certain if this was the most practical solution to fulfill their mother's wishes to prevent the girl from falling back into the foster system. They would deliberate together over long-distance calls to Vancouver and Florida, trying to figure out how to balance family unity with the advice of the estate lawyer and pressing concerns about the health and safety of the vulnerable residents. The attorney expressed concern that if they confronted Keri, it could result in restricted access to the property and potential complications during the probate process. The lawyer also advised that Keri had a fiduciary responsibility to look after the estate as per her one-year interest in the property provided in Karen's will, and if there were damages above normal wear and tear within that year, then she would be responsible and that could be dealt with in a future suit if necessary.

William decided to follow the advice of the lawyer and minimize contact with Keri to avoid provoking any altercations that could be taken as grounds for a possible harassment claim or trespass notice, but it still didn't leave him feeling good about the situation. Later, William said to the police detectives who were investigating Guy's death that "you're sort of torn in that dynamic of, do you want to rip the family apart or find a solution to move it forward when you don't really know what the issues are other than the fact that you're not given access to see what the conditions are. Are you then going to automatically be in a worse place because you don't have evidence otherwise, or what?"

One condition of the estate was to have an appraiser visit to perform an inspection to determine a value for the house and property. But, like everything else, it seemed, setting a date to complete the inspection proved difficult. Meetings were scheduled and cancelled at the last minute without much notice. On one occasion, William showed up at the house but there was no answer at the door. He checked his voice mail and there was a message. "According to Keri, the appraiser cancelled it," William told the police. The appraisal was rescheduled for a week later. William showed up first, but decided to remain in his car until the appraiser arrived to avoid a possible confrontation that might jeopardize the appointment. Jennifer ran out to greet him. "You might want to be careful," Keri hollered from the door. "Jennifer was sick last night, and I'm cleaning it up right now." It could have been a friendly warning, but few friendly words ever passed between the siblings in the preceding months.

The appraiser's car pulled up shortly afterward, and they all proceeded into the house. William never lived in the house he helped his dad build, but it also wasn't his first time stepping foot inside. Some clutter and mess was normal in the Santor house when Karen was alive, but this was different. "It was apparent that attempts to clean up had been made, but those had fallen short," William told the jury. "It smelled of urine and feces. You could see stains throughout. As we were going through Jennifer's room, there was vomit on the floor and there was a scrub brush still within the vomit on the floor. It was just in a general state of disarray." As Jennifer's room was finished in laminate flooring, William wondered why it took so long to clean up a mess like that, especially if it had been there since the previous evening. William said the top loft space where Guy and David slept smelled of urine and feces. "I didn't see any, but it definitely smelled," he told the police. "I don't recall there being sheets on the bed," he later added for the jury. William recalled that after Karen died, both Guy and David would soil themselves, but understood this was a coping mechanism in response to stress. "They would have issues from time to time with soiling themselves. You know, you clean it up. But nothing that it should be engrained into the room," said William to the police. Descending the house from the top floor, the smell of urine and feces was gradually masked by disinfectant.

Keri had arranged for Diane and Dave to come by later that day for an Easter dinner with Guy, so she likely cleaned the areas where they were expected to be. The smell of bleach blanketed the area, insulating the guests from an entirely different scene on the upper floors. "It was somewhat awkward," Diane remembered about the dinner. Guy was in high spirits to have his mom and stepdad there, but normally Diane hardly made it past the front door when she was picking up or dropping off Guy, so it was common for her not to see the inside of the Santor house for weeks or months. In this rare opportunity to observe the living conditions, Diane noticed nothing out of the ordinary, the general state of disarray by now an unremarkable feature of the house where her son had grown up. She had never seen William's pictures of her son and the house, and it's uncertain why he never shared his concerns with Diane, especially after the recent inspection of the house with the appraiser. Diane didn't use any of the kitchen facilities, and the short amount of time she was present was spent in the dining room. She did note that the toilet flushed, but it's possible the tank was manually preloaded with water for that purpose. She initially had doubts about the Santors, but was reassured by Karen's successful help in raising Guy. Now, with Keri, new worries had arisen, but Diane remained steadfast in her belief that Guy just needed to endure the next few months until the Santor house was sold and he found a new home. As Diane kissed her son goodbye and closed the front door, she had no idea this would be the last time she would step foot inside the Santor home.

Later that month on April 20, 2012, William received an email from the secretary at Glenwood school on behalf of the principal, Keith Muldoon, asking William to call him regarding Jennifer. He called right away and learned some disturbing news. Apparently, Jennifer was frequently absent, including that day, and the school often couldn't get in touch with Keri — and possibly hadn't ever been in touch with her — to determine the cause of her absences. There were also concerns about Jennifer arriving to school with no lunch on multiple days and issues with especially poor hygiene. Muldoon would later walk back some of these statements, but attendance records indicated she was absent thirty-five days since she began at the school in October 2011. "And they said it had been getting progressively worse," William told police. "I think they said in February she had missed twelve days. I don't know how much of that is actual illness or sickness, but at the end of the day it was enough for the principal to bring it up in conversation." At a special needs school such as Glenwood, absences due to doctor's appointments and behavioural issues are not necessarily uncommon, though the school's administrators would normally be kept in the loop as to why.

William called his sisters and recounted the conversation for police detectives. "Look, I just had this conversation with the principal. I think this is the final straw. We need somebody who's not emotionally attached to the situation and has a more professional outlook on what the situation might be." They decided that if the school wasn't going to contact the Children's Aid Society (CAS) about the situation, then they would. They reached an after-hours worker who said they would only speak to one caller, so William lodged the complaint. He relayed the issues about Jennifer's absences at school and their concerns about the suitability of Keri as her guardian. It wasn't until a week later that a CAS worker called William back to say they didn't feel it was an emergency or warranted an immediate investigation. It was upsetting news for William, who felt his concerns weren't being taken seriously enough, so he offered to share the pictures of the home he had previously taken as evidence of a pattern of neglect. After reviewing the pictures, the CAS responded by opening an investigation, but categorized the response time at the lowest priority level. That meant there would be no unannounced visit and that someone would check up on the house in a week's time, in early May. "It was only after we basically had to force them to look at the photographs that they agreed there would be a visit. And that was a week after our first phone call," William stated to the jury.

William had complained to the Choices CEO, police, social workers at the hospice where his mother died, his lawyer, and now the CAS regarding his concerns about what was going on at the Santor farm and his sister's lack of capacity to care for the vulnerable residents there. William hadn't lived on the property for many years, was not directly involved in any of the caregiving relationships, and was also going through a tough time in his own life; he had gone above and beyond what might be expected of a reasonable person in his circumstances. But instead of being rewarded for doing his best to prevent something terrible from happening, the information he kept feeding into the system seemed to yield no results. The experience left him feeling defeated and disillusioned. "To me, it felt like not just one safety net fell down, but every single public safety net across the board collapsed in its entirety. It felt as though we had to force ourselves upon them for any action to be considered."

ooooo

William learned of Guy's death from the estate lawyer. "We ended up being as much passengers as everybody else, you know, getting information from *The Spec* [newspaper]," he recalled to the jury. "The whole time, we tried reaching out to Keri and she never responded to us, never answered us, never reached out to us to even tell us Guy had passed." The omission was stinging, and perhaps telling. Keri and William couldn't agree on much, but they both grew up with Guy and considered him to be their brother. If the death of their mother couldn't bring them closer, it was unlikely the death of a mutually beloved sibling was going to be any different.

Of course, William wasn't the only set of eyes on the Santor farm during that tumultuous time, and as much as his part of the story exposed certain fault lines, knowledge of how much other people knew about what was going on only served to reveal just how deep those flaws ran and how the system itself helped create the conditions for a tragedy that would rock the community.

6.

THE HELPERS

"All rise," the bailiff instructed everyone in the courtroom. "This inquest is now resumed."

Dr. Stanborough nodded towards Crown Attorney Shea. "Next witness, please."

"The next witness is Stephen."

"Do you swear that the evidence you will give at this inquest into the death of Guy Mitchell will be the truth, the full truth, and nothing but the truth, so help you, God?" the bailiff recited.

"Yes," Stephen responded softly.

"Please be seated, sir."

"Good afternoon, Stephen," Shea began. "My understanding is that you are an educational assistant at Glenwood school? Tell me a little bit about the school."

Stephen described the special day school where he worked. He was quickly recruited by Karen to help her at home. Despite her experience and strong character, Karen knew she couldn't handle everything on her own after Bill died, so she would hire assistants like Stephen to help her around the house and supervise the residents when she had meetings outside the home.

"And how did you come to work for the Santors?" asked Shea.

"I mentioned to Karen I needed a part-time job, so she hired me." Stephen started by looking after the dogs, sheep, goats, and horses.

He spoke softly and slowly, occasionally pausing between thoughts and sentences, his measured tone perhaps honed by years of working with children and adults who needed extra time to process information. "Organized chaos" was how Stephen described the Santor home at the best of times. Donations of clothing, incontinence products, food, and toys sometimes piled up around the house, adding to the normal accumulation of clutter in any busy household. But this wasn't just a matter of a few dishes left on the counter or clothing on the floor. Eventually, there was so much stuff in the house that some of it needed to be stored in the barn. Besides the needs of Guy, David, Jennifer, and two other foster children, there was a large property to look after, horses and other animals to feed and groom, a large lawn to be cut, gardens to tend, snow to be cleared, and appointments with doctors, specialists, and social workers at all hours of the day.

"When did you start working inside the home?" Shea asked.

"Periodically, Karen would have a meeting in the afternoon after school, so she would ask me to come up for a couple hours to feed them dinner and get them ready for bed, so that's what I would do."

"So you were looking after the residents?"

"Yeah."

"Did you do any work in terms of maintenance or cleaning?"

"No, Karen tried to get me to paint walls a couple of times, but I did such a crummy job she didn't ask me to do it again," Stephen admitted to a round of low chuckles.

"What was your relationship with Guy?" Shea asked.

"We got along well. He was a very happy-go-lucky guy. I enjoyed spending time with him."

ooooo

The lawn mower roared, sowing a gust of tiny green blades across the front lawn that filled the air with a sweet scent. Stephen spun the steering wheel wildly to manoeuvre around the rough terrain. Guy would follow Stephen around the property, a willing pair of hands always ready to collect branches, feed the dogs, take out the recycling, or help with odd jobs. Guy knew the area where the old farmhouse once stood was unsafe, full of unseen sinkholes and crumbling remnants of the stone foundation of the house that was torn down some time in the early 2000s, and Stephen would remind him to be careful whenever he was out with him in the area.

"Stand back over there, Guy. It's not safe here," Stephen called out as the lawn mower chewed up the long grass.

"Okay!" Guy hollered back as he stood patiently by the driveway, ready with a rake in hand to help collect the grass clippings.

Most nights, Guy and the other housemates would retreat to their bedrooms soon after dinner, ready for bed as early as seven o'clock when the summer sun was still low in the sky. But things were different when the helpers were there. They'd order pizza, watch a movie, and hang out together in the living room for a few extra hours. "Don't tell Karen I'm having pop and chips!" Guy would whisper gravely, as if making a pact with the devil. As soon as he spotted Karen's headlights coming down the driveway, Guy would be up like a shot and race to his bedroom. He was never one to be caught breaking the rules.

Annual inspections by service agencies were occasions to enlist extra help to clean the house. "I would use a putty knife to scrape dried feces off the wall," another helper named Peggy moaned, adding she had done so on at least a dozen occasions. Peggy remembered the house as always cluttered with boxes, garbage, and dirty clothing. She testified that the foster children and adults tended to have body odour due to a lack of regular bathing. Peggy had a complicated relationship with the Santors. At first, she was just the bus driver who regularly frequented the property from around 2002 to transport the residents to school or programming. Peggy was a horse lover but lived in the city, so she would board her horses at various farms. In conversation one day, Karen agreed to allow Peggy to board her horses in their barn in exchange for help looking after Guy, David, and the foster children.

The arrangement worked well until Keri threatened to kill Peggy's horses over an argument about Peggy's choice of parking on the Santor property. Peggy alleged she began finding nails scattered in areas frequently trod by the horses, and the horses out of their stalls without her permission. Keri allegedly fed pine needles to one of Peggy's horses, a poisonous substance that apparently resulted in the horse being euthanized. According to Peggy, Keri later threatened to kill another of Peggy's horses, and a month later the horse was found to be very sick for unknown reasons and had to be euthanized on site. The remaining horse was removed from the property by the SPCA, which ended Peggy's troubled relationship with the Santors. Later, Peggy would tell police that besides her problems with Keri, she never liked the way Karen treated some of the foster children. "She ran that house like it was a jail, and she was the warden," Peggy said, alleging that teenage foster children would be forced to scrub the grout in the bathroom with a toothbrush, boys and girls were instructed to sit on opposite sides of the room, no one was allowed to play outside, and meals and early bedtimes were strictly enforced. "There was no love or joy in that house," Peggy lamented, adding that she would take every opportunity to play with the children or take them outside for fresh air against Karen's wishes. While some of the children were sick or lived with various disabilities, others rotated through the foster system, so it is entirely possible Karen's strict orders were based on information and experience Peggy lacked in running a home with so many moving parts. Peggy admitted she had no formal training working with special needs children and at first went along with whatever Karen told her to do because she didn't know what was normal in such a house, and Karen was the relative expert in the situation.

Stephen was less descriptive about the social conditions in the Santor house, possibly because he spent far less time inside the house with the residents than Peggy, who was there on a near-daily basis for several years. But he also found the place always cluttered, and it was often his job to remove items from the house to the garage, and when that space filled up, he would be directed to store things in the barn. Sometimes he would repair sections of scuffed or chipped drywall. He never knew whether this was in preparation for an inspection by social agencies, but there were periods of intense activity to spruce up the place. Of course, Guy would often be right beside Stephen to lend a hand. After a while, Stephen earned a good reputation as a dependable person, so Diane also hired him to take Guy to bowling on Saturdays when she was away during the winter, an arrangement that continued for several years. "He was a good bowler," Stephen told police. "He got some strikes and spares in."

Stephen got to know Guy well in all the time he spent with him. Stephen explained that Guy wasn't someone who would volunteer information easily. "If you asked him, 'Guy, do you have any problems?' he'd say 'No,'" Stephen told jurors. "But if you asked him a specific question like, 'Guy, does your knee hurt?' he would answer truthfully." Even then, Guy never wanted to get in trouble or break the rules, so if a trusted person told him to keep something a secret, then he likely would, without necessarily understanding whether it was right to withhold that information from others. Stephen described Guy as a people pleaser, someone who genuinely wanted to help others and could be counted on if asked for help. "He would follow 99.9 percent of your direction all of the time," Stephen told police. If Guy was told to get ready for bed, he would get into his pyjamas and go to bed without complaint. If he were asked to take the recycling to the end of the driveway, he would do exactly as you told him, exactly the way he was instructed. Guy knew what was safe and what wasn't, according to Stephen. He knew not to cross the road because his vision was poor. He knew not to enter the area around the old cistern because it was dangerous.

"Would he play around the cistern?" Crown Attorney Shea asked Stephen at the inquest.

"Absolutely not," he replied. "He knew he wasn't supposed to be there. And once he was told to do something, he wouldn't do it."

"So how can you explain the fact that he was found in the cistern?"

"The only possible explanation to me is that he was asked to go there," Stephen concluded.

Stephen watched Keri grow from a troubled teen into a troubled adult. He helped at the dance studio Karen allegedly bought for her until Keri's mismanagement led to its demise, and he alleged Keri would steal money from Karen. Stephen feigned surprise when Keri lost her licence due to impaired driving. "She did drink a little. I think she drank to cover her anger," Stephen speculated, pointing to the tragedy of losing her father at such a young age. But Stephen typically kept his head down and focused on the job of looking after the vulnerable residents, noting that Karen would call him in to do so even if Keri was home. Stephen was there when Karen got sick and was perplexed as to why Choices saw fit to allow her to continue looking after Guy and David, even after she was forced to step down from the board of directors and all the foster children were removed from the home. "Why weren't they [Choices] doing more then? If they were concerned about her [Karen's] role in the organization, where was their concern about the people in the home?"

After Karen died, Keri fired all the helpers, including Stephen, who had been a presence in the house for over a decade and even looked after her when she was just a teenager. Frank, a long-time family friend and former president of the Choices board of directors, visited the Santor house after Karen's funeral. Despite their history, Keri refused to let him past the front door. It was a stark departure from their previous interactions, where Frank was always welcomed into the home. He attempted to visit a few more times, but Keri refused to come to the door, leaving him feeling rejected and confused. Stephen also went to the Santor farm to offer his condolences. "Keri, I'd like you to know I am here to help you." He was met at the door by Keri's boyfriend. "You are no longer needed here," the man muttered before shutting the door. Months later, Keri called Stephen one night to ask if he could watch Guy, David, and Jennifer. Stephen declined. "I just didn't feel comfortable," he said. Keri screamed at him. "Keri was sometimes hard to talk to," Stephen began. "And when stuff didn't go her way, she would throw a little tiff."

Stephen continued to return to the Santor farm to take Guy to bowling on Saturdays, as per the separate arrangement he had with Diane. But Keri wouldn't let him in the house. One time, he made it as far as the front door before Keri called out for him to stay there. Stephen didn't think anything of it at the time. "I just thought he was organized and ready to go," he suggested. "But I did smell bleach."

7.

THE NEIGHBOUR

"I feel so guilty," Susan whispered on the stand at the inquest. Her raspy voice was barely audible through stifled emotion. She sniffled, holding a worn tissue to her nose as her face contorted into an expression of pained mournfulness.

"No," Dr. Stanborough replied. "I think you've done more than what most people would have done." The statement was delivered matter-of-factly to provide comfort and reassurance, but it also highlighted a troubling realization about how an average person would have reacted if they were in Susan's position.

"I should have thought more about the people in the house," she responded pensively, lost in thoughts of what might have happened if things had played out differently.

"I think your actions were quite commendable," Dr. Stanborough offered.

ooooo

Susan's relationship with the Santor family began and ended with death. A plainspoken woman with a folksy accent and long brown hair streaked with strands of white, she had a charming rural quality about her. She is an avowed animal lover and self-described "tree hugger." Susan's fifty-acre farm bordered the Santor property, their houses separated by a few subdivided lots at the road, but there were clear lines of sight from the back fields. She moved there on a whim in the early 1990s to start a horse boarding business that eventually grew to over thirty horses.

In the area, relationships between neighbours tended to develop slowly over time even if both parties were welcoming and hospitable. "If someone comes knocking, it's actually considered rude to make someone get up and come to the door," Susan explained. "People assume you're either a salesman or you're lost." But Susan made an effort to be friendly with her neighbours and developed a reputation as someone who could be counted on to lend a hand in times of need.

Susan learned early on from other neighbours and her own experience that the Santors were a family that preferred to keep to themselves, which wasn't necessarily an uncommon trait in those parts, but it ultimately meant they were disconnected from the local community. A few friendly words might be exchanged from time to time, but that was it. According to another long-time neighbour, the Santors allegedly told people not to bother them, perhaps because they had safety concerns for their wards or because they valued their privacy. Susan was from a small town where nobody locked their doors and everybody knew one another's business, so this kind of intentional isolation struck her as rather odd, especially in a rural farm setting where functional relationships with neighbours are sometimes a necessary lifeline.

On July 10, 2010, scorching temperatures ushered in a blanket of hot, humid air that made southern Ontario feel like a bayou bordering the Gulf of Mexico.[34] While people scurried to air-conditioned spaces or splashed in backyard pools, farm animals baked in paddocks or super-heated barns that were transformed into giant ovens. At the time, the Santors' long-term helper Peggy was still boarding horses on the farm. One of the horses was dying after an attempt by Peggy's husband to forcibly rehydrate it, and the practicalities of how to dispose of the body was what drew Susan to the property. Earlier, Peggy came by Susan's house to use the phone to call a veterinarian. "I heard her phone several vets who refused to come, and I knew what that meant," Susan recalled, suspecting the property had developed a poor reputation among the small number of veterinary clinics in the area. Susan called a trusted vet herself who agreed to come out. Susan's husband later drove their tractor the short distance down Jerseyville Road to the Santors'. Waiting at the

Santor property were a veterinarian who euthanized the horse, a police officer who was there to resolve a verbal altercation between Keri and Peggy, an officer from the SPCA, and Karen Santor.

It seemed to Susan that Karen was someone who was used to being in charge. But on that day, it was clear that the Santors weren't experienced horse owners. "They didn't seem to know much about caring for horses," she concluded. After the animal was buried rather unceremoniously, Susan proceeded into the barn. "The state of the barn was horrific," she recalled. She observed the Santor ponies had not seen a farrier in months, their hooves having grown to distorted proportions that caused pain and eventually would have led to lameness. One of the ponies was elderly and completely blind. Susan helped draw water from the old cistern to water the horses, but just two days later, a second horse was euthanized, and the SPCA seized the final horse belonging to Peggy. The Santor ponies remained in the barn with an SPCA compliance order that required them to meet certain standards of care. Susan offered to take in the remaining ponies, but the Santors refused. Seized by her concern for the ponies, Susan returned to the Santor property that December under the guise of offering Christmas presents so she could check on the animals. As she descended the driveway after dropping off the presents, she veered off to peek in the barn where she discovered the ponies lacked water and food. Keri witnessed the detour and later drove over to scold Susan for looking in the barn. Susan could handle herself in a confrontation, but there was something about Keri, a scrappiness mixed with volatility, that Susan found intimidating, so she stayed away.

For eight months, there was no communication between the neighbours, although Susan would occasionally monitor the property from afar. This continued until August 2011 when Keri unexpectedly arrived at Susan's doorstep to inform her that her mother had passed away and requested to borrow a lawn mower. Susan obliged, and when her husband went to collect the mower, which hadn't been returned a few days later, he met Guy and David sitting idly on the front steps. Keri answered the door, but her words were drowned out by screaming and banging coming from somewhere behind her. "That's just Jennifer," Keri allegedly said as toys started flying down the stairs. "She gets locked in her room when she has meltdowns but must have gotten out. I have to go check on her." Between the declining state of the property and fresh concerns about what her husband witnessed, Susan grew increasingly concerned about the situation at the Santor property.

A few days after the mower was returned, Susan visited the Santor farm and was shocked to discover the state of the barn and animals. Empty food and water dishes, huge piles of manure, and both ponies covered in burrs indicated a serious lack of regular grooming and general care. One of the ponies was blind and wandered aimlessly in the muddy paddock while another was kept tied up in its stall. Susan made her way up to the house and knocked on the door.

"Yes?" Keri answered.

"Hi, I was just stopping by to see how everything is going and if you might need some help with the horses?" Susan asked gently.

"Nope, we're good," Keri shot back.

"Are you sure?" Susan began, trying her best to contain her anguish. "I noticed they haven't been out in the field much. I just stopped by the barn and saw they're out of water and could use a brushing."

"Really, we're fine. We don't need any help," Keri bristled, closing the door.

Over the next few days, Susan noticed the horses still weren't out in the pasture. It gnawed at her, the knowledge that just a few hundred yards away there were animals that needed her care and attention. Eventually, her concern got the better of her, and she crept back onto the Santor property to peek in the barn. Nothing had changed. The horses were still standing in piles of manure with no food and no water. She rushed back to her own farm, desperately grabbing armfuls of hay and buckets of water to provide to the ponies. Later, she lodged a complaint with the SPCA.

Vivian, the SPCA officer who attended the property, concluded the ponies were not in immediate danger, a determination due in part to Susan's sustained intervention with supplies from her own farm. It was an untenable trade-off for Susan: leave the ponies to suffer from neglect so the SPCA could bear witness or continue providing emergency food and water thereby artificially improving their presentation. Before leaving, however, the officer put a compliance order in place that, if contravened, would result in the immediate seizure of any animals found to be in a state of neglect. Vivian testified at the inquest about her interaction with Keri, stating, "I discussed with her at length her ability to care for the existing children [sic] in the home and the animals. I told her I believed she was overwhelmed and encouraged her to think about placing the ponies in new homes." Keri rejected any claims she was unable to shoulder all her responsibilities and emphasized the importance of the ponies to her adopted sister, Jennifer, and her continued well-being.

Vivian later made an unannounced visit and discovered the compliance order was not being followed. She issued Keri a stern warning. "I warned her of the Ontario SPCA order she received and if she failed to comply could result in the removal of her animals, as well as possible charges." Keri deflected, complaining about Susan entering the property, but Vivian had heard it all before. "I told her it was her responsibility to supply the ponies with appropriate food and water, and that I should not be attending her address to find them without proper care."

Susan was equally undeterred. She kept returning regularly until one day when Keri caught her going into the barn. Keri went back inside and called the police to report Susan trespassing. She told the police she worried Susan might be overfeeding the ponies. A police officer showed up at Susan's house the next morning to advise her not to trespass on the Santor property. But it didn't stop her. She kept showing up every day with food and water, lodging complaint after complaint with the SPCA. When Keri put a lock on the barn door, Susan enlisted a friend of small stature to slide underneath the door to secure video evidence of the lack of food and water before tending to the animals against the SPCA compliance order. When Vivian made another unannounced visit, she discovered the barn door locked. Keri gave her the code, but when Vivian returned a few days later, she found a new lock on the door, and no one answered the door at the house.

This continued for another month until October 2011 when Susan called police to report she could hear the Santor ponies screaming, a high-pitched squeal horses make when they are particularly distressed. Police attended the barn to discover the ponies without hay or water standing in filthy stalls. Keri told police she fed them earlier, despite evidence to the contrary. The SPCA was then called in, and Vivian noted, "I entered the barn and found the ponies' water buckets completely empty and no hay was provided nor was I able to observe any reminisce [sic] of hay in amongst the manure to indicate they had been fed recently. I took pictures and proceeded to give them food and water. While feeding the ponies they continually called out as I approached them with hay. This left me to believe the ponies were left without food and water for an extended period of time." Vivian decided to lay animal cruelty charges against Keri and seized the ponies, who were relocated to an animal rescue organization. Two emaciated dogs remained on the property, which resulted in another SPCA compliance order to ensure their well-being.

Vivian documented the resulting exchange she had with Keri, which was highly illustrative of Keri's deceptive approach to dealing with those who challenged her. "At approximately 5:11 p.m. I drove to the house and met with K. SANTOR who signed the surrender form. I explained to her and told her she left me with no other choice but to remove the ponies as I had found them again to be without food or water. I further told her I believed the complainant [Susan] was truthful and that on several of my visits, I myself found the ponies to be without food or water and had to supply it myself. I continued to tell her that I had given her the benefit of the doubt and felt sorry for her and that on occasion I felt she was being harassed, but now believe she failed to care for the ponies properly. SANTOR told me she attended the barn this morning at 6:00 a.m. I told her I did not believe she had attended the barn since I called her yesterday to come to the barn and fill Frosty's [one of the ponies] water bucket. SANTOR reports she is afraid to go to the barn and since I would not tell her who the informant was she could only attend twice daily. I told her I believed she was using the neighbours as an excuse and if she was not going to the barn more than twice a day she should have supplied the ponies with a lot more food and water than what they had and that I would not be attending the address to care for the animals. I cautioned her and told her she failed to supply proper standards of care to her animals and that I would continue to monitor the address and if I found her dogs losing weight or not being cared for properly they too would be removed. SANTOR started to cry and stated she had others to care for and returned inside her home and shut the door."

Vivian attended the property later and found one of two border collies tied up in the backyard out of reach of a water dish, noting, "I identified the dog as Sara and could see she did not have any food or water nor were there any bowls to indicate she did have any. I could see she was thin and proceeded to feed her. When I approached with the water container, she continued to walk on her hind legs as it she was trying to reach the water. Once I placed the water in front of her she continued to drink for a four (4) minute period non-stop." Vivian confiscated the dog but was unable to locate the other dog on the property or neighbouring properties.

Susan's initial concern was for the animals. As an equine expert, the proper care of horses was her bailiwick. She knew what animal neglect and abuse looked like and she spent her professional life caring for horses and teaching others how to care for them. But she knew nothing about the proper care and treatment of people with developmental disabilities, other than what her gut told her what was right or wrong. But there were other things that disturbed her too. One time, Susan went to the Santor house, and there was no answer and no car in the driveway. When she turned to leave, she spotted David in the window. It seemed he was home alone in the middle of the day and he didn't seem like the kind of person who should be left unsupervised. Another time, Susan happened to be there when Guy and David arrived home on the DARTS bus, but they wouldn't go inside until Keri allowed them. "She [Keri] told me that they had to ask permission to go into the house and that they're not allowed to answer the door," Susan testified at the inquest. "I guess that's why I assumed Keri wasn't home the time they were home alone because she may have rules about answering the door when no one else was home." Then there was the drinking. With a clear line of sight between their properties, Susan noticed Keri had plenty of outdoor bonfire parties. When approaching the house, Susan had seen empty beer bottles strewn on the ground near the front door, and one morning she arrived to find Keri drinking beer on the front porch.

Susan didn't know much about the people who lived in the house, but she did know the Santors took care of various adults and children with disabilities. Concerned about what appeared to be a deteriorating situation since Karen died, Susan started making calls and taking notes, a tenacious if accidental advocate propelled by a strong suspicion that something was wrong. She decided she needed to let the authorities know what she had seen, trusting they would do something about it. But who were the authorities for Guy and David? "I didn't really understand the different organizations. I just felt I should be ringing some bells," she stated at the inquest. She called the SPCA about the animals. She called the CAS about Jennifer. She eventually called Choices, but only after a bit of a runaround since it wasn't clear which agency was responsible for Guy and David. She even called police when one day she heard shots fired in the vicinity of the Santor property. An officer arrived to find the front door unlocked and nobody home. The officer discovered squalid conditions inside the house with cigarette butts and empty beer bottles littering the floor and dirty clothes scattered throughout. The missing border collie, now frail and unkempt, was located locked in a filthy room with no water.

Susan was there another time in October 2011 with a police officer to help provide water to the dogs, which they drew from the old cistern together. Covering the opening was a single flimsy piece of plywood with a handle screwed into it that they both agreed was unsafe. Susan had a cistern on her own property with a solid concrete lid that needed at least two people to lift out for safety purposes. "When we went to put the cistern lid back on, it barely caught the edges," she explained at the inquest. "If you put any pressure on it, it would fall right into the cistern. So, we decided to turn it cockeyed so it would catch better on the edges." Susan was aware of the cistern since the first time she stepped onto the Santor property for the horses but didn't realize until now just how dangerous it was, especially to the vulnerable residents who lived there. The police officer may have noted the dangerous cistern opening, but never mentioned it in their notes despite the existence of a 2010 municipal bylaw requiring cisterns to be properly secured by a fence with a warning sign, neither of which were present.[35] Regardless, Susan decided to call Choices on October 11 to notify them about the cistern lid. She left a voice mail and later spoke with Sylvia, the manager of associate living. "The purpose of my call was about the cistern lid, but I also mentioned about the fella [David] being there alone, which seemed to be of concern now that I realized that they were developmentally challenged, and they probably shouldn't be home alone as far as I was concerned."

Susan told anyone who would listen what she had seen, including her concerns about the state of the home and the care of its vulnerable residents. "I didn't expect I would be kept in any sort of loop. I was trying to make sure that I described the situation with enough strength that they would pursue it and someone would actually visit the house and ensure everything was okay," she testified.

So, when Susan heard sirens and saw flashing blue and red lights coming from the Santor property one April evening in 2012, she thought maybe somebody finally decided to do something about the vulnerable residents who lived there. Even in her worst nightmare, she couldn't possibly have imagined they were there to recover a dead body and a team of forensic specialists were already trying to piece together what happened. Susan wandered down to the property and started talking to a woman who turned out to be a local reporter who published their conversation. When Susan's name and picture appeared in the newspaper the next day, online comments pegged her as the nosy neighbour and how awful it was for people like her to be so intrusive in a police investigation of a tragic death. "It was just so crazy and upsetting for me to hear this because without somebody sticking their nose in, God knows what else might have happened," she concluded, adding that she wasn't the only person concerned about what was happening at the Santor farm, despite her being the only one to act on it. "People don't get involved, but you should know your neighbour and if they're safe. Hopefully, what happened to Guy will make people think twice about someone who is vulnerable. You know, it takes a village to take care of people."

ooooo

Despite her experience, which she described as the failure of every oversight body including the police, Susan still believed in the power of institutions and government to do good. "I have faith in what the institutions are designed to do, but the people who run them are really the key in terms of whether you have honest and competent people or not," she later concluded. But it wasn't enough to ease her feeling that she could have done more.

"I feel guilty," Susan cried to the police detective who questioned her in the days following Guy's death, dabbing her swollen eyes with tissue.

"Why do you feel guilty?" asked the detective.

"I feel like I didn't pay enough attention at the house. I was so focused on the animals."

"You made calls though. I think you acted reasonably."

"I don't," she shot back. "The boy died. And I knew that cistern wasn't safe. I was willing to trespass to feed the animals, but not to see if the cistern was covered properly. I've gotta live in my own skin, right?"

"I know this is upsetting. Somebody died."

"Three horses had to die before we rescued the other one. Now this boy had to die before someone decided it's not safe for them to live there. That just seems wrong."

8.

THE SUPPORT WORKER

"How can you explain the fact that two days later there is an overwhelming stench that was not there on April 27 when you were last there?" Crown Attorney Shea questioned Choices support worker, Jennifer, on the witness stand. As the front-line worker responsible for overseeing the homesharing arrangement, it was Jennifer's job to ensure the Santor home was a safe and healthy place for Guy to live. As the last worker inside the home before his death, her testimony promised to shed light on the situation in those final critical hours.

"I'm not sure why," Jennifer shrugged. She was a young woman with an angular face and long blonde braid who sat with her legs and arms crossed tightly as though her entire body were braided together. "If I had smelled something I obviously would have addressed it. But I didn't smell anything out of the ordinary." She spoke quickly with a slight lisp, a high-strung sort of person with a squirrelly energy producing rapid-fire responses that almost comically outpaced her questioners.

"I find it so incredibly astounding that someone could not smell something that two days later was knocking people off their feet," Shea marvelled sardonically. "There was obviously an accumulation over time of feces, vomit, and urine. How could you not detect that within the home?"

"I didn't smell anything," Jennifer responded, a defensive tone creeping into her voice. "It's a very large house. If I smelled anything, I would have reported it immediately."

ooooo

Jennifer was the last in a long line of support workers Choices tasked with overseeing the homesharing arrangement between Guy and the Santor family. Unlike a group home with round-the-clock staffing, Jennifer acted as a resource liaison between the agency, client, and home provider. It was her job to ensure the placement was operating effectively and act as the first point of contact with the agency. There were monthly visits, quarterly meetings with day-program staff, annual inspections, checklists, forms, policies, and procedures to follow. The aim was to offer a system of checks and balances in the absence of day-to-day supervision, one that was flexible to the needs of the client and home provider with the goal of supporting a family-home environment that was more natural than group-home living. Early in the development of the home-sharing program, Choices decided to prioritize the privacy and needs of the home provider. Surveillance, including unannounced visits, were seen as an infringement of homeowners' rights and ran counter to the idea of a natural home setting, which might scare away potential home providers. Workers like Jennifer, then, were taught to be nonintrusive and provide a basic level of support to ensure all parties were happy with the home-sharing arrangement.

Home providers like Karen and later, Keri, signed a contract that was renewed each year in conjunction with the annual inspection. Home providers were treated as independent contractors hired by Choices to fulfill certain obligations at a per diem rate of $41, including an extra 1.17 days per month that could be used to pay an approved respite provider, normally Choices' own limited network of group homes or casual home providers. Home providers were fully reimbursed for any days the home sharer — the person in their care — spent with family. As outlined in the Choices standard home-provider contract, other obligations included

> 1. The Provider will provide each Homesharer the best possible care, skill-based training and opportunities for personal development in a method that is as non-intrusive and non-threatening as possible. Providers will

support this process by respecting the dignity, value and individuality of the Homesharer.

2. The Provider will participate in the Person Centered Planning process for the ongoing development of the Homesharer and will strictly adhere to the implementation requirements of any programs developed for the purposes of supporting the Homesharer.
3. The Provider will seek out and arrange for appropriate support for each individual in collaboration with the Choices support staff for scheduled respite and vacation days. The Provider will only use Choices approved Respite Providers.
4. The Provider will inform Choices support staff as far in advance as possible of any stays outside of the Provider's home, including details of where the Homesharer is staying and for how long.
5. The Provider will be responsible for food, housing, and household operation, safety, laundry costs, normal wear and tear and depreciation of appliances; personal care and toilet articles, such as soap, shampoo and toothpaste and normal family transportation costs.
6. The Provider will not engage in residential supports, also to include rental agreements, with any other person/agency without first receiving the written approval of Choices. Choices reserves the right to deny approval or rescind approval at its discretion.

In exchange, Choices promised to support home providers in becoming and remaining familiar with all necessary regulations by providing training and ensuring support staff conduct monthly meetings and maintain regular contact for any issues that arise in relation to the agreement. Termination of the contract was also clearly outlined, leaving little room for interpretation:

1. Choices may terminate this Contract for Associate Living Support Services at any time without written notice if sufficient cause exists to believe the care and/or treatment the Homesharer is receiving in the home does not warrant the Homesharer remaining.

2. Choices may terminate this Contract for Associate Living Support Services, at its discretion, for any reasonable grounds (such as repeated non-compliance of the Associate Living Provider Responsibilities or loss of funding for the Homesharer). In this circumstance, thirty days written notice will be provided to the Homesharer/Guardian and the Associate Living Provider.

3. Either the Homesharer or Provider may terminate this contract with thirty days written notice provided to all other parties to this agreement.

Karen renewed her contract in December 2010 prior to her illness, and it's uncertain whether a valid contract existed between August 2011 and December 2011 when Choices allowed Keri to take over, but she did sign an identical contract with Choices in January 2012 at the annual inspection.

But, as would later become clear, there was a significant disconnect at the Santor home between what happened on paper with support workers and what actually occurred. The Santors understood the role support workers played in the home-share program better than anyone, but it appeared they seemed to resent the intrusion of workers in their home. As a co-founder of the agency, Karen might have felt such support was unnecessary or that it didn't apply to them given her knowledge of the process and her oversight position on the board of directors. A former support worker stated they found it difficult to work with Karen and noted her predecessors also had problems dealing with her. Another worker stated home visits with Karen were often cancelled. "Home visits are so infrequent it is very hard to give a thorough evaluation," the worker wrote. "The residents attend our day program and sometimes this is the only way we know how they are."[36] As to the reason for the cancellations, the worker commented, "mostly they all seem legitimate," adding that a significant conflict of interest existed trying to ensure compliance with any policies given the role the Santors played in executive positions within the organization.[37] The worker observed they had never contacted on-call support staff, and any emergencies or situations that came up tended to follow different backchannels instead of normal policies and procedures. "They tend to take care of their own difficulties," the worker concluded. In response to the question, "Do the home providers follow Familyhome policies and procedures?" the worker placed a question mark with no additional commentary.

This indifference to support workers was an established practice by the time Karen became sick and appeared to continue with Keri after her mother died. Karen was a highly experienced caregiver and trained special-needs educator whose legendarily assertive personality and role as a founder provided her with a level of unparalleled authority and influence at Choices. But Keri held no advisory or employment role at Choices, had no special education training, no background in social work or developmental services, and was allegedly unable to support herself, as made apparent by unpaid fines and bills, and a suspended driver's licence. Despite this, there was little pushback when she repeatedly rescheduled or cancelled home visits or failed to show up to important meetings and training sessions. In the six months prior to Karen falling ill and Keri effectively taking over responsibility for the residents, there appeared to be only one complete monthly home visit and several cancellations, including one day in May 2011 when Jennifer was turned away at the front door because Karen forgot about a visit that was rescheduled four times. When Jennifer returned two weeks later in June, she noted, "Karen not ready for home visit. Financials not completed since February . . . House unkempt. Karen sleeping when staff arrived for home visit." Ten days later, some of the foster children were removed from the home by the CAS after Karen forgot to give them their medications. A few days later, Jennifer arrived for a home visit and noted, "Karen not at home when staff arrived. A woman, Carla, was watching Guy and David. Guy's clothes were dirty." Jennifer informed her supervisors of the incident, all of whom were aware of the fact CAS had removed foster children from the home. But since neither Guy nor David took any medications, Jennifer was instructed to simply book another home visit.

This pattern dramatically escalated when Keri took over. Between June 2011 and April 2012, she cancelled or rescheduled approximately twenty times, and Jennifer was only inside the home to conduct a monthly visit six times during that period. Sometimes there were excuses, the variety of which seemed too random to be true. Food poisoning due to bad sushi. Stomach flu. Miscommunication about an impromptu visit to the disability benefit office. Misremembered scheduled visit times. Injuries that required hospital visits. An injured cat that required surgery. Schedule conflicts. Medical appointments. A grandmother who had a stroke. Another (or the same) grandmother who died. More often, it seemed there was no excuse at all. Getting in touch with Keri often meant several calls, emails, and text messages. Sometimes her voice mail was completely full. During one weeklong stretch in mid-December 2011, days went by with Guy and David absent from the day program and Keri unreachable with the home phone off the hook and her cellphone turned off. Apparently, everyone in the house was sick. Unscheduled visits, as it would become apparent, were not performed as a matter of policy to protect the privacy of home providers, an expectation Keri became very adept at exploiting. When a staff member dropped off Guy and David at home the following week, it was noted that "the house was a mess; paperwork everywhere." Keri requested to delay the annual inspection, which was granted, then subsequently rescheduled four more times.

The consensus among Choices management was that Keri was a grieving daughter who had undertaken an enormous workload, and her willingness to look after Guy and David meant front-line workers, such as Jennifer and other day-program staff, should endeavour to work with her to become a more successful home provider. Keri later indicated she had requested more training in her onboarding as a home provider, but she never showed up to mandated home-provider training sessions despite being repeatedly provided the opportunity to do so. In fact, when Jennifer emailed Keri about a mandatory training session in April 2012, she used bold font because of Keri's history of skipping meetings when it was her responsibility to attend regularly. Keri didn't attend that session either, and there weren't any consequences for not showing up. All this meant that Keri did not receive sufficient scrutiny, beginning with the ill-fated decision to grandfather her in as the home provider and continuing with a laissez-faire approach to enforcing certain policies when dealing with the Santors.

Caught between a lack of effective intervention from management and a litany of excuses from Keri, Jennifer was put in an unenviable position, forced to reconcile whatever feelings she may have had about the situation with the limited tools she was given to rectify the problems she was witnessing. It was a position many front-line workers in social services come up against and that lead so many towards burnout and dissociation from their work, a heavy cloud of mismanagement overshadowing the realities faced in the field. Jennifer's response to the inaction of her superiors was to simply do her best within the restricted parameters of her role even when her actions defied logic or even basic common sense. Given the gaps between home visits, when they did occur, Jennifer would take the opportunity to sign off on multiple months at once. "I know I did a home visit every month, even if it was done at the beginning of the next month," she testified at the inquest. Her evaluation of her own records was nonsensical as it revealed sign-offs for monthly reports were frequently one or two months overdue with multiple months signed off on the same date after repeated cancellations. Sometimes Guy was present at these mandatory visits, sometimes he wasn't, with Keri informing Jennifer about things that should have come from Guy's mouth.

During her visits, Jennifer utilized a monthly report form that was specifically created to gather precise, real-time information about the home-share arrangement. This information was then used to provide feedback to the organization as a component of the person-centred planning process. The day program had a monthly balance sheet of expenses drawn from Guy's disability benefit cheques and a detailed chart of daily activities accompanied by copious notes observing his behaviour, attendance, participation level, and any incidents. Jennifer was similarly required to fill out a detailed monthly report form noting any incidents, goals, accomplishments, changes in health status, home provider concerns, and support worker follow-up responsibilities, including a monthly accounting of expenses drawn against Guy's account. The form was prepopulated with some typewritten answers that corresponded to quarterly updates to his person-centred plan with spaces for additional comments. While the day-program reports told a fairly complete story about how Guy was getting on there, the home-share reports left much to be desired, with just a few supplementary notes indicating the report had been filled out.

Meetings at the Santor house always took place in the dining room, a straight line from the front door and through the hallway. Jennifer never checked to see what was in the refrigerator or cupboards, or tried the faucets to see if they worked, or if the toilets flushed. According to her training, that would have been an invasion of the home provider's privacy. In fact, none of these items were even checked at the annual inspection, also performed by Jennifer, an event scheduled well in advance at the convenience of the home provider. This policy provided ample opportunity to stage the home to present an inaccurate version of what day-to-day living looked like, and the visits to the Santor house bore little resemblance to reality. A narrow section of the main floor became like a stage, its featured characters trotted out to perform the "monthly" ritual in spaces cleaned specifically for the visit. Jennifer rarely, if ever, left the dining table to investigate the rooms beyond the immediate area.

Annual inspections were a time for a more fulsome assessment of the property and home-sharing arrangement with a detailed checklist to fill out prior to renewing a home provider's contract. The inspection should have taken place at the beginning of December, but cancellations by Keri pushed it to the end of January. Instead of using a qualified third party or even a senior staff person to perform the inspection, Choices had the assigned support worker do it, even though the job involved assessing adequate ventilation, heating and electrical equipment, fire prevention (functioning smoke detectors and fire extinguishers), fuel storage, fire exits, and emergency preparedness. Jennifer testified that she received no training to do home inspections, only a briefing on the checklist and requirements.

The problematic procedures around the annual review process led one juror at the inquest to question Jennifer about the quality of her inspections. "You said the appliances were in working order, but you didn't look in the fridge?" the juror quizzed her regarding the kitchen section of the checklist that asked whether all appliances were in good working order.

"No," Jennifer responded.

"But you marked that you did."

"Yes."

"That doesn't seem right. And what qualifications do you have to examine heating and electrical equipment?"

"I just looked at it."

"That doesn't make any sense," the juror replied. The checklist required further inspection of the condition of wiring, including proper fusing, appliance cords, circuitry and receptacles, shut-off and safety switches, all of which received a check mark.

When asked if there was any impediment to conducting monthly inspections of the home, Jennifer replied, "It was just not something we were supposed to do."

The annual inspection report began by outlining concerns about Guy and David's hygiene, inadequate lunches, frequent absences, and communication issues. When Keri was informed of these concerns, she suggested that she would get "call waiting," as if that would help. Rather than investigating these issues further, Jennifer repeated the narrative that justified Keri taking over where Karen had left off, even though it appeared Karen had never expressed a desire or expectation to anyone for this to happen. "Keri has been in the home since Guy and David came into care and has grown up with them," Jennifer wrote in her report. "Guy and David seem to enjoy Keri as the home provider. Keri does have a lot on her plate. Both Guy and David are a part of this family, from outings and [illegible] to family gatherings. Keri tries to keep everything as normal as possible since the passing of Karen." Later, Jennifer offered some justification for Keri's poor performance as a home provider over the preceding five months. "Keri has been under a great deal of stress since the passing of her mother in Aug. Due to this there were missed home visits, concerns with Guy and David at WF [Westfield day program]."

The remainder of the inspection involved a checklist that seemed more like a box-ticking exercise than an attempt to address the issues regarding the home-share arrangement that were brought up in the opening remarks. For example, when asked "Is there appropriate and satisfactory communication/visits between Associate Living Provider, Homesharer and Associate Living Support Staff?" Jennifer checked "Yes." She also checked "Yes" to Keri following all policies and procedures, offering no caveats to this assertion. She wrote "N/A" in response to whether there was a woodstove despite the featured presence of a gigantic fireplace in the centre of the house that was used regularly. The report also indicated that Keri lacked a valid first aid and CPR certificate. Apparently, Keri practised fire exit plans with the residents, though no evidence exists to indicate that ever happened. The floors throughout the house were given a pass as being clean and free of any hazards, particularly tripping hazards. And amazingly, Jennifer marked "Yes" to the statement "furnishings and housekeeping standards shall be such that a Familyhome presents a comfortable, clean and orderly appearance," something contradicted by her own assessment of the home in various case notes.

There were times when Jennifer commented on the fact that the home appeared unkempt, but no action was taken to hold Keri accountable. "There are so many red flags with her," Jennifer privately confessed to her coworker in a series of texts presented at the inquest. Following the cancellation of yet another scheduled annual inspection date, there were allegations Keri drunk dialled another home provider at 3 a.m., an allegation the home provider later denied. Jennifer testified that she never saw evidence that Keri may have had a drinking problem, though did admit there were times she presented as very tired and dishevelled. In one text chain, Jennifer wrote that Keri had cancelled yet another home visit apparently because her family had been visiting for the past month. "I know that's bullshit," she wrote. Another time, Jennifer noted the Santor house was extremely cold, but Keri had an excuse at the ready. Apparently, the fireplace backed up, so she had to open all the windows. If it seemed strange to Jennifer that all the windows had been opened, effectively airing out the house immediately preceding a scheduled home visit, she didn't mention it in her notes or on the witness stand. Nor did she mention whether the house smelled of wood smoke, a distinct scent that would have most certainly lingered even if a window was opened.

Crown Attorney Shea interrogated Jennifer about her failure to submit a serious occurrence report regarding Keri. Shea raised a hypothetical scenario, asking Jennifer if, as a teacher or educational assistant, she would consider a child arriving at school smelling of urine, with feces under their fingernails, and inadequate lunches. "Wouldn't that fit the definition of neglect?" Shea asked.

"Yes," Jennifer replied.

"So why wasn't a serious occurrence report filled out?"

Jennifer stated that they were attempting to address the issue with Keri before resorting to filing a report. Shea mentioned that the board of directors received copies of all serious occurrence reports each month to keep them informed about any issues. Had Jennifer and her managers adhered to the established protocol and promptly submitted a serious occurrence report to the Ministry of Community and Social Services, there might have been a quicker intervention. The act of filing a formal report had the potential to trigger required actions, and the board of directors could have stepped in earlier if they had been informed about the situation through such a submission. Regrettably, due to Jennifer and her managers' failure to follow this procedure, Choices missed an opportunity to address the situation sooner, possibly preventing additional harm to the vulnerable residents at the Santor home.

Finally, a red flag surfaced that caused Choices management to begin to seriously consider terminating their contract with Keri. One day, Jennifer received a voice mail on her work phone from a loan company asking for Keri. Jennifer called back, advising it was against policy to share any personal information over the phone, then looked up the company and discovered it was a payday loan firm that typically preyed on people in dire financial straits. To qualify for a loan, Keri would have to prove her income and place of employment; she must have misrepresented herself as an employee of Choices despite her contract as a home provider clearly indicating she was not. Further, the $41 per diem she received from Choices was for reimbursement of expenses for Guy and David, not a wage for Keri to claim as her own income to qualify for a loan. Families who applied to become home providers were assessed for their financial stability, a process Keri never went through, and there was no evidence to suggest Keri earned income outside of whatever her mother's estate may have disbursed to her. Financial records for Karen's estate later revealed her account to be highly overdrawn in late 2011 with numerous charges for insufficient funds. The only deposited income came from Choices for Guy and David. It wasn't long before collection agencies started sending threatening letters to Keri.

Jennifer told her managers about the voice mail, which prompted an emergency meeting. They decided that this was the last straw. After months of problems, they started to develop plans to permanently remove the men from the home. But even with ample evidence to demonstrate Keri was unfit to be a home provider — including repeated violations of her contract responsibilities with Choices, an unprecedented number of home visit cancellations, lack of communication, and months of reports from the day program indicating serious concerns about Guy's and David's hygiene, inadequate lunches, and frequent absences, including more than half of March — a senior manager in charge of the associate-living program decided they would use the emergency meeting not to cancel the home-share arrangement with Keri, but to "open up dialogue." The meeting was scheduled for April 20, 2012, but Keri failed to show up. It was rescheduled for May 4. Until then, it was business as usual. On Friday April 27, 2012, around 2 p.m., Jennifer arrived at the Santor house for the monthly visit. It had been rescheduled a few times like so many visits that preceded it, and it happened to fall on a day when Guy was with his mother attending a bowling league dance. Although home visits required all home sharers to be present, Jennifer met with only David and Keri. Walking in the front door, Jennifer looked to the left to view the living room and proceeded down the hallway to the dining room where she could also see the kitchen. She observed nothing out of the ordinary, the house in its usual cluttered state and "normal" smell. "Every house has a different smell," she later testified. They sat down at the dining table and spent the next forty-five minutes filling out a checklist of questions. Jennifer noted David was in good spirits and participated in the conversation. Two months earlier, he was temporarily removed from the home for respite against Keri's wishes, possibly because she couldn't afford to lose the daily allowance that came from supporting him nor pay for respite with money she had already spent. While David was in respite, day-program staff reported he seemed well-rested, clean, and had proper lunch food, but when he returned to the Santor home, he presented as tired with strong body odour and inadequate lunches.

But according to Jennifer, everything seemed fine now. "I remember calling my manager afterwards and saying that was a really good visit," she exclaimed. The checklist included a review of the safety and security plan. Written in bold and underlined was "Guy needs to have close supervision at all times." Although Guy wasn't present at the home visit, Keri updated Jennifer on what he had been up to that month. His accomplishments included getting the gardens ready for spring, helping hide Easter eggs, and collecting branches for their campfires. There were concerns about his weight loss that required follow-up since he had little weight to lose on his lanky frame. Keri and Jennifer signed the checklist but left a blank spot for Guy, a line that would never be scratched in with his signature. It is uncertain whether Jennifer informed Keri about a developing plan to remove the men from the house the following week, though Keri must have been somewhat aware how her conduct jeopardized the home-sharing arrangements. Or maybe she was simply running out the clock before she was forced from her family's property. When Jennifer gathered up her paperwork and left the Santor house, it was with high hopes. She anticipated reuniting with everyone at the Santor residence after a week to resolve issues with Keri, oblivious to the fact that she would return to the farm within two days, under drastically different circumstances.

Jennifer knew about the old cistern. As early as September 2011, she identified the cistern opening as an area of concern if the lid wasn't properly secured. The horrible irony was her concern wasn't for humans but for cats. Jennifer had visited the Santor property in her capacity as a volunteer with a cat rescue agency. She and another volunteer were looking for the mother of kittens found in the barn when she came upon the old cistern. The plywood cover was in place, she testified, but the set-up gave her cause for concern. Amazingly, she failed to make the connection to the safety hazard it presented to the vulnerable residents she was responsible for monitoring.

"In September 2011 you knew the cistern existed, but in January 2012, you didn't feel it was appropriate to inspect the area?" Mr. Manishen asked Jennifer at the inquest in reference to her annual review, which did not include a section for assessing the property beyond the home.

"It was far away from the house," Jennifer answered.

"But you knew Guy went to the end of the driveway for the recycling and would have passed by the cistern on a regular basis."

Jennifer was unfazed. "It was farther away from the driveway, and Guy did what he was supposed to do and came back."

"But you also knew Guy couldn't be left unsupervised," Mr. Manishen reminded her.

"But it was covered," she retorted. "There was a piece of plywood."

Her answers were guarded and unemotional, lacking any acknowledgement of wrongdoing on her part or that of Choices; they were still her employer at the time of the inquest, although she had switched positions and was working in a group home. Hers was the story of so many who follow orders and are later forced to explain actions that can appear utterly indefensible to others. How could she not smell things others could barely stand? Not see red flags and act upon them immediately? Why would she continue to do things by the book when the book was so obviously deeply flawed? Immersed in the dysfunctional culture of the agency where she worked, Jennifer was guided by faulty policies and received direction that ran counter to reason, effectively prioritizing a homeowner's privacy over a vulnerable person's safety and dignity or identifying safety concerns for cats but not human beings. For people like Jennifer who work on the front lines in social services, it is often easier to follow orders than question the rules. It also takes their special knowledge and close attention to a person or situation to sound the alert when there are problems, but this closeness has drawbacks.

Jennifer knew that the arrangement with Keri had deteriorated, but she couldn't see it as neglect bordering on abuse because the situation had become normalized to her. The smell and clutter inside the home was normal. Guy and David's body odour was normal. The cancellations of mandatory visits were normal. It is a dangerous game when standards meant to protect the health and safety of vulnerable people are routinely ignored or passed off as "normal." For too many years, abhorrent conditions inside residential hospitals and the isolation of people with developmental disabilities from mainstream society were considered normal. That is, until people on the front lines, namely the parents of children with developmental disabilities and disability rights activists, helped the rest of us see that it was, in fact, cruel to allow vulnerable children and adults to live in a place that violated their dignity.

"What if a fresh set of eyes came in to do an inspection?" Dr. Stanborough mused.

"That would be a good idea," Jennifer agreed.

"If you saw a child who looked neglected or abused, what would you do?"

"Call the CAS."

"Why?"

"Because that's the appropriate place to go when you see a child like that," Jennifer said confidently.

"If you saw an animal that was neglected or abused, what would you do?"

"Call the SPCA."

"Why?"

"Because that's who we're supposed to call when we have issues with animals," she proclaimed.

"Right. A third-party agency that comes in that has certain powers."

So why didn't anyone reach out to the equivalent agency meant to protect Guy from neglect or abuse? Probably because no such third-party agency for vulnerable adults exists. No arms-length inspector to hold agencies and the government accountable for their actions and no advocate to protect the rights of vulnerable persons. Instead, front-line workers like Jennifer are simply expected to identify neglect or abuse and report it to their managers. The police have a role to play too, but it is ill-defined, and it is hard for workers to tell when to invite them into the internal workings of social service agencies. But what happens when an agency is unable to effectively respond to red flags, when its work environment is so toxic and dysfunctional that it pushes the organization into a state of crisis? Whose needs come first then?

9.

THE STAFF

"In one year, I had eleven different managers," testified Christina, one of the day-program staff who was employed by Choices and remembered the turmoil that frustrated her ability to protect clients like Guy from the clear and present danger of neglectful treatment they received at home. "It's different now, but back then it was a very autocratic workplace." Certain people, such as Karen Santor, were considered "untouchable," she said. "There would be recourse if you did speak out."

"What would happen if you brought an issue to management?" Mr. Manishen asked.

"It would get swept under the rug, and you might get written up," she sighed. "I was written up three times for expressing concerns about Guy and David's care."

"Are you aware of the photos produced as part of this inquest in regards to the conditions in which Guy, David, and Jennifer were living?" Crown Attorney Shea asked.

"I'm aware of the photos, yes," Christina replied, shuddering at the visual confirmation of the dysfunction she witnessed written daily about Guy's body and behaviour at the day program.

"As one of his primary support people, how did that make you feel?"

Christina swallowed hard, trying her best to stifle her emotions. "I regret I didn't, um, go to the police or call MCSS [Ministry of Community and Social Services]."

"If you as a worker weren't getting the response from management that you wanted, what would be your next step?" Shea asked.

"That would be it [go to police or MCSS]. But because of the culture of the agency at the time, people like Karen Santor were untouchable. You couldn't voice your concerns because you'd be penalized. People didn't want to lose their job, but they also couldn't not support people like Guy."

"After Karen died and people in your circle weren't getting what they needed from management, where would you go? What would you do if you didn't get the response from management?"

"The leadership team beyond the managers at that time was the same culture as Karen Santor and Hal Bushey. So, if managers went to their leadership team, they wouldn't get any answers or were disciplined for bringing up something nobody wants to talk about."

"Do you know why that is?"

"The multitude of people coming in were interim people. They were more focused on fact finding and dealing with immediate issues. They weren't people who were dedicated to the agency for the long term. But change doesn't happen overnight."

ooooo

Christina saw Guy nearly every day for a decade. She started at Choices in the day program in 2002 as a support worker working alongside four other full-time staff and a revolving door of part-timers. It was a good job for people who wanted to work in developmental services with a set schedule and have opportunities to work in a variety of settings. There were classrooms for individual and group programs, recreation and leisure activities with outings into the community for swimming and basketball, and a work program. Although Guy loved the work program in the Hut, he also cycled through the classroom and rec programs. Groups were big enough to require multiple staff to lead programs while managing behavioural issues, but also small enough for the support staff to get to know everyone well. To outsiders, it could appear quite chaotic with little sense of purpose or structure. It sometimes felt like that on the inside too, especially when there were staff shortages. The additional responsibility of overseeing several individuals with varying needs and little backup support led to high turnover and burnout rates.

To Christina, Guy was a constant source of positivity in an often-stressful day that began early and ended late in the afternoon. The job required a high level of patience, empathy, and compassion, traits that could be tested daily by many factors outside her control. A typical day could vary based on the program and client behaviours, but it tended to follow a certain pattern:

1. Arriving at the program site and preparing for the day, which might involve reviewing any individualized care plans or activity schedules, setting up equipment or materials for activities, and checking in with other staff members.
2. Greeting the participants as they arrive, helping them with any personal care needs, and assisting them with any mobility or transportation requirements.
3. Conducting group or individual activities designed to enhance their physical, emotional, cognitive, and social skills, such as arts and crafts, exercise routines, music therapy, cooking, and games.
4. Monitoring the participants to ensure their safety and well-being throughout the day, including supervising their interactions with one another, managing any challenging behaviours, and administering medication or other treatments as necessary.
5. Providing emotional support to participants who may be feeling anxious or upset, and communicating with families or caregivers about any concerns or updates.
6. Assisting with mealtimes and snack breaks, ensuring participants receive proper nutrition and hydration.
7. Cleaning up after activities, sanitizing equipment, and maintaining a safe and hygienic environment.

8. Documenting participant progress and behaviour, writing daily reports, and participating in staff meetings to discuss individual progress, challenges, and solutions.

9. Escorting participants to their transportation at the end of the day, ensuring they leave with their personal belongings and any necessary information for their caregivers or families.

Guy was usually the first person to greet Christina each morning and the last to wish her a goodnight. "What did you have for dinner?" he'd ask, bounding off the bus in the morning. Waiting to leave in the afternoon, he'd turn to her again. "What are you going to do tonight?" he would say and throw a parting high-five as he boarded the return ride to the Santor farm. The next morning, he'd ask how her previous evening went and how she was doing. Monday to Friday, 8 a.m. to 4 p.m., Christina worked with Guy for over ten years. At one point, she would even see him on Saturdays, picking him up at the Santors to take him to bowling. "I probably knew him better than anyone," she said, fighting back tears.

Christina knew Guy's wants and needs, likes and dislikes. "He loved to be out in the community. He loved to feel like he had a job. He felt like he was an office worker, always looking for papers and staplers and hole punches just to feel like he had an office job," she told the police. Every morning, Guy was eager to head out into the community or interact with people at the Hut. He would grab his backpack with purpose and set out as if on a mission to find something to do, eager to feel productive and useful. He was always scanning his environment for papers or anything else that he could use to simulate the feeling of being an office worker. Sometimes he would come across old radios, which he loved to take apart and inspect, as if searching for hidden secrets inside. Whenever he crossed paths with anyone, he would stop and eagerly share his latest findings or ask about their day. He spoke often about his mother and stepdad, telling slightly embellished stories about all the wonderful things they had done together. When his mother went to Florida, he would eagerly await her postcards, rushing to show Christina and anyone else who paid attention.

As the holiday season approached, he could hardly contain his excitement for the annual Christmas party thrown by his mother and stepfather. He would talk about it for weeks in advance, making sure everyone knew how much he was looking forward to the festivities. And during the summer months, he would retreat to Honey Harbour, a place that held a special meaning to him, where he could relax and enjoy the friends and neighbours of the area.

Christina recalled that Guy was friendly with everyone but also had a small group of friends at Choices. Guy would walk into his all-male classroom, hoping to catch sight of some familiar faces. He would quickly spot his friends and join them in a conversation about their shared interests. They all seemed to love the same activities — swimming, basketball, and walking down to the bayfront. Guy loved nothing more than spending time with his buddies. Being a natural helper, he consistently sought opportunities to assist others, whether it involved improving their swimming technique or passing the ball to a fellow teammate. His helpful nature didn't go unnoticed at Choices. Staff picked up on Guy's willingness to assist others, and he was often given extra tasks to complete. For Guy, these little jobs were just as important as participating in the recreational activities he loved so much. They allowed him to show his dedication and contribute to the group in his own unique way.

As a person with a developmental disability, Guy tended to become frustrated when anyone interrupted him. He would become intensely focused, his attention fixated on one thing alone. Christina had observed this countless times, and as a result, became an expert in anticipating Guy's meltdowns. Sometimes, even she couldn't prevent his outbursts. If he was left on one task for too long, like his "paperwork," he would erupt if someone tried to redirect him. Christina remembered a time when Guy was so absorbed in a task that not even personal injury could deter him. He had picked up something sharp, and before anyone knew it, blood was dripping down the walls. "He didn't even acknowledge that he was bleeding. And we said, 'Guy, you're bleeding! Let's take care of this. Let's do first aid.'" When Christina and others tried to take care of his wound, Guy became even angrier because he couldn't complete the task he had started. When something caught his attention, Guy couldn't easily be diverted.

If Guy wasn't given enough time to answer a question, he would get upset. It wasn't that he didn't want to answer, but it took a lot of time for him to be comfortable and get out what he wanted to say. And when he couldn't give the reply people expected to hear, he would become very frustrated. With new and unfamiliar staff cycling through the environment, often Christina was the only one who could provide him with the patience he needed.

Seeing Guy every day meant Christina was one of those who knew what Guy could and couldn't do, when to push him on things and when to hang back. Guy had difficulty with reading and writing, though he had a strong sense that he could write. He relied on reminders and prompts for everyday tasks such as cooking, doing laundry, and getting dressed. While he could dress himself, he required reminders to put his shirt on the right way or to zip up his pants. Tying his shoes was also a challenge for him. Additionally, he had trouble differentiating between hot and cold water for washing. Despite needing glasses, he didn't like to wear them. He had a high pain tolerance, which meant that he might not always notice when he was injured.

For an objective assessment of how Guy spent his days at the day program, we may look to a 2005 report from an occupational therapist who undertook an assessment of Guy. The assessment noted that Guy ate his lunch extremely fast, putting huge pieces of food in his mouth and not always swallowing before putting more food in. He put away his own plate and utensils. Guy often mumbled to himself. When he recognized people he knew, he'd say hi to them. He would successfully comply with requests given by a worker. He walked very quickly and sometimes ran, although he appeared lost. In the classroom, he went straight to the cabinet to get his paper and organize it. His work consisted of drawing lines on paper and scribbling in between them; the result looked like notes a person might take, but they were illegible. He had trouble sitting still, constantly getting up and down out of his seat. He would spontaneously speak about other people, what they were doing, or what was in their cabinet. When asked a question using simple words, he stared at the questioner blankly.

The report went on to say that Guy was very task-oriented and always busy doing something, although not necessarily productive. He left class without letting the worker know and went to the next classroom to ask if he could go into the Snoezelen room, a multisensory environment designed to provide relaxation and sensory stimulation for individuals with cognitive, developmental, or sensory disabilities. He laid in the Snoezelen room and seemed very comfortable and calm. When it was time to go home, he immediately got himself ready and helped out his friend. He was a very good helper, but found it difficult at times to understand questions being asked of him. Guy continually entered and left the room and, after about two minutes, expressed that he was looking for his friend when the worker asked him a few times to tell her what he wanted. He did not stay in the hallway to wait for the bus, constantly walking around until his ride came for him.

The next day, the observation period continued with Guy initiating conversation, understanding some questions but not others. There was approximately a two-to-three-minute gap between his statements. He unstacked chairs and didn't have a specific task to complete, so he wandered around a bit. Eventually, he decided on his own to sweep the classroom. Later, he set up Christmas lights and exclaimed, "I finally did it!" Guy collected blankets, folded them, and put them away. He continued to wander a bit and kept himself busy by rearranging lights and blankets. He also plugged in and unplugged the lights, rearranged the cabinets, and rearranged the couch and chairs. He made his own corner with a chair, cabinet, and pencil crayons. Eventually, Guy left the room to get a drink of water before continuing to arrange things. He seemed to have an unending source of energy that never depleted.

Another assessment completed in 2011 reached similar conclusions about Guy's abilities. "I went over his rights and responsibilities with him using the pic symbols," the assessor began, referring to the system of pictorial symbols used to communicate complex concepts to children and adults with developmental disabilities. "Guy understood a fair amount of it but doesn't have the understanding that when he gets injured at work or home that he needs to tell someone." In fact, the assessment report indicated Karen Santor raised concerns about Guy's desire to be trained to operate a push mower at the day program. "Karen has some concerns with Guy using the push mower as he tends to be a bit clumsy and could injure himself . . . Karen also stated that if Guy gets an injury that staff here will support Guy if he needs medical attention."

ooooo

While things got worse once Keri was running the household, Christina had been concerned about the level of care Guy had been receiving at home for as long as she had been working at the day program. In her statement to police, Christina recounted her experience seeing Guy coming in to the day program with hygiene issues. "I would see him every Monday morning and Monday to Friday, and I was doing duties that should have been completed at home," she explained. She described a disturbing list of hygiene and clothing issues: ill-fitting clothes, shoes with holes, tattered socks, and dirty fingernails with feces underneath. Christina would shower Guy before he could go swimming and provide him with fresh clothes to change into afterward. "None of it was acceptable," Christina stated. She made it a habit to wash and dress him in new clothes from the donation bin before he started his day with the others. On Fridays, when Guy's mother came to pick him up, Christina went the extra mile to make him look presentable. She shaved his face and put him in clean clothes, knowing that it was a special occasion for him to spend time with his mother. Christina attended to Guy's hygiene needs, such as cutting his dirty fingernails and brushing his teeth. However, this extra care may have unintentionally shielded Guy's mother from the reality of his daily condition, reinforcing her belief that Guy was receiving appropriate care. It was not Christina's responsibility to perform these tasks, but she did them anyway.

Tensions ran high during lunchtime at the day program, especially when it came to Guy's insatiable appetite. Christina vividly recalled the struggle of trying to keep him fed during the long hours he spent at the centre. "I'd write notes to Keri, begging for a couple more drinks. We're constantly on the go, swimming, walking, you name it," she recounted. "It wasn't uncommon for me to have to give him extra snacks because there was never enough food for him." But Keri refused to budge, insisting that Guy must have eaten his lunch on the bus ride to the centre. As a result, Guy would sometimes resort to stealing lunches from other participants. The situation escalated when Guy and David began showing up with inedible lunches consisting of mouldy sandwiches, stale muffins, and burnt popcorn. That's when Christina and the other staff members took matters into their own hands, whipping up hearty meals or rummaging through the donation bin to ensure that the men didn't go hungry.

Then there were the increasing number of absences. Under Karen's leadership, it was rare for Guy or David to miss the day program, but when Keri took over, their absences increased significantly. When Keri took the men down to the disability benefit office without notifying anyone at the program, it caused confusion and concern. Staff wondered if Guy and David were okay and if there was an emergency. They called Keri but the phone just rang and rang. They called Diane, but she had no idea where Guy was or why Keri wouldn't notify the day program. For Christina, unexplained absences like this caused stress given her sense of responsibility for Guy's safety and well-being. Another time, Keri said family were visiting for a month and she decided to keep them home. Then there were multiple absences for "food poisoning," accidents, unapproved trips to the doctor, and a litany of other excuses.

Christina knew how to ask Guy if he was in pain or something was wrong, but it was usually a dead end if she tried to prod for more information. "He didn't want to say much unless it was something positive," she told police. "He would shut down when you asked him something that maybe he didn't want to answer. Guy shut down when he thought he was in trouble so he would not talk. And he would go through phases of not talking." Sometimes Christina need only read Guy's body language to know he was off. "You can just tell," she explained. "Two very talkative people [Guy and David] and then when things change, they get very quiet. I mean everyone goes through stretches and whatnot, but the change in the demeanour, becoming very quiet, was a sign."

During her testimony, Christina stated Karen had expressed concerns regarding their support for Guy in the day program, but usually it was the other way around. Yet, when concerns were finally raised, Christina would either be disciplined with a note in her file, or there would be no follow-up. "Basically, the concerns were brushed under the rug. I went to my manager, wrote incident reports that never went anywhere. It was never dealt with. Bringing it to the attention of the caseworkers and bringing it to my direct supervisor. Nothing was done. I'd contact Karen, and she'd say, 'Oh, Guy was smearing BM [bowel movement]. That's why he has BM on him. He spent the weekend cleaning his room because he defecated in his room.' I was with him for ten years and he never defecated in his pants. That's something he didn't do. If he had a mess where he was sick, that was one thing, but it wasn't a regular occurrence." Christina learned that nothing good or productive ever came from speaking out against Karen Santor, so the issues she witnessed and reported on for years remained unresolved.

Though she was never inside the Santor home, Christina was one of the helpers Diane hired to take him to bowling when she was away. Christina's winter visits to the house were often uneventful. When she arrived to pick up Guy and he was not yet ready, she would wait outside for him. She noticed a large amount of cat feces on the ramp leading to the side entrance, where Guy would eventually emerge. Sometimes, she would catch a glimpse of David sitting in a rocking chair amid a sea of toys. However, since her interactions with Guy were privately organized by Diane, she was often not greeted by Karen or Keri, and she was not welcomed inside the home despite her frequent visits.

A regulation (Regulation 299/10, s.8 (4).) was passed in 2008 requiring agencies in Ontario to call the police if they suspect neglect that rises to the level of a criminal offence. However, determining what level of neglect constitutes a criminal offence is not easy in practice. The burden falls to front-line workers, who have to navigate these legal complexities while also ensuring the safety and well-being of the individuals they support.

Without adequate training to identify and respond to neglect with confidence and in the context of a dysfunctional administration, front-line workers like Christina had few options other than simply giving Guy extra attention that he clearly lacked at home. Each day Christina cleaned Guy up, fed him, and helped him get on with his day. Keri tended to use the rifts at Choices to her advantage, pitting the various departments against one another. When concerns about Guy and David's mouldy lunches were raised by Christina, Keri would spin the situation by telling Jennifer that the day-program staff were out to get her, leveraging the sense of mistrust and division between the different departments. By deflecting attention elsewhere, Keri contributed to the atmosphere of conflict and tension that ultimately impacted the quality of care provided at Choices.

ooooo

With Karen's passing, a new chapter began in the Santor house, ushering in a period of decline and turmoil matched only by what was happening at Choices. Despite enormous growth in the previous fifteen years, the organization was facing an existential crisis as staff turnover reached an all-time high. Morale among front-line staff was low, and a unionization drive promised to organize them. Managers were constantly being shifted from one program to another, leaving gaps in continuity of supervision. "It became a running joke," Christina testified about the turnover in managers. Whenever a new manager was appointed, there would be all sorts of promises of change, Christina recalled, but they often weren't around after a month or two, so they couldn't implement any of the promises. Front-line staff stopped trusting managers, concerned complaints might come back to haunt them when a manager moved into a different role.

Soon, Choices staff in different programs stopped trusting one another too. If day-program staff raised concerns about how clients from the family-home or group-home programs presented when they arrived at the day program, or vice versa, such concerns were treated with suspicion instead of cooperation. Over the years, this long-standing strife fractured the organization into silos, each department its own echo chamber of grievances gumming up the proper functioning of the organization. Government audits later concluded that leadership formed its own niche, insulated not only from staff but also proper board oversight.

As the overseer of the day program and Christina's manager at Choices, Sarah gave her testimony at the inquest about the organization's dysfunctional work environment. She spoke about the high turnover rate, communication barriers between programs, and fear of punitive action that prevented front-line workers from sharing their concerns about clients. "Back then it was all about what we weren't doing, or what they weren't doing instead of agreeing and collaborating together," she said. She noticed that there was a hostile relationship between programs within the organization, leading to deficiencies in the assistance given to clients. This damaging dynamic had persisted for a while and diminished the efficacy of the support provided. Sarah traced much of this dysfunction back to the CEO, whom many at Choices argued contributed to a toxic work environment. In 2009, a government audit scored the agency poorly on human resources, governance, service delivery, stakeholder satisfaction, and public perception. The board removed the CEO in September 2011 due to his refusal to answer questions and work with the board. However, his decision to grandfather in Keri as home provider for Guy and David, which had been approved by his director of operations, had disastrous consequences that outlived his tenure.

Sarah saw Guy every day but didn't have a direct working relationship with him. Yet, Guy's cheery morning greetings were always a welcome interruption in Sarah's busy schedule. "I would see him every day, but I wouldn't be working directly with him. He'd be running down the hall, 'Good morning, Sarah!' and I'd invite him into my office for a visit." During an interview with police, Sarah shared her observations of Karen Santor, a woman she observed to always be on the move and with an unwavering, strong-willed demeanour. "She was a very, very strong-willed person. It was her way or the highway." Karen's approach, and perhaps her personality, clashed with Sarah's, but the power differential between them in the organization kept Sarah in her lane. After Karen died, Sarah didn't have significant interactions with Keri, except for dealing with the constant complaints from day-program staff. "She was very difficult to get a hold of, and I know that, for me, the way they looked when they came in indicated that she was having a hard time and she was struggling." Sarah was surprised Keri had taken on such responsibilities given her age — she was only in her early twenties. "It was difficult because we were trying to get Keri to say, 'I need help. I can't do this.'" But she never did.

Keri wrote a letter to Choices a few months after becoming a home provider, responding defensively to the concerns expressed by Choices staff. Despite any flaws she may have had in her role, Keri was adept at crafting a convincing rebuttal to refute allegations that she was not fulfilling her responsibilities properly. With confidence, she stated what she had done and what others had not, which cast doubt on the legitimacy of Choices' worries about her home-provider performance, while redirecting attention to the deficiencies of others. Whether Keri's complaints were grounded in reality remained debatable, especially since many people within and outside of Choices contradicted the information she presented about herself and the quality of support she provided Guy and David. Nevertheless, Keri's letter provides a glimpse of the woman who had been relatively successful at convincing others to believe her.

> Since concerns about David were mentioned last month I have taken the time to document both of the men's showers, laundrying and lunches, including making banana muffins with Guy last week, them becoming stale in two days does not seem likely. I have also documented the state David and Guy are in when they leave the house in the morning as well as what they look like when they return. I find it odd, that if hygiene is taking such a huge part of David's day at Westfield [Choices day program], that he returns home with lunch remains all over his face and clothes. I have also voiced in Guy's communication book about his clothes being ruined by markers. When he returns from Westfield it has become routine to wash his hands for at least 30 minutes to remove the marker stains. I mentioned concerns about these issues to [Jennifer, Guy and David's home-share support worker] numerous times in our monthly meetings.
>
> I have sent 3 outfits to Westfield in the past 7 months for David in case of accidents. Confirmation of this is in his communication books. On top of this he now has 18 pairs of underwear at Westfield. This is a gross misuse of his monthly allowance. I have asked for some of these items to be returned to him and have yet to receive a response. More often than not, he comes home without his hat and mitts in cold weather. In the past 3 months I have spent over 100 dollars out of my own pocket on winter wear for David due to staff misplacing his belongings. This does not bother me, his welfare and missing belongings do. He also has three work bags, and communication books, due to the

amount of times he comes home with not a single article he left with outside of his coat.

When I attended another client's PSP [person-centred plan] last year David was sitting with his button up shirt completely undone. I, rather than staff redressed him. The response from staff was, "David does that." I find it disgusting that he was left practically topless in front of clients of both sexes. If there was a wardrobe issue I should have been notified; more so staff one table away should have addressed the issue. After seeing the situation I changed David's choices in work clothing. Staff lunch breaks should be taken in shifts separate from the clients. The clients lunches should not be ruined by distracted staff and it certainly puts the clients at risk.

OT [occupational therapy] has been requested for David due to his issues with walking. Numerous times I have commented in his communication book about changing him into his running shoes that were suppose to stay at Westfield. They come home in his bag everyday and are obviously not being used. Every time I have been at Westfield he is trudging around in his boots which has caused blisters. This needs to be remedied.

There has been a continuous issue with communication from Westfield. Reviewing David's communication book from his two weeks in respite shows this is not an issue only I have suffered.

David had an accident at Westfield in September due to being pushed by another client, staff has lied about this. Even more concerning is that they stated he did not have any allergies to the hospital staff, when it turns out he does. Granted as a home-share provider I should have known even though I had only officially been caring for David for a month (a proper home-share provider investigation and file on the client would have solved this). I have lived with David for many years, essentially as a respite worker for him, but to me as a sibling, it never came to pass that

I needed to know these things. His staff MUST! The constant change of staffing at Westfield is not putting the clients best interests at stake. For the sake of all clients, the staff must know the medical, and all of the clients history. The fact David's information was not passed on to the staff that took him to the hospital is a huge error. I hate to imagine what could have happened. Thankfully that was not the case — this time.

When Darts drivers commented to me that Sonja [another day-program member] was dragging David around and causing him harm I voiced concerns to Jen. At David's PSP it was addressed that David has been working on telling Sonja "NO." This is not acceptable. Clients should not be doing staff's work and David's safety should not be degraded in such a manner.

As for David being tired, I have no response. David sleeps very well at night and when he returns home from Westfield is very energetic and enjoys spending time with the family. Perhaps a lack of stimulation/supervision at Westfield is an issue. This is yet another concern I voiced in the August PSP meeting.

David and Guy have been sent with the same lunches I have made for them the past 4 years; two sandwiches, a water bottle, a juice box, fruit, and a sweet snack. When Guy was given too much freedom at Westfield, lunches started to go missing, including that of his worker. During the August PSP I witnessed a client coming into the meeting room and taking random lunches with none in the room commenting or rectifying. Guy's behaviour issues seem to come from being accused of things he did not do. When David's bag was kept in the classroom his lunch did not disappear. How this relates to Guy eating lunches on the Darts bus is for us all to contemplate. When Vanessa [day-program staff] voiced concerns to Jen but not me about David's bowel movements and other bathroom issues I started sending him prunes to show acknowledgment of concerns and an attempt to work with the Westfield staff. Again I have documented what is sent and the prunes were most definitely not dried.

On top of all this, due to the lunch issue I sent extra canned food to ensure there was always something available to them. Other home-share providers have informed me of the other means of extra food donated to Westfield. The fact that Guy's incentive money has been spent without permission on buying others replacements for food he supposedly stole is not acceptable. Especially when incentive money cannot be left at Westfield due to staff stealing from clients.

Guy was removed from the Hut and this led to 5 months of his PSP being useless. I was told numerous stories as to why Guy was removed as was Jen. His communication book says it was due to behaviour; his behaviour seems to be due to lack of supervision and being condemned for acts he did not commit. Regardless of Guy's behaviour the official story to his removal has yet again been changed to allowing other's a chance to experience the Hut. That would pass as valid had it been the original story. I have heard from other sources it's, to quote, a load.

Guy has recently started working in the Mulberry bush. How watching National Geographic DVDs relates to crafts or work placement I do not comprehend. Regardless both myself and Guy's mother have voiced we would like to see Guy back in the Hut. I have suggested ways to aide in his behaviour, if that is the real issue, and we have yet to get a concrete response to a timeline for him.

Every time I have tried to reach Westfield minus one day in January, I have not gotten a response. When Darts informed me they were not bringing Guy and David home one day in December I called Westfield many times unsure if I should leave home to go get them or wait for them here. Thankfully they made it home okay. I have found the best and only route of communication to be letting

Jen know of our family plans or days off. She is the only one I have received consistent responses from. My endless attempts to get a proper response out of Westfield staff as to why Guy is not in the Hut or for the LINKS program is proof of this.

Over the past 7 months I have asked endlessly what else is needed of me. All of our concern should be focused on the clients. When I officially took over David and Guy's care there should have been a proper new home-share provider inspection. I voiced this concern. I offered up police checks. None of this was taken nor looked into. For months I have been asking for dates of the training sessions and anything else I can do to ensure Guy and David are getting precisely what the ministry mandates for them. I have yet to receive any concrete answers. Jen should not be held accountable for this as it is apparent she has been mislead [*sic*] as much as I have by CHOICES staff.

I am concerned that the August PSP was never signed off on, yet in February we were asked to sign August's as if it were February's. I am more concerned that David stated he did not want his PSP shared yet staff encouraged and redirected him into saying yes. This does not seem appropriate nor respectable. I do not see how David's PSP being shared is harmful to him, yet his choices should be respected.

In August I sat back while voicing my concerns but as it was a new role for me agreed to try the staff of CHOICES ideas in relation to Guy and David. This has proven detrimental to both of their lives. After spending a few months observing I started to be more adamant in voicing my concerns. As soon as this happened Guy and David's home life came into question. I would like to think this is a coincidence. Past history in CHOICES minutes shows this is not the case.

I hope from here on out we can all work together for the betterment of these men. My parents spent much of their lives building CHOICES and much of my childhood was spent there as well. I would like to see it be built up, rather than torn apart.

Regards,
Keri Santor

Keri's letter did little to resolve concerns about her ability to care for Guy and David, even if it did raise certain questions about the veracity of some of Choices claims about her. Later, Sarah shared her perspective as an experienced front-line manager with police detectives. Sarah felt it was important to be careful about balancing one's morals and values when it comes to intervening in an individual's living situation. Sarah questioned whether she had the authority to judge someone's cleanliness or the quality of their lunch and remove them from the home based on those factors alone. "To me, you have to be very careful where you're balancing your morals and your values. I come in and my hands are clean. Someone else comes in and their hands are dirty. Do I have any authority to go into that home and say I don't like the way that you're dirty or have inadequate lunch so I'm pulling you out? I don't have any authority to do that."

"And what about the wishes of Guy and David?" Choices attorney Manishen responded. "They're developmentally disabled and it may well be that they don't fully appreciate that they could have clean clothes and better lunches. As far as they like being where they are, if you ask them, 'How are things going? Do you want to move out?' they would have said they wanted to stay with Keri." Sarah acknowledged that Guy and David may not have fully appreciated the concept of cleanliness or quality of food, but she stated she had spoken with other managers who reported that Guy and David were happy living in the Santor home. But previous testimony by Stephen, a long-time helper at the Santor farm, confirmed Guy would simply answer in the affirmative if asked if he liked where he was living, so his responses should not have been taken at face value. Nevertheless, Sarah concluded her deposition by stating her belief that removing Guy and David would have gone against their rights and choice as individuals.

"It may very well be that self-determination is very important," began Crown Attorney Shea, "but for people like Guy and David on a day-to-day basis, what about their dignity? What about the fact that they may say they're happy where they're living, but they're being provided with mouldy food, burnt popcorn, inadequate amount of food, expired food products; they're in filthy clothing smelling of urine; they have fecal matter under their fingernails. When is it that someone says there's no dignity here? They may say they're happy where they are, and this is the condition they're in. Where's the dignity? How do you balance that?"

To help make her point Shea offered the example of the Santors' neighbour, Susan, intentionally trespassing on the Santor property to provide care to neglected horses and was told by the SPCA that so long as she continued to do that, there wouldn't be signs of neglect to act upon. "The same thing was happening at day program, and staff were cleaning them up so even Guy's mother, Diane, wouldn't know the true extent of neglect. What would have happened if your staff stopped cleaning them up and providing food?"

"I don't know, but I couldn't imagine them not doing it," Sarah said.

"Because it's the right thing to do."

"Yes."

Christina vividly remembers the last time she saw Guy at the day program. Though it had been a typical day, their interaction left a lasting impression. Notes from the day indicate he enjoyed being with his peers and that he was quick to start his routine and was working on maintaining eye contact and personal space with customers. Apparently, his anxiety levels had lately improved. As the day drew to a close, and Christina began the task of cleaning Guy up before his mother arrived, Guy inquired about her weekend plans and, to Christina's surprise, he excitedly shared his own plans to attend a dance. With great care, Christina made sure that Guy was looking his best for the occasion, ensuring that his clothes were clean, his teeth brushed, and his fingernails trimmed. Before he left, Guy insisted that Christina pass on his greetings to her daughter, and they exchanged a heartfelt, farewell high-five. It was a moment of bittersweet tenderness between two dear friends, one that would forever be tainted by the tragic loss that followed. Christina's sadness soon gave way to frustration and anger. She had been advocating for years to have Guy and David removed from the Santor home, but every time she raised the issue, the response was the same: "Where would you put them? There are no family home providers available."

When police brought Christina in for questioning, she did not hold back. She described the filthy, disgusting living conditions that Guy and the other residents were subjected to. They were not being taken care of properly and were given food that was not fit for human consumption. "Stuff from dollar stores," she recalled with horror. It was a horrible situation, and Christina was determined to do something about it. "If you were to rate based on your experience the level of care Guy received from zero to ten—" the detective began before Christina interrupted.

Christina was unequivocal in her assessment of the living conditions that Guy and other residents were subjected to. "Zero. Without a doubt," she said when asked to rate the conditions. "You wouldn't raise animals that way. Disgusting." She expressed embarrassment that the agency where she worked had continued to allow people to be housed in such unacceptable conditions. Christina had a reputation for being outspoken, and she couldn't imagine going into monthly visits at that home and not speaking up about the conditions. But it wasn't her role to do so. She and others repeatedly asked, "What is it going to take for something to happen to pull them out of the house?" It seemed that nobody cared about the residents, and that the agency's focus was solely on making money. Christina's voice grew louder as she spoke, her outrage and regret evident. "Nobody gave a shit about them, really. Nobody cared for them. It was just about the paycheque."

Christina was one of the closest people to Guy, other than his family. She even spoke at his funeral. The injustice of his death weighed heavily on her. "He didn't deserve this," she said, her voice trembling with emotion.

10.

THE MANAGERS

By day three of the inquest, Choices was on the defensive. Inquests are not criminal or civil processes so there is no finding of guilt or legal responsibility, but much of the presented evidence pointed to serious problems with agency oversight of the home-sharing arrangement. In response, Choices appeared to attempt to minimize damage to their public reputation given the role they played in the circumstances around Guy's death. This approach was on display when, one morning during the inquest, a lawyer for Choices' insurance company appeared at the table. Only parties with standing — that is, those with a direct connection to the death — may participate in an inquest, and that certainly did not include Choices' insurer. The insurance lawyer struggled to explain why they were there, explaining they were representing Choices in another ongoing civil lawsuit. Dr. Stanborough was furious and ordered the lawyer to leave the table immediately. "This is a death investigation and has one mandate: to answer five questions," Dr. Stanborough began. "Witnesses are not on trial, nor should they be made to feel defensive. They are here to help the jury understand the death and not to be cross-examined for any other purpose than to assist the inquest."

"Just as the witnesses are not on trial, I'd ask to point out that Choices is also not on trial," Mr. Manishen responded, his voice rising in defence of what had just occurred. "A lot of the evidence here seems to have the flavour of directing towards Choices being at fault, or Choices' responsibility for this or that, when it turns out that to some respect they were not responsible. It's not an exercise in trying to cast aspersions in relation to Choices, but in a fair and impartial manner, develop what role Choices did or didn't have in these proceedings."

The following day, it was discovered Choices was vetting documents subject to the production order before they were released to the coroner's office, rather than following procedure by allowing the coroner to decide which documents would be vetted for examination at the inquest. Crown Attorney Shea indicated there were documents that should have been received but weren't, including a 196-page report on a comprehensive internal review conducted in the months following Guy's death. Choices argued it wanted to protect the privacy of its clients, but Dr. Stanborough was incredulous. "I'll have my staff generate another copy of the Coroner's Act to help you out, so you can read it and get some clarity with it. The way this works is that material coming in as evidence comes to me first and then it goes to the parties with standing for exactly the reasons you've described. Privacy and relevance that is material to the scope of this inquest. That is *my* role, *my* job, and having it served by the party with standing is not only inappropriate but counterproductive."

"It sounds like Choices is on trial!" Mr. Manishen cried out.

"You know what, sir, I'll tell you something. Sit down for a second," Dr. Stanborough hissed. "The reason why people bow when they walk through that door, the reason why people stand up at the beginning and end of the day is out of respect for this process, out of respect for society, out of respect for the procedures we're going through here. Out of respect for each other. When I've asked for something for the purposes of this inquest, there is an associated respect, not only just to me and the coroner's office, but to the person who has died, to his or her family who are grieving, and all the parties and people who are going to be in this courthouse. There is a respect that you're going to comply and you're going to be taking this seriously on behalf of the coroner's office, and on behalf of the family, and on behalf of Mr. Mitchell, who's dead. When I teach death investigations, I say, 'Can you imagine what this person's gone through?' This person [Guy] was at the level of a five-year-old. He couldn't see well. He couldn't walk well. He was in a well and died by himself. Can you imagine that? The family, the friends, everybody who's gone through this."

Dr. Stanborough continued, "We're doing this inquest because of what this poor fella has gone through. And the disrespect for ignoring the process I find shameful. I think Choices and their conduct in not producing, assisting, and complying with this inquest is quite frankly shameful. Not only to me and the people here, but to the family of the deceased and Mr. Mitchell. I find it discreditable. I don't know what the game is, I don't know why you do this as counsel, but Choices' conduct to have the material requested from them specifically at a case conference three years ago and for me to receive it twenty-four hours ago, quite frankly I find that shameful."

"Can I speak?" Mr. Manishen interrupted.

"No! Let me finish. On a go-forward basis, I don't expect to have this happening anymore. When we're requesting things, I expect them to be produced. I expect to have cooperation here. I have never requested to have a party removed from an inquest, but I've been giving it consideration in the last twenty-four hours. I've never had, in my thirty inquests that I've done, where I say to myself, 'Do I need to have this party removed as a party with standing at this inquest?' That is embarrassing, inappropriate, and not a route I ever want to go down. But when I ask for stuff for this inquest, the spirit of cooperation has clearly gone out the door when a 196-page report has been three years in the coming. I don't understand that. I don't understand the lack of cooperation. And I don't understand the disrespect to Guy Mitchell, to his family, to his friends. The reason why Mr. [William] Santor was up here in a jacket and tie giving his testimony, when his voice was shaking and tears in his eyes, is because he respects the process. I think that degree of respect has to be across the board, especially from the organization that provided oversight to Mr. Mitchell. Am I upset? You're darn right I'm upset."

Mr. Manishen tried to explain the internal review was not specifically about what happened to Guy and included confidential information pertaining to other clients and home providers of Choices' associate-living program.

"Do you think any of that has to do with oversight?" Dr. Stanborough asked. "Because I don't think that is getting through to you."

"Yes."

"I don't understand the confusion."

"How other homes are monitored is irrelevant to these proceedings," Mr. Manishen asserted.

"Whose decision is that? Is there not a whole chapter in there addressing the death of Guy Mitchell and the response to that death? And somehow, [Choices] didn't figure that a review done in November 2012 following the death of Guy Mitchell was relevant to the inquest?"

Mr. Manishen redirected, commenting that the review was mandated by the ministry and the resulting report was sent back to them. He questioned why the ministry didn't produce their copy of the report since it was also in their possession, a valid deflection that conveniently redirected attention about Choices withholding information from the inquest.

"I don't know if you folks understand the principles here," Dr. Stanborough sighed, now addressing all the lawyers at the table. "Whether we have the material or not, or going to use the material or not, whether it's relevant or not, is *my* decision. This is why it takes two to three years for an inquest to be prepared. This is a discretionary inquest because I have very little confidence that there is sufficient oversight for people who are handicapped in society in group homes and private homes. And you know why I don't have much confidence when you see the material that came in the last few days. Horrific. There's a reason why we're doing this inquest, and to hide material and produce it halfway through an inquest is shameful."

Diane watched the heated exchange with a combination of confusion and disappointment. She had few expectations about what an inquest was supposed to be like, so she thought maybe it was normal to have these kinds of procedural disagreements. But she also thought that Choices should have known better than to withhold important information. "Why would they do that if not to hide something?" she thought to herself. As the atmosphere in the room eased after the tense exchange, Diane realized, perhaps for the first time, just how high the stakes were in this fraught journey to find justice for her son. As Choices fought to protect its reputation, Diane lamented how the focus had shifted away from the real issue at hand. Guy was already a victim of a broken system, having paid the ultimate price with his life. Diane feared he might be forgotten, as if falling through cracks in the system yet again, his story ultimately overlooked amid complex legal proceedings, power dynamics, and big personalities. For the grieving mother, justice was not just about holding those responsible accountable, but also about ensuring that Guy's life was not lost in vain. She hoped the process would honour his memory by propelling change and raising awareness of the issues that led to his tragic death. Diane's quest for justice, then, was about keeping Guy's memory alive and to prevent others from experiencing the same pain and loss. As the outcome of the inquest remained uncertain, all Diane could do was wait to see how the rest would unfold, hoping for a positive result but resigned to accept whatever answers it could provide.

ooooo

"Can you explain why there weren't unscheduled visits at home where Guy lived?" Crown Attorney Shea asked Sylvia. As the manager who oversaw the host-family program at Choices, Sylvia was responsible for supervising front-line support workers who were entrusted with upholding home-sharing arrangements between Choices clients and families in the community.

"It's a private residence," Sylvia responded. "It's not a facility run by our agency so we can't just go in unannounced."

"I always think, if you're not doing anything wrong, then you have nothing to worry about," Shea declared.

"Exactly," Sylvia agreed. "But even now, there would be some resistance to the idea."

"Well, it would appear Keri was being allowed to get away with what her mother had done in the past. And cancellations were at critical times when you were going to inspect the home."

"It would give her more time, but the visit would eventually take place."

ooooo

As winter settled over the Santor home in January 2012, Sylvia paid a scheduled visit to the house. For months, she had been hearing complaints about Guy and David's presentation at the day program. Little did she know that this would be her one and only visit to the home before tragedy struck. Sitting down with police, Sylvia recounted her brief view of the home, remembering how immaculate it looked. "I didn't do a tour of the house," she confessed. "I just went to the table in the dining room. But it was very clean and looked well-kept." Despite her limited visual survey, Sylvia couldn't help notice that the garden looked a bit rough, but concluded Keri had a lot on her plate, and that it obviously wasn't a priority for her. Sylvia wasn't there for a full inspection. That would take place later by support worker Jennifer, and direction from upper management at Choices was that only support workers were to do inspections. She admitted Jennifer wasn't trained to do proper home inspections. "And I wouldn't know either," she stated at the inquest. "But I was told we would check it off." Although Sylvia may have had reservations about the methodology or standard of home inspections, she approved the report that declared the Santor home acceptable since Jennifer had not reported any problems with it. This allowed Keri to renew her contract as a home provider, as if the inspection was simply a routine task to be checked off.

Sylvia was one of the key witnesses summoned to testify at the inquest, shedding light on the tumultuous inner workings of Choices, an organization she had been a part of since 2008. As an experienced middle manager who had worked at other developmental services organizations, she was shuffled from one portfolio to another at Choices, never staying long enough to fully comprehend or resolve any of the issues that plagued the agency. Articulate and poised, her testimony painted a grim picture of Choices, which had been in crisis long before Guy's untimely death. The months preceding his passing were marked with labour strife and managerial turnover. Sylvia's time managing the home-share program exposed her to the organization's many inadequacies. As she assumed her role managing the program, she quickly discovered that certain families, like the Santors, seemed exempt from the program's policies and rules. Eager to learn more about her responsibilities and the family homes under her supervision, she requested permission to visit each of them. However, she was informed that that was not allowed. Only the support worker was authorized to make home visits, and only at times convenient for the home provider.

As Sylvia began to receive complaints from day-program staff about the poor condition in which some of the home-share participants were arriving, she knew she needed to act. Instead of calling the police, she decided to first work with Keri to address the issues. Unfortunately, her efforts were in vain. Despite the numerous problems that had arisen with Keri since she took over from her mother, Choices still renewed its contract with her in February 2012, which stipulated that she would continue to provide a safe home with adequate food, toiletries, and personal care.

Crown Attorney Shea was keen to understand how Choices ensured home providers were fulfilling their obligations. Sylvia explained the screening process for new providers was thorough and included a termination clause in their contract. However, she acknowledged that determining whether providers were meeting their obligations was not always straightforward. Sylvia explained that the people they supported often tended to wear the same clothing day after day, and that it was not uncommon for clothes to have food stains on them. Shea was insistent and asked whether, in cases where home providers were not ensuring that the home sharer was presenting themselves appropriately, it became Choices' responsibility to clean them up. "This is a contract. If the home provider is not ensuring the home sharer is arriving as they should, then it just becomes your obligation they're cleaned up?" Shea asked. Sylvia replied it was Choices' responsibility to ensure that clients were presented in the best possible way. "However, it's the home provider's responsibility pursuant to their contractual obligations to make sure that they have clothing in good repair and suitable," Shea responded. "And in terms of hygiene, the home sharer is to have their personal rights respected, and that's why the home provider is to ensure there is acceptable hygiene. And the home provider is to ensure the eating habits and special habits are considered." Sylvia agreed with Shea's line of questioning, but it was clear that the issue of ensuring that home providers were meeting their obligations was a complex one that required careful consideration.

Shea devoted considerable time and effort to combing through the case notes and was dismayed to find there was no record of any inquiry into the reasons why Guy was consistently unkempt or what caused his bouts of food poisoning. Baffled by this oversight, she raised her concerns with Sylvia on the witness stand, who suggested the inquiries were made orally and not documented. But Shea was not satisfied with this explanation. "All I've heard for the last two weeks is about person-centred planning and lots of talk about goals, but I see nothing about the safety and well-being and nothing that reflects monthly meetings to ask clients why they might be tired or dirty, etc." Sylvia conceded there was no standardized form to document such inquiries, but she assured Shea that the team always made a concerted effort to ensure their clients' welfare. Despite her reassurances, Shea was deeply troubled by what she saw as a lack of concrete measures to safeguard the clients' well-being and felt strongly that such measures should be given greater importance in their planning processes.

During Sylvia's questioning, Shea expressed concerns about the call made by the neighbour, Susan, to Choices in October 2011. Susan left a voice mail with Sylvia's supervisor and later discussed her concerns in a return phone call from Sylvia. However, Sylvia disputed this claim during her own testimony, stating emphatically that Susan never mentioned the cistern during their conversation. Sylvia went on to say that had she known about the cistern's potential danger, she would have taken immediate action to rectify the situation. "She never mentioned the cistern," Sylvia stated emphatically. "I don't want to be dramatic, but I am absolutely positive she didn't mention the cistern. Had we known, we would have been out there in a flash. I would have been in the car right then." Sylvia also stated that Susan confirmed that she had never witnessed any neglect or abuse of the residents. With both women insisting on different versions of the conversation, it would become yet another missed opportunity to intervene in the deteriorating situation at the Santor property.

When asked if she had contacted the SPCA or police after this call, Sylvia admitted that she discussed the issue with her supervisor, Andy, but they decided not to contact the SPCA as their focus was on the clients. Shea probed further and pointed out that the decision not to contact the SPCA seemed odd given that a neighbour had called with concerns about the property. "So you've got a neighbour calling in with concerns about the property and you determined not to contact the SPCA for an independent version?" Shea asked.

Sylvia defended her decision, stating, "I didn't try. I didn't think it was relevant to the gentlemen on the property." Of course, had Choices managers contacted the SPCA for an independent version of events, they may have discovered clear evidence that the person they entrusted with the care of two vulnerable adults was incapable of providing even the barest of necessities to various animals on the property, animals that were eventually seized and relocated to others who could provide adequate care while Guy, David, and a young girl remained on the property.

During the inquiry, Shea suggested that if Sylvia had contacted the SPCA, she might have discovered that Susan had also contacted CAS about her concerns. This information was not shared with Choices, indicating that important details were missed during the investigation of Susan's complaint. Shea noted that had Choices discovered this information, they might have acted sooner to remove Guy and David from the home. Choices attorney, Mr. Manishen, interjected, arguing that Choices managers were not on trial. However, Shea pointed out that her recommendation would address the issue of silos within the agency and developmental services sector more broadly, including the problem of agencies that do not communicate with each other as they might in other sectors. Shea emphasized the importance of taking complaints seriously and following up on them, highlighting the need for better reporting and communication between agencies. Dr. Stanborough allowed Shea's comment, recognizing the importance of addressing the breakdown in communication between agencies and the need to improve reporting processes. Sylvia later noted there had not been any contact with the CAS then or since regarding the matter, adding, "I was under the impression that we weren't supposed to discuss this with anyone or take any further moves until the inquest was over."

ooooo

In 2008, Bill 77, Services for Persons with Developmental Disabilities Act, was enacted with the goal of empowering and protecting individuals with developmental difficulties. The Act made it clear that, unless they had been deemed mentally incompetent, an individual had the right to make their own decisions. In the Act, neglect was included as a form of abuse and was defined as the failure to provide necessary support and assistance that is required for the person's health, safety, or well-being, including inaction or a pattern of inaction that puts their health or safety at risk.

The regulations gave developmental services agencies until 2011 to meet the new standards of support. These measures represented a significant change from how things were done in the past; compliance with the legislation would have been a challenge for any agency, let alone one like Choices dealing with so many internal problems. Among other things, agencies were now required to immediately report suspected criminal abuse to the police before conducting any internal investigation.

To educate workers in the sector about the new regulations, a training video was released. However, confusion persisted about when to involve the police in cases of suspected neglect and how to respect the autonomy of individuals with developmental disabilities. The regulation also required an individual's permission to speak with their family or a trusted third party about any investigation. Because of this, some Choices staff believed they were not allowed to communicate with Diane about Guy's well-being without his consent, except during the quarterly meetings that Diane attended to discuss Guy's progress and goals.

The implementation of the new regulations highlighted the complexities involved in balancing the need for protection with respect for autonomy in the care of individuals with developmental disabilities. The legislation unequivocally stated that clients had the right to make their own decisions, provided they had not been declared mentally incompetent. Guy, despite his developmental disability, had not received such a declaration of incompetency. It was the agency's responsibility to uphold his rights while also ensuring his safety and protection from harm. The dual responsibility proved to be a formidable challenge. As one executive at Choices later reflected, "This dual direction often results in a very challenging balancing act."

Crown Attorney Shea posed a difficult question to Sylvia on the stand. "What if the person is functioning at the level of a five-year-old?"

Sylvia answered, "They would still have to give us permission."

"So, in the case of Guy Mitchell, his mother wouldn't have known," Shea said.

"If Guy said no, then no," Sylvia replied firmly.

"But doesn't that go against the idea of protecting vulnerable individuals?" Shea asked.

Sylvia sighed. "The spirit of the regulation gives people with a developmental disability personhood. Unless they've been declared mentally incompetent, we have to respect their rights."

Shea was shocked. "Even if it means they could die?"

Sylvia thought for a moment. "It would depend on the situation. If there was an imminent danger, then I would take it to my superiors for their input." Normally, the answer to such a question would prompt a straightforward answer: safety always takes priority over autonomy. But the new regulations and lack of adequate training caused front-line managers and workers to pause to ensure they were acting in compliance with the client's wishes and the principles of autonomy. This discrepancy not only ultimately undermined the safety of clients but also potentially created a new loophole: front-line workers and paid caregivers could now say they were respecting the autonomy of clients if or when they failed to safeguard clients from harm.

Shea persisted. "So, if someone like Guy, who has a mother who loves him, is in a neglectful situation and his mother doesn't know about an investigation because Guy won't provide the information, she can't even make a decision for him?"

"According to the law, no," Sylvia replied regretfully.

Diane's attorney wondered why Diane was not included in discussions among Choices managers about the future of Guy's living arrangements. Despite the new regulations, there is no evidence to suggest Guy ever expressed his desire *not* to include his mother in his personal support plan or discussions about his care. "Why was Diane never notified about the meeting on April 20 and the decision to remove the men from the home?"

"We would have notified her once we had a plan in place," Sylvia explained. "We had to find somewhere for the men to live and verify whose furniture belonged to whom. It can be complicated, and we had no idea about the condition of the home."

The attorney pressed on. "But did you consider that Diane would have taken him in?"

Sylvia replied, "Diane had previously stated that she wouldn't be able to accommodate Guy for any length of time." An assertion made by Jennifer but denied by Diane.

"But not to you?" the attorney asked.

"No," Sylvia admitted.

"So you made the decision, and Diane was never notified," the attorney concluded.

"Yes," Sylvia said with a sigh. "We were working through things, but we just ran out of time."

Sylvia explained how other jurisdictions have successfully managed to address the dilemmas at hand and offered them as examples for the jury to consider. She described how, in British Columbia, home-sharing arrangements are becoming more prevalent, and agencies subcontract home providers, who are then held to a higher contractual standard in the event of any transgressions in the provision of services. In Europe, adults with developmental disabilities have teams of trusted individuals who advocate on their behalf at substitute decision-making meetings. Sylvia emphasized that these measures should be given greater consideration to bridge the accountability gap that exists between individuals who have been declared mentally incompetent by a court and those who simply require assistance with decision making. The process of declaring someone mentally incompetent involves going to court, which can cost upwards of $5000 — a significant amount of money that many low-income individuals and families cannot afford. It may also be unnecessary or counterproductive.

The concept of legal incompetency is a complex issue that has been present for centuries. Individuals who are deemed incompetent, due to various reasons such as mental illness or developmental disabilities, are often stripped of their ability to make decisions about their own lives. This can include basic decisions such as what to eat or wear, as well as more significant decisions such as where to live or who to associate with. The consequences of this lack of control can be far-reaching and can have a significant impact on the individual's mental and emotional well-being. They may feel powerless and isolated, with little say in the direction their life takes. Decisions made on their behalf may not always be in their best interests, leading to further frustration and a sense of helplessness. It is for this reason that it is so important for individuals who are declared incompetent to have a voice, even if it may not always be the most informed. By giving them some say in the decisions that affect them, we can help to restore a sense of autonomy and dignity. This can be achieved through various means, such as involving them in the decision-making process as much as possible or appointing a trusted representative to act on their behalf.

While adult protective service workers exist, they are typically reserved for those with the highest needs or the least available support, and there are often long wait-lists. Sylvia also argued that government overseers should conduct home inspections since nonprofit agencies are often cash-strapped and ill-equipped to perform proper inspections. Sylvia suggested adopting such alternative approaches to decision-making assistance and accountability need to be explored and implemented to support individuals who require them. And these measures don't involve reinventing the wheel. By looking to successful models in other jurisdictions, there may be opportunities to improve the current system and ensure that vulnerable individuals receive the support they need.

ooooo

Sherri was the director of operations at Choices and held a position of authority over Sylvia. As with many other management positions, Sherri's job was constantly evolving, and she was always adapting to meet the demands and priorities of her role. However, at the time of Guy's death, Sherri had only been responsible for the host-family program for a short three months. Despite this, she brought a wealth of experience in developmental services to her new position. Sherri was a strong advocate for home sharing and its benefits for individuals in need of support. She believed that the family-home program provided more personalized opportunities compared to group living situations. In her own words, "The family-home program is fantastic because individuals get more personalized opportunities as opposed to living in a group situation where everything is done as a group." However, she also recognized the challenges that came with home sharing, especially the demands it placed on families. She noted that home sharing was a 24-7 job, except for when individuals attended day programs. As a result, finding suitable families for the program had proven to be a difficult task.

Upon receiving complaints from day-program staff regarding the lunches and hygiene of the men in the program, Sherri was informed of the situation. However, she didn't view these issues as major concerns, especially since the most recent annual home inspection had not revealed any problems. She believed that the complaints were solvable and could be addressed. Sherri also testified that Sylvia had informed her of "a difference of opinions about the food" among staff members and that Sylvia believed that the lunches provided to the men were adequate. Despite the differing opinions, Sherri believed that the issues could be resolved with communication and cooperation between the parties involved. Regarding the issue of cancelled appointments, Sherri preferred to support home providers in becoming compliant rather than using punitive measures. She believed that finding balance in messaging was essential in addressing the problem with Keri. "Whether Keri was turning down support or being evasive at that time was really just coming to light," she told the jury. "The next step was convening a meeting with her to open lines of communication and be supportive of her because perhaps she was overwhelmed." However, Sherri's lack of awareness of the escalating problems with Keri may have influenced her lenient handling of the situation. She was unaware that Keri had only until August to live in the Santor home before it was sold.

Diane's lawyer pressed Sherri about her knowledge of previous concerns with Keri, particularly regarding Guy's insufficient lunches and her application for a payday loan. "So the fact that you had information previously that Guy was coming to the day program with insufficient lunches and not enough lunch to eat and then you're getting a phone call that Keri might be having some financial issues . . ."

Sherri interrupted, "That doesn't necessarily indicate she was having financial issues. It looked like she wanted a loan of some type. I wouldn't suggest that all of a sudden I get an email like that, that a person has financial issues." Sherri concluded no one could possibly consider the stipend Keri received for the care of Guy and David as a wage. "If you can only support one or two people, there is no money in providing care for somebody for 24-7. Forty-two dollars a day? It's not a wage," she argued. "You want to do it so you're not deterring people from becoming a family home because it really is an excellent quality of life that you won't get in group situations."

"But this was about the time you had a lot of concerns with Keri, correct?"

"I was just starting to get the information related to concerns, which were being addressed by myself and Sylvia," Sherri explained, adding that Sylvia had reviewed the lunches and found no issues.

Prior to meeting with Keri about all this, a pre-meeting was arranged with workers and managers from the day program and associate-living program, but Diane was not notified. "So for all of the people who were to attend, why was Diane not notified?"

Sherri clarified that it was related to home-share responsibilities and the purpose of the meeting was to open communication with Keri, addressing concerns about both Guy and David.

"So if there's concerns and it's significant enough to have a group of people at hand to meet with the home provider, would it not be good practice to have the natural family member notified?"

"It would depend on the situation. If it was specifically about Guy, then that would make sense. If it was a person-centred planning meeting, then that would make sense."

"But this meeting was to address concerns about Guy as well, right?"

"Guy and David. It was more to open the communications between the programs and Keri."

ooooo

Following the departure of the long-serving CEO at Choices, an interim executive director named Catherine was hired in October 2011 for a six-month contract to give the board time to find a permanent replacement and begin the process of setting the agency back on the right track. Catherine wasted no time in getting to work. She immediately began a comprehensive review of the agency's operations, finances, and programs, identifying areas that needed improvement and implementing corrective measures. She also met with staff members and stakeholders to gather their feedback and insights into the agency's strengths and weaknesses. Catherine faced the daunting challenge of tackling multiple issues at once. A severe staff shortage resulting from numerous staff on stress leave, a toxic work environment, and an underdeveloped policy framework added to her already heavy responsibility. With a pending strike vote, she had to prioritize and allocate her attention to the most pressing concerns.

Catherine was fully cognizant of the ongoing challenges faced with the Santor home-share arrangement, and she deemed them to be "significant" rather than "immediate" in the larger context and therefore did not feel the need to escalate these issues to the board of directors. She provided testimony to this effect, stating that the difficulties did not appear to be so pressing as to require immediate action by the board. Rather, she felt that the team was managing the situation in a responsible and proactive manner, and that the situation was under control. This approach was evident in a letter penned by the executive team in the aftermath of Guy's death in which they concluded, "This was a sad situation for our agency, however we acted responsibly and continued to move forward to support service recipients in all of our programs." In her testimony, Catherine emphasized the importance of taking a measured and prudent approach to problem solving, particularly in situations where multiple factors are at play. She recognized the significance of the difficulties faced by Choices staff with Keri, but believed her team was addressing them in a thoughtful and thorough manner, and that there was no need for further intervention.

Dr. Stanborough was not pleased with Catherine's assessment of the situation at the Santor home. As he began his questioning of her, the tension in the room grew palpable. "You're the boss and the buck stops with you, the way the organization runs," he began. "Did you feel that the delivery of the programs, including the residential programs, was effective?"

"Yes," she responded.

"Was this the sort of residence you thought of as the product of an 'effective' associate-living program?"

"No."

Dr. Stanborough wasn't satisfied with her response. "On the one hand, you're telling us the program was effective, but then when you look at the product of an effective delivery, I don't think you're terribly happy with the product."

"I didn't say the programs were delivered perfectly," she explained. "We had mechanisms in place that we thought were reasonable to monitor program delivery and to address issues by way of rules. I met with the program managers every two weeks, and we had agendas and we took minutes and we discussed issues and there were managers—"

"That's what you were doing," Dr. Stanborough interrupted. "But you know what the outcome was."

"In terms of that home? Yes," Catherine said, struggling to defend what seemed indefensible. "And as I said, there was nothing on my radar to suggest that home was in the condition it was."

Dr. Stanborough wouldn't let her off the hook. "So that's the point I'm trying to get at. You just hit the home run issue right here. You're the executive director. This is your baby. You're in charge. And nothing was on your radar about the home."

Catherine tried to explain that there were concerns brought to her attention, but Dr. Stanborough wasn't having it. "Where was the deficiency? Where was your supervision of the system and operations for these six months when things clearly deteriorated in that home?" he grilled her.

Catherine stammered, unsure of how to respond. Dr. Stanborough continued, "How is it possible the executive director has no idea the programs under her watch are being delivered in this fashion and says three years later she still thinks the programs were being delivered effectively?"

"I couldn't know everything that was going on all the time. I was dealing with . . . there were a lot of issues we were dealing with that were critical—"

Dr. Stanborough interrupted again. "Pardon my bluntness, but I think death is pretty critical. In fact, we're doing this whole process because death is critical. So let's explore that answer again. What do you think was the deficiency when an executive director thinks that a program is being delivered effectively when the house has no heat, no water, marijuana is being grown on the property, horses are being removed because there is no oversight, no care, no compassion?"

Catherine conjured an explanation. "I think, for me, some of the deficiencies were the nature of inspections and the way inspections were done, the whole property and not just the house itself, and the vetting process. In retrospect, these are things that would need to be improved."

Dr. Stanborough continued to push. "You were in a good position to be the outside eyes and ears to assess whether something more needed to be done."

"Yes," she agreed.

"You discussed red flags, given what you were learning about this home; there was also food poisoning. You can't look at information in isolation, but there are all these additional issues."

"It could be . . . I wasn't aware they weren't coming to the program. All I knew was they were coming to program with hygiene and food issues."

With the knowledge that even the executive director at the time seemed oblivious to what was happening at the Santor home, Dr. Stanborough concluded there was nothing further to hear. "You are excused," he declared frostily.

11.

THE BUREAUCRATS

As the inquest continued, it became clear that Guy's tragic death was not just the result of one caregiver's incompetence, nor of one dysfunctional agency, but an outcome of larger systemic issues. During the proceedings, the Crown attorney questioned Patti, program supervisor for the Ministry of Community and Social Services, the government department overseeing Choices, and asked her a pointed question: "Would you anticipate that an agency would raise general concerns with you about someone like Keri?"

"They could have easily come to us," Patti replied.

Shea followed up, "What would you have been able to provide them?"

"We could have brainstormed solutions and supported them to arrange respite. If respite wasn't available, then they could have been connected to another agency."

Shea then asked if Patti was aware of Guy and David not attending the day program or arriving filthy with inadequate food. "No, that's within the mandate of the agencies to manage themselves. If there are staff who are concerned, they should inform the agency. I told them it doesn't matter how many issues there are, they just need to report it," Patti explained.

The Crown attorney nodded but sought further clarification. "So, if something doesn't constitute a criminal offence, who do they call?"

Patti replied, "The agency is responsible for fixing the problem, and if they can't, they are to call the ministry."

"Even if the client wants to stay in the home?"

"Yes. It's a difficult balance. It has been for a long time," Patti began. "It requires that the agency work very well and have lots of skills within the agency. But it also requires that they reach out beyond their own agency. So, in this example, to talk to family of Guy and have those people help them to convince those individuals that at least on a short term it isn't a good idea."

"Are you aware of the Provincial Advocate for Children and Youth?" Shea asked.

"Yes."

Shea discussed the need for an independent office to protect the rights of vulnerable individuals, pointing out that while an advocate existed for children and youth, no similar office existed for vulnerable adults. Patti explained, "When adults are accessing services like Choices and they are not in care, they are considered autonomous individuals who can make their own decisions."

However, the question remained as to whether it was necessary to declare someone mentally incompetent to enable them to access trustworthy substitute decision makers or protective services workers. Shea expressed concern about this issue, questioning whether staff who have worked with vulnerable individuals for a significant period of time should be responsible for influencing them to make decisions. Patti suggested that this may make the most sense. "The staff who work with him on an ongoing basis for a number of years would be the people who would be more likely to understand him and influence him to make the decisions rather than someone that he's just met or that he sees once or twice a year." Patti emphasized that legislation intended to support the social inclusion of vulnerable adults is geared toward ensuring that vulnerable individuals have a network of support and a range of people involved in their lives, not just one caregiver or agency. "The intent is to keep people embedded in their communities, so there is a number of people, like neighbours, officials in other capacities who recognize who they are and can speak up on their behalf. That they have 'a home, a job, a friend.' So that there is a lot of sets of eyes on them."

Shea wondered how to prevent misuse of funding allocated to support home-sharing arrangements. "I don't think the family-home program was ever intended to be a source of income to support the family," Patti began. "The program grew up out of the foster system and it was done by families who frankly wanted to make a difference in the community or the individual's life. It's not intended to be an income source. In the guidelines, families are being screened, selected, and monitored on an ongoing basis to ensure there is a stable income apart from this so they are not reliant on the individual."

ooooo

Patti's office provided supervision and funding to local and coordinating agencies supporting enough people to fill a medium-sized city spread out over an area the size of the US state of Rhode Island. Hers was just one of several offices overseeing a much larger developmental services sector that provided residential, day program, vocational, family support, and behavioural services. Patti developed a relationship with Choices back in 2009 when an audit determined they had an unusually high level of risk and were out of compliance in several key areas. It was Patti's job to work with the board and CEO to bring Choices back into compliance before more serious steps were taken to protect clients. She discovered the board did not have much understanding of front-line operations, nor the concerns of staff or the public. A board member testified that theirs was a policy-oriented board responsible for setting the direction and overall strategy of the agency through high-level decision making, as opposed to an operational board that gets involved in the day-to-day management and implementation of policies and strategies.

At Choices, the disconnection between the board and operational matters facilitated the development of a toxic work environment. Eventually, the board recognized the severity of the situation and sought advice from a legal consultant. The consultant advised that the board was at fault for allowing the CEO to behave in this manner and reminded them they had a responsibility to the agency to ask tough questions and hold the CEO accountable for his actions. Despite this advice, the situation persisted for many years, until 2011 when the CEO was finally forced to step down from his position, his tenure serving as a cautionary tale of the importance of effective oversight and accountability in organizations, and the potential dangers of allowing power to go unchecked.

Patti worked with the board to develop better governance practices. "I told the board they were stretched beyond capacity, and I removed funding for a program," she said, adding she had the authority to take over the agency if needed. In certain circumstances, such as serious financial difficulties, operational mismanagement, public safety, legal action, or accountability issues, the government can take over a social service agency. Such measures are typically a last resort and would involve working with other agencies to ensure that the agency's services continue to be delivered without interruption. The government would appoint a supervisor, such as Patti, to oversee the agency's operations, assets, and finances with broad powers to make decisions on behalf of the agency, such as hiring and firing staff, renegotiating contracts, and selling assets. In some cases, the government may also appoint a board of directors or an interim management team to manage the agency until it is stabilized or a suitable replacement is found. Such drastic measures are not just theoretical as there are numerous instances worldwide where developmental services agencies have had their funding rescinded or been taken over by governments for various reasons. There was no immediate threat of Patti's office taking over Choices, but to prevent this possibility from becoming a reality, Choices would have to prove that it could properly govern itself.

The situation at the Santor home could have been addressed earlier if Choices had taken the appropriate steps to involve the ministry. Patti acknowledged that there were several missed opportunities to file serious occurrence reports in relation to Guy and David. For instance, when William Santor reported his concerns about Keri and shared photos of the home and Guy with the CEO in July 2011, a serious occurrence report should have been filed, but it wasn't. Similarly, when Diane reported her concerns about Keri yelling at Guy in September 2011, a report should have been filed, but it wasn't. In October 2011, when the neighbour, Susan, raised concerns with Choices about the home, the complaint should have been reported to the ministry. Staff members also complained endlessly about Guy and David's poor hygiene and inadequate food when they arrived at the day program, but no report was filed. Patti explained that the serious occurrence reporting procedure requires that any serious occurrence be reported within twenty-four hours. A follow-up investigation by the agency might not be completed within that time frame, but a report detailing what was done should be submitted within seven days.

Shea probed further. "So it's not a matter of the agency determining whether it's a credible complaint or investigating and coming up with a solution, it's about reporting in the first instance?"

"That's correct," Patti nodded. "It's the complaint itself that requires a serious occurrence, and the forms allow them to explain it."

Shea also inquired about what the ministry would have done if Choices staff members had reported concerns about poor hygiene and inadequate food. Patti said that she would have reminded them of their contract for services and urged them to enforce it, regardless of how long Guy and David had been in their care. She would also have put them in touch with another agency that runs a family-home program and may have had a similar experience, providing them with some insight on how to handle the situation. While it was not the agency's responsibility to investigate complaints, it was obligated to report them immediately to its government overseers.

Patti explained that the ministry can enter any premises owned by an agency, including its day-program and group-home facilities, but that did not include any private homes where clients resided with a caregiver from the associate-living program. This presented an accountability problem that stems from the fact that host families are not necessarily held to the same standards as other providers of care. Unlike group homes or other care facilities, host families are often not required to undergo extensive training, and their qualifications are not necessarily well scrutinized. Moreover, host families are not subject to the same level of monitoring and evaluation as other care providers; there is often little to no oversight of their activities, which can create an environment in which abuse or neglect can occur without detection, as happened in the case of the Santor residence.

Patti was determined to do her job well, but the limitations of her contract with Choices made it challenging. She could only check on the homes of the host families in accordance with the agreed-upon terms, which meant no surprise visits or inspections. It was a delicate balance, as Patti didn't want to undermine the trust between Choices and the families they served, but she also had a duty to ensure the safety and well-being of people like Guy. In the autumn of 2010, a complaint was lodged against one of the Choices home providers. Patti reviewed the complaint along with a list of home providers to determine if internal complaint policies were being followed. It seemed everything was in order, but her peace of mind was short-lived. The following spring, another complaint was filed, and this time Patti wasn't satisfied with the response. She directed the ministry's compliance unit to review the agency's family-home program, but since any facilities not owned by Choices could not be inspected, very little could be done to ensure a thorough review.

There were other missed opportunities to escalate issues with the Santor home to authorities. None of the information about child protection investigations into the Santor household, animal welfare compliance orders served to Keri, nor police involvement at the house were shared with Choices. Reporting protocols between the Children's Aid Society (CAS) and the police, or the Society for the Prevention of Cruelty to Animals (SPCA) and the police, may vary depending on the specific laws and regulations of the jurisdiction in question, but in general, there are certain protocols that are typically followed in such cases. When CAS receives a report or suspicion of child abuse or neglect, they are obligated to investigate the situation thoroughly to determine if the child is in danger or not. If they determine that the child is in immediate danger, they will contact the police and request that they intervene to protect the child. Additionally, if the abuse or neglect involves criminal activity, such as physical or sexual assault, CAS will also contact the police to report the crime. Similarly, when the SPCA receives a report or suspicion of animal cruelty or neglect, they will typically investigate to determine if the animal is in danger or not. If they determine that the animal is in immediate danger, they may contact the police to intervene and protect the animal. Additionally, if the animal cruelty or neglect involves criminal activity, such as intentional abuse or neglect, the SPCA may lay its own charges against the offender or contact the police to report the crime. In cases where the police are involved, they will typically work with CAS or the SPCA to ensure that the situation is handled appropriately. The police may conduct their own investigation to determine if criminal activity has taken place and may work with CAS or the

SPCA to ensure that the child or animal is protected and receives any necessary medical care or other support. These agencies work together to ensure that children and animals who are at risk of abuse or neglect are protected and that any criminal activity is reported and prosecuted.

But no such protocols existed between police and social service agencies such as Choices, nor government oversight bodies, including Patti's office. Instead, Keri's interactions with police, CAS, and SPCA authorities were treated as one-off events, leaving Choices in the dark about the specifics of complaints and compliance orders. It's not a giant leap to imagine how these knowledge gaps impair an agency's ability to gather information and respond to developments that might compromise the safety and security of vulnerable adults. Suppose the trespass order Keri had police lay against the neighbour wasn't just an attempt to prevent her from snooping around the property, but rather a reaction to a legitimate threat to the safety and security of the vulnerable residents in the Santor home. Or consider how the SPCA compliance order revealed a pattern of neglect on Keri's part that might have attracted greater attention to the safety of the property or condition of the residence under normal, unannounced circumstances. Or how the multiple police interactions with Keri over the preceding months helped paint a portrait of her that differed from the stories she passed off to front-line workers at Choices. In none of these cases was information shared with Choices or Patti's government office as a matter of rule. Consequently, Choices managers saw the deterioration of the Santor home-share arrangement as something that happened quickly, as the Choices director of operations, Sherri, put it, rather than the culmination of a long-standing and more established pattern of behaviour.

In the quiet courtroom, Patti sat on the witness stand and recounted the disturbing details of a tragedy that could have been prevented. She spoke of missed opportunities and raised voices that went unheard. Despite multiple complaints from concerned individuals, including Diane, day-program staff, the neighbour Susan, and William Santor, the agency failed to file a serious occurrence report. Each time a complaint was raised, it should have been escalated to the board and ultimately to the ministry.

"The circumstances around Guy's death are very unfortunate. It should not have happened. There are some deaths in developmental services that are expected, but this is not one of those. Circumstances in the family home were very bad, and the agency providing oversight was in a bad situation at the time, so things conspired against Guy in the family-home program. For an agency to arrive at the point where they are dysfunctional — and I would suggest the agency was at that time — takes a little while. When I contract with an agency, I'm contracting with the board," she said, her voice firm and steady. "The board's job is to set the directions for the agency, to hire an executive director, and to monitor the executive director's performance. In the case where there are problems in the running of the organization, it's the board's responsibility to deal with that."

Dr. Stanborough listened carefully, but he wasn't quite satisfied. "I'm going to ask you a harder question," he said, leaning forward in his seat. "The ministry provides the funding for these agencies, but where is the oversight on the ministry's or society's level that those funds and resources are actually allocated in the right direction?"

Patti paused for a moment, considering her response. "The ministry is in partnership with the board of each agency," she said finally. "One of the things that I went to the board and requested they do is to hire a third party to do an outside review of the agency, including their executive director. It was based on the complaints that we received and the concerns that we had. But there was no requirement that the agency do that." Dr. Stanborough nodded thoughtfully, but Patti wasn't finished. "I think when we have an agency that's been identified as other than low risk, there should be identified sanctions applied that may include things like a requirement they engage in a third-party review."

ooooo

The jury needed to comprehend the challenges of creating policies to oversee numerous agencies responsible for delivering essential services to the public because the policy framework sets out the relationships between supervisors, like Patti, and local agencies, like Choices. Christine was a manager of policy development, and she knew all too well the intricacies involved in managing such a vast network of agencies. She explained how since the establishment of Ontario's Family Home

Program in 1984, agencies were given best practice guidelines but left to develop their own internal policies and practices. The aim of favouring guidelines was to provide agencies with the flexibility to attract and retain home providers without subjecting them to the stringent monitoring and inspection procedures that are typical in group-home settings. However, in the absence of clear policy directives, the program lacked accountability. Family-home programs differed significantly from one agency to another, and services were inconsistent. Even government officials were unaware of how the program was being implemented locally, and without clear criteria for measuring the effectiveness of services, it was difficult to assess the agency's impact and recommend improvements.[38]

The existence of the family-home program was just one outcome of a decades-long social movement to create space for people with disabilities outside of residential hospitals and other marginalized spaces in their communities. Since the 1980s and 1990s, Western societies have passed progressive legislation meant to promote the rights of individuals with disabilities and protect them from discrimination in employment, public services, transportation, and other areas of public life. Together, the Canadian Human Rights Act (1977) and Charter of Rights and Freedoms (1982) created the legal framework to prohibit discrimination on the grounds of disability. Elsewhere, the United States passed the Americans with Disabilities Act (1990), the UK had the Disability Discrimination Act (1995) and now has the Equality Act, which consolidated anti-discrimination law in 2010, and Australia has the Disability Discrimination Act (1992). These acts reflect growing international recognition of the goals of anti-discrimination, accessibility, and ensuring people with disabilities can access support services they need to participate fully in their communities.

In Ontario, Canada, where Guy lived, it was the introduction of new legislation in 2008 meant to promote the social inclusion of people with developmental disabilities that helped usher in a new era in the developmental services sector. The Services and Supports to Promote the Social Inclusion of Persons with Developmental Disabilities Act shifted the focus towards community-based services and individualized funding to give individuals greater control over the services they received, further decentralizing governance to five regional offices across the province and enhancing accountability. The act introduced a more person-centred approach that emphasized social inclusion, individualized support, and community-based services, reflecting a more modern understanding of the needs and rights of individuals with developmental disabilities.

When regulations concerning agencies under the new act came into force in 2011, Christine and other members of the policy unit circulated a training video aimed at ensuring agency staff knew how to recognize signs of abuse. The video, which was played during the inquest, showed staff how to identify and report instances of suspected abuse, and indicated the goal of providing individuals with developmental disabilities with the tools they needed to protect themselves. While the video was meant to be paired with additional training, the content lacked clarity about what constituted neglect and in what circumstances police should be involved. "Whereas previous legislation protected people with developmental disabilities, under new regulations they will be given the tools to protect themselves," the presenter in the video stated. The video went on to explain that people with developmental disabilities were up to ten times more likely to be physically or sexually abused than people without developmental disabilities. To create a more uniform approach, staff were instructed to report to the police any suspected or witnessed abuse, which would then be followed by an internal investigation by the agency. "Individuals with developmental disabilities have independently advocated for the right to be safe in their homes and the right to be educated about abuse. Now, they've been heard," the presenter concluded magnanimously.

The video served as a powerful reminder that individuals with developmental disabilities have the right to be safe and protected from harm, and that it is up to all of us to ensure that these rights are upheld, but it also sent mixed messages about how to respond to incidents of suspected or actual neglect below a criminal threshold. The regulations stated that police should be contacted only when suspected abuse or neglect constitutes a criminal offence, but Christine argued that anyone watching the training video should walk away feeling that any suspected abuse or neglect should be reported. "There are two kinds of abuse," the video announcer began. "That is to say, abuse that constitutes a criminal offence, and actions that may still be abusive but not criminal. Abuse must be reported to the police and the regulations clearly outline how agencies are required to respond. Should the police determine a criminal offence has not occurred or upon the conclusion of their investigation it is determined the Crown will not proceed with charges, the agencies should still take action. All agencies will need to have policies and procedures that clearly state the zero tolerance for abuse and how they will respond to the individual who has been abused and the abuser. Generally, there needs to be consequences depending on what occurred. On minor infractions, more education or training. For instances of a criminal nature or repeat offences, consequences may include termination of employment for the abuser. Regulation 299/10 requires zero toleration for all forms of abuse."

Later, the announcer amended this instruction to specify when police should be called. "Suspicions of abuse must be warnfully considered before action is taken. Reports of suspicion must be validated only by having direct evidence. Not just concerns or worries. Direct evidence is tangible, defined as seeing and having documented, such as bruising, torn clothing, bleeding from vagina or anal orifices. Should someone arrive to a program with clear evidence of abuse, such as a black eye or torn clothing even though there are no witnesses or disclosure, you must report to the police. Should someone's behaviour change in a way that leads to concerns, then it's important to become even more observant. Looking to see if there is more direct evidence of abuse. However, behavioural changes alone are not considered violence because police are unable to investigate on that basis alone."

The training video admitted only 3 percent of abusers are ever convicted due largely to underreporting or misreporting. "Why don't people with developmental disabilities tell us when they're being abused?" the announcer asked. "There are many reasons: they don't recognize they're being abused; they fear the abuser; they fear getting in trouble for reporting; they are never believed so why report; they don't know how to tell." The presenter recognized that individuals with developmental disabilities tend to be overly compliant, which poses challenges in training because they are more likely to agree with anything communicated to them compared to other populations. In fact, many people with developmental disabilities, including Guy, were subjected to "compliance training" as children, a method of behavioural therapy that aims to teach them to follow rules, instructions, and social norms. The focus is on reinforcing positive behaviours and discouraging negative behaviours. The approach typically involves breaking down a task or skill into smaller, achievable steps and using positive reinforcement techniques, such as praise, rewards, and tokens to encourage compliance with those steps. The goal is to promote independence, improve communication, and enhance the child's overall quality of life. Compliance training is often used in conjunction with other therapies and interventions to support children with developmental disabilities to achieve their full potential.

While compliance training has been found to be effective in promoting independence, improving communication, and enhancing the overall quality of life for children with developmental disabilities, it also has its drawbacks. For example, compliance training can place a strong emphasis on obedience rather than creativity and individuality, which can limit a child's flexibility and adaptability in real-life situations. Additionally, the use of rewards in compliance training can lead to a situation where the child only behaves appropriately when they know a reward is coming, rather than for their own enjoyment or satisfaction. This can limit their intrinsic motivation and ability to problem-solve or advocate for themselves. Studies have also found compliance training can be stressful and frustrating for some children, especially if they are repeatedly corrected or do not receive rewards. This can lead to negative emotions such as anxiety, sadness, or anger.

Growing up in the Santor household, Guy Mitchell was trained to be obedient, training that eventually became a defining aspect of his personality. Those who knew him and provided testimony during the inquest or spoke to the police remarked on his helpfulness, suggesting that he had an intrinsic drive to be of service to others. Karen Santor learned how to apply compliance training techniques in her early-childhood education courses while attending college and eventually earned a well-respected reputation for her skill in handling challenging cases. While Guy may have possessed a naturally caring and easygoing nature, the compliance training he experienced from a young age may have further developed these qualities, shaping him into the person he became. Unfortunately, this training also made him more susceptible to abuse and neglect, especially among people who knew him best. By her own account, Keri grew up with Guy and caring for him was second nature for her. Although she never received any formal education or training in social work or developmental services, she felt that watching her mother run their busy household taught her everything she needed to know. Keri knew what reward system worked best for Guy and would presumably know how to convince him to tell others how much he loved living there, even as the home-sharing arrangement became increasingly problematic and conditions inside the house deteriorated. Tragically, it seemed the compliance training Guy received worked too well, so much so that he may not have even understood what neglect looked like and that he was a victim of it.

Guy never told anyone about what life was really like at the Santor home during the final months with Keri. The training video shed some light on the matter. "Most abuse involves some kind of threat," the video explained. "Threats aren't always about violence. 'I will hurt you if you tell.' Threats are also about other kinds of hurt. 'I won't like you anymore.' 'I won't give you special gifts.' And, 'I won't take you to special places anymore.' Whenever threats are combined with a lifestyle of compliance training, this means too many individuals with developmental disabilities simply allow the abuse to continue." In her statement to police, Keri admitted she told Guy on the afternoon before his death that he would not be able to participate in karaoke until he could demonstrate he was well enough to go, a warning that immediately prompted him to pretend as if he were magically cured of his nausea and diarrhea. What else might he have done, or agreed to do, to prove he was all better?

The video went on to explain that over time, individuals with developmental disabilities learn that there will sometimes be hurtful consequences to telling others about abuse or neglect. "Teaching assertiveness so individuals with developmental disabilities know how to speak up will improve their lives in so many ways," the video suggested. "It will allow people to determine their own direction and give their lives real meaning." Whatever assertiveness training Guy may have received, it was clear he did not feel empowered to tell others about his living conditions or whatever other treatment he received at home. Unfortunately, this meant that the regulations that were meant to protect him also allowed him to remain in an increasingly dangerous and unfit living situation.

As Crown Attorney Shea listened to the training video, she couldn't help but notice the lack of tools provided to front-line staff to recognize and act on signs of neglect. "There seemed to be a misunderstanding or inability to grasp the fact that what was occurring with Guy Mitchell was neglect that constituted abuse," she pointed out, suggesting that the training program needed a major revision to correct this omission.

"We subcontracted the training to a vendor," Christine explained. "But we agree there's little on the issue of neglect."

Choices' lawyer, Mr. Manishen, spoke up, frustrated with the language used in the video. "The video suggests that all abuse should be reported to the police, but the regulations only qualify incidents that 'may constitute a criminal offence,'" he observed. This disconnect was a major concern for him. "But with Guy, here's a situation where there is poor hygiene and inadequate food. That is not a criminal offence, so staff should have to investigate?"

"If you're not providing people with adequate food and water, it might be criminal," Christine replied.

"But there is nothing to train staff about what might or might not be criminal," Manishen commented.

"The ministry didn't develop the training material," Christine deflected. "It was subcontracted to an agency."

"But if the agency has to investigate after police have handed it back with a finding of noncriminal abuse, they still need to know how to investigate," Manishen observed.

Christine attempted an alternative approach. "The case of Guy Mitchell demonstrates the need for community involvement. When people with developmental disabilities are integrated into the community, they are also safer."

Shea nodded in agreement, adding, "If there are concerns that are being brought forward by staff, the public, or police, I'm not satisfied that service agencies are in a position to adequately address them," she observed. "Agencies should focus on service delivery, not non-criminal investigations of abuse or neglect."

ooooo

As Diane sat in the courtroom, a tumultuous mix of emotions washed over her. She was captivated by the exchanges taking place, yet simultaneously bewildered and horrified by what she was hearing. Throughout her life, she had entrusted "the experts" with her son's well-being and relied on doctors, teachers, social workers, policy-makers, and law enforcement to help her and her son. All she had ever wanted was to work with these professionals — she trusted their expertise — to help her raise him, to help him realize his full potential, and to safeguard him from harm. But as she listened to those same experts speak about the system that had failed Guy, she was filled with doubt and regret. How had she ever placed her son in the hands of these people? She had convinced herself that she would be able to detect any potential problems by remaining actively involved in his life. Yet, when Choices workers, managers, and their lawyer suggested she was at fault for not being more aware of the danger, Diane was left feeling betrayed. How could a mother have possibly known that the agency she had trusted was in crisis? The circle of support around Guy had been filled with holes, with countless red flags ignored or overlooked. Even law enforcement had been powerless to stop the situation from spiralling out of control at the Santor home, as the agency's workers were themselves unsure of how to deal with the situation. Diane couldn't help but think she had failed her son by trusting in a system that had ultimately let him down. The pain of knowing that her precious son had suffered and died as a result of these failures was almost too much to bear.

Diane grappled with an all-consuming sense of guilt and despair over what had happened to Guy. She found herself constantly wondering what she could have done differently to prevent the tragedy, her sense of grief compounded by the growing realization that Guy's death was the result of a confluence of factors. Diane wondered whether anything could have been done to alter the course of events and she couldn't shake the feeling that there was more to the story than what had been revealed by the police investigation. But it seemed the quest for justice was just as elusive to her as the truth of what really happened to Guy that night. The night that changed everything. The night that haunted her dreams. The night that only one person could explain. Diane believed that if this person were to step forward, the truth could finally be revealed, and justice could be served. It was a chance for closure, a chance for healing, and a chance for Diane to find the peace that had eluded her for so long.

12.

DEATH OF AN INNOCENT

On Friday April 27, 2012, Guy was excited for a dance party for the bowling league. Diane always made sure he was immaculately dressed and groomed for these kinds of events, so after picking him up from the day program she took him to the barber for a haircut and goatee trim. Guy always knew he looked good in a suit and would tell people as much. "Don't I look nice?" he'd quip, proudly presenting himself for inspection. He had a great time at the dance, but there was something different about him. Diane noticed it first. He'd usually be bouncing from one end of the place to the other, hardly pausing long enough to lend his attention to anything. That evening, however, he was much calmer and sat down with a group to do a springtime craft activity, something that rarely held his attention. He slept soundly that night, and the next morning, after breakfast, he sat down to do his "papers," but instead of the normal scatter of papers and pens, he selected just a couple sheets and a pen. Diane wasn't sure what it meant at the time but remembered it as one of the most peaceful mornings she ever enjoyed with him. Later that afternoon, she drove him back to the Santor home and kissed him goodbye. It was a beautiful early spring weekend, a cool breeze rustling the waking crocuses and snowdrops as squirrels and chipmunks dashed through the grass unearthing their winter stores. What began as a quiet and peaceful weekend took a sudden turn that Diane could never have predicted.

That Sunday nearing midnight, Keri followed Detective John Tselepakis to the police station to provide a statement. The detective was handsome, clean-shaven with jet black hair and well-dressed in a black suit and expensive watch. He had conducted countless interviews in rooms like this and knew how to begin, slow and measured, sensitive and calm, especially since there were not yet any grounds to hold Keri. She was led into a grey carpeted interview room, a metal chair bolted to the floor with built-in microphones and a camera poised to capture every word. This was likely not her first time in a room like this. Wearing a pink jacket and jeans, an Adidas ballcap pulled low over her forehead, she looked deeply uncomfortable. Her arms and legs were crossed defensively, her voice apprehensive. The interview began around midnight. "Guy apparently showed up on my first birthday," she mused. "Growing up, he was a playmate for me."[39] Keri proceeded to give the detective a description of Guy. She said he lived a simple but routine life that brought him comfort in its familiarity. He loved the sound of pens scratching on paper, and the satisfaction of crossing items off his to-do list. In the mornings, he would take a bath, devour his breakfast, and head out to his day program. He took pride in his work and would even have business meetings with himself, a mysterious self-contained discussion that could last longer than most meetings. At home, he was always eager to lend a hand, picking up toys when Jennifer would throw them and completing various chores. He cherished his Saturdays, spending them with his mom or helpers at bowling. It was a tradition that had lasted from September through April, and next week was meant to be his last for the season. Sundays were reserved for family time, which could mean swimming at the aquatic centre or watching a movie. With the weather warming up, they enjoyed picnics at the Jerseyville playground, soaking up the sun and relishing the simple joys of life.

The detective sat across from Keri in the brightly lit interrogation room. He could sense the tension in the air, like a live wire waiting to snap.

"The past two years have been very difficult for you, I'd imagine," the detective said gently.

Keri's eyes remained fixed on the floor, her arms and legs still folded. "It's been something," she muttered softly.

"Who's been helping you out since your mom passed?" the detective pressed on, carefully reading her body language.

"Various friends," Keri replied, her tone guarded.

"I've got to commend you for your hard work," the detective said, his voice filled with genuine admiration. "It must have been very difficult to take care of three people like that."

Keri shrugged. "Not really," she responded. "They're my family."

The detective leaned forward, his eyes intent. "So, what happened today?" his voice low and urgent.

Keri's heart pounded as she recounted the events of the past twenty-four hours. After Diane dropped off Guy on Saturday afternoon, they decided to have a bonfire. As the sun set behind the old barn, someone fetched a safety bucket of water from the old cistern to later extinguish the fire. The flickering flames illuminated the group, casting an orange glow that danced across their faces, the warmth pushing out the crisp evening air as they toasted marshmallows. Later, the cozy ambiance gave way to a sickening dread as Guy began to vomit and experience diarrhea. Keri could still smell the acrid stench of it, the putrid odour of sickness that filled the air of the house and still clung to her clothes in the interview room. As the night wore on, Guy grew worse. He lost all control of his bodily functions, unable to make it to the bathroom in time. Keri stripped his bed and cleaned him up as best she could, but it was clear that something was seriously wrong. The next morning, Guy was still in bad shape. He refused breakfast and stayed in his room, resting fitfully. As the morning wore on, Keri watched him grow weaker.

By midday Sunday, Guy showed no signs of improvement. Keri's boyfriend went to Tim Hortons to get a treat for everyone, and soup for Guy to see if he could keep it down. She took everyone out of the house so Guy could rest, but he soon had another bout of diarrhea. He had another bath and returned to his room to play the song "Ice Ice Baby" repeatedly, but not loud enough that he didn't overhear Keri telling the others, "Maybe we won't go to karaoke tonight because Guy's not feeling well."

As soon as he heard that, Guy jumped up and told Keri he was all better. "Go get some rest and if you're not sick again, then maybe we'll go for a bit, or we can go somewhere else on Tuesday," she told him.

While he rested, Keri called Diane to ask if anyone else at the dance had been sick. "Well, he was around everyone else," Diane replied. "But I don't know if anybody was sick. Do you want me to come get him?"

"No, no. I just wondered," Keri said. Diane assumed it must have been something he ate and thought Guy would be fine.

Meanwhile, Guy spent the rest of the day trying to prove he wasn't sick so he could go to karaoke. He changed into his jean shorts and a short-sleeved grey shirt and went outside to soak up the sun, sitting next to David on the porch listening to music before returning inside to do his "paperwork."

Around five or six o'clock, Guy declared, "Keri, it's Sunday. I have to get the flyers."

"You're right. Good memory," Keri responded. Apparently, pizza and Chinese food had arrived for dinner.

It had already cooled down from earlier in the day, so Guy grabbed his jacket from the corridor of overstuffed cubbies, scattered shoes, and debris, and bounded out the door heading towards the long driveway that insulated the house from the road. He inhaled deeply, clearing his lungs of the eyewatering stench of the house that stained his clothes.

Keri alleged that he couldn't have been gone more than ten minutes before she left the house to check on him. She went down the driveway calling his name, and that's when she noticed the lid on the cistern was off. She looked down and saw his body floating in the dark water, his face half submerged. He was unnaturally still and unresponsive. Keri tried to pull him out but couldn't, so she ran back to the house and called 9-1-1 at 6:52 p.m.

"9-1-1. Police, fire, ambulance?" answered the dispatcher.

"Um, ambulance, please."

"Stay on the line."

"What is your emergency?"

"Um, I have somebody who fell in a well."

"Is that person inside the residence right now?"

"No, he's in the well," Keri cried out.

"And when you looked in, you just called in and you couldn't get his attention?"

"I couldn't get any response from him. I tried to pull him out on my own so I could do CPR and couldn't get him out."

"Okay, how deep is it?" asked the dispatcher.

"It's a cistern. It's very deep and he's floating at the top."

"Okay. All right, listen. I'm going to get some extra assistance, okay? So, you tried to pull him out and you could not?"

"I couldn't lift him out on my own, no."

"Okay. Just stay on the line with me for one moment, okay? Don't hang up. Are you there by yourself?"

"Yes," she answered after a brief pause. Jennifer screamed in the background as Keri asked David to pull up his pants.

Keri then called her boyfriend who had already left the house. "Please get over here now. Guy's in the well. I think he's dead!"

By the time she made it back to the end of the driveway, the siren of the first responding officer announced his arrival. The officer leapt out of the squad car, and Keri frantically directed him to the cistern. The officer looked down and saw Guy floating face up in the water, unmoving, his eyes and mouth slightly open. He did not answer when his name was called. The officer lay down next to the opening and stuck his head into the cistern and, bracing himself, pulled Guy out onto the grass, leaving his jacket and shoes floating in the water. Keri performed mouth-to-mouth while the officer started chest compressions, each exertion causing water to seep out of Guy's mouth. He was very cold to the touch.

Before long, the area buzzed with first responders, their flashing blue and red emergency lights slicing through the tranquil countryside evening, radiating an urgent and eerie glow as they raced to perform an unlikely miracle. Fire and EMS took over resuscitative efforts. An air ambulance was called to rush him to the nearest hospital, but the minutes ticked by, and Guy remained VSA (vital signs absent). The helicopter was cancelled as the paramedics exchanged a regretful, knowing look. Everyone knew the time for miracles had passed.

It was still a VSA emergency response, so Guy was transported to the emergency room at the nearest hospital, in the nearby town of Brantford, where doctors and nurses began resuscitation and body warming procedures. With his slight build, his body temperature had reached hypothermic levels in the cold water more quickly than someone with a heavier body mass. Guy arrived at the hospital with a body temperature of 21.8 degrees Celsius with no vital signs; however, hypothermic patients cannot be officially pronounced dead until their body temperature is warmed to approximately 37 degrees Celsius. Less than an hour after arriving at the hospital, Guy was officially pronounced dead at 9:18 p.m.

∞∞

"Did Guy ever mention needing water from the well?" the detective asked Keri, leaning in and clasping his hands together, his elbows resting on his knees.

Keri furrowed her brow, trying to remember. "No," she replied.

"Take us back inside the house," the detective instructed. "I know you were having some water issues. How long does it take to fill a bottle of water?"

"A few minutes," Keri replied. "It's just a thin stream." She explained that the water pump kept overheating, so she had been flipping it off periodically to let it cool down.

"Do you think Guy might have gone to get water without your permission?" the detective probed. "He seems like a caring and thoughtful man."

"It doesn't seem likely," Keri said, unconvinced. "Why else would he—" She paused, maybe realizing something, or stopping herself from revealing more details than requested. She had been at the old cistern the previous night to retrieve a bucket of water for the bonfire they had behind the barn. Halfway down the long driveway sat a seemingly abandoned camper trailer behind the barn. A circle of ashes in the grassy area indicated the place where bonfires were sometimes lit. There didn't appear to be any bucket left behind, though a similar one was found floating next to Guy's body in the cistern.

"And where did you go check for him?" the detective asked.

"I went down the driveway, and the flyers weren't there," Keri began. "And that's when I saw that the lid on the well was off."

"Was it normally on?" the detective wondered.

"Yeah, but it doesn't sit snugly because of the guards, so I had taken them out," she replied, referring to the sump pump electrical cords and hoses once used to pump out water for the horses when the area was still serviced with electricity for the old farmhouse that once stood nearby.

"And what happened after that?" the detective pressed.

"I went and . . ." Keri paused and began to cry softly. "He was floating in the water."

The detective circled back to the issue of the water supply and old cistern several times, but each time Keri said Guy would never go there on his own, even if it were without her permission. The interview then pivoted towards the state of the house. "Did we catch you on a bad day? Is that why the house looks the way it does?" the detective questioned her.

"No, Jennifer was on a rampage this morning, screaming and throwing things, which is why you saw the landing trashed," Keri explained. "Guy was puking everywhere and had been throughout the night. I brought him downstairs, cleaned up the mess upstairs, and gave him a bowl for being sick. He had a few more and then went back up to his room to his chair and then, I guess, went back to bed after I stripped it and was sick again."

"The toilet on the second floor, there were some pants on the ground. What bathroom is that? Is it used by everybody?" the detective asked.

"Usually, the boys use the ones downstairs. Today, to give Guy his bath, I used that bathroom, and when I went to clean him up again, I saw that he had diarrhea as well and sat him on the toilet and didn't have a chance to clean up the mess from it."

"I think it's a lot of work. Wow," the detective said. He then circled back to the first few minutes after Guy disappeared from the house. "So, Guy didn't end up getting the flyers? Or were they not there?"

"They weren't there," Keri replied.

"You said about ten minutes that he was out of sight."

"Roughly," she said. "It wasn't very long."

The detective leaned forward. "What triggered you to think something was wrong?"

"That's exactly it," Keri replied. "It just doesn't take that long to walk to the end of the driveway and back."

"So the flyers would be dropped off at the end of the driveway in a plastic bag?" the detective asked.

"Yeah," Keri confirmed.

"So you came down to the end of the driveway, and there's no flyers and no Guy. So you turn back, right?"

"I looked down the road a bit first. I thought maybe he'd gone in the ditch or something," Keri added.

"At what point when you were walking back did you see that the well cover was open?" the detective asked.

"As soon as I hit the trees lining the side, the bushes," Keri replied.

"So you look over to your left and you notice the cover's open. What was your first thought?" the detective asked.

"Just to put the lid back on," Keri said.

"Because of the night prior?" the detective probed.

"I guess," Keri replied.

"So you walk over to the well and that's where you see Guy floating in the water," the detective said. "And you run back to the house after you tried to pull him up. His jacket comes off, and you run back to the house? And you call 9-1-1 and you're on the phone with 9-1-1 and you call your boyfriend and tell him this is what's going on. Did you wait at the house?"

"I called him and then I came right back down," Keri said.

"You're off the phone and you run back to the well," the detective said.

"As fast as my smoker's lungs let me," Keri replied.

After nearly an hour of questioning, her eyes red and swollen, her voice hoarse, Keri decided to end the interview. "Can we finish this another time?" she asked.

"Would you like to step out and take a break, and we can continue?" the detective asked.

"I'd like to have a moment, some time to grieve and process. I'd rather come back another time if that's okay." The detective assured her she wasn't under arrest, so she was free to leave. It was never intended to be a final statement, but rather the beginning of a longer process of questioning to get to the bottom of things. But for now the detectives were left wondering, did she know more than she was letting on? Or was she truly innocent, caught up in a tragedy that she couldn't have prevented? Only time would tell.

ooooo

As that Sunday evening crept on, Diane sat out on the balcony. She had an unexplained feeling of nervousness and tried to calm herself with the view of the forested ravine below. Suddenly, the phone rang. Dave answered it. "It's Choices," he called out to her.

"Choices? What?" Diane asked, taking the receiver from him.

A voice on the other end told her there had been an accident. "An accident? A car accident? What are you talking about?" Diane's voice quivered.

"No, Diane. Guy fell in a well. He's at the hospital," the voice explained.

Diane's head spun. "What? What are you talking about? What's happening?" she shouted. For a moment, the world around her vanished, and time seemed to stop. Then, with a rush of adrenaline, she sprang into action. They had to get to the hospital quickly. Dave's eyesight prevented him from driving at night, so Diane took the wheel. The thirty-minute drive felt like an eternity as Diane's mind raced with worry. When they finally arrived at what they thought was the hospital, they realized they were in the wrong place. In a panic, Diane drove to a nearby police station, but no one was at the front desk. She drove onto a main street and suddenly recognized the hospice where Karen had died the previous year.

Diane pleaded with the staff at the hospice. "Can you tell me where the hospital is? My son's been hurt. I have to get to him, and I don't know how to get there!" After getting directions, she raced off to the hospital again.

When they finally arrived, Diane rushed up to the triage nurse. "My son Guy Mitchell is here, and he's been hurt," she told the nurse frantically. The nurse looked down at her computer screen and her eyes widened.

Two women from Choices were waiting for Diane in a small room. "Is Guy all right?" Diane asked, desperate for answers. They had none to give.

A few moments later, a doctor entered the room. "We did everything we could, but he's gone," he announced bluntly before turning to leave. Diane stood up and drew in a long breath, the breaking of her heart nearly audible. "I want to see him," she cried out, grabbing at the doctor's arm.

"That won't be possible because the coroner is coming," the doctor replied coldly. "It'll be several hours, so you might as well go home. He'll be going back to Hamilton tomorrow for an autopsy, so you can see him there."

"Well, I'm not leaving," Diane retorted. This was her son they were talking about, flesh of her flesh, not some stranger on the street. She wouldn't be put out by some doctor she'd never met, not before she had a chance to say goodbye to Guy and kiss his cheek one last time. But it was not to be. There were well-established procedures to follow, and no one would make an exception for Diane, the terrible irony being that she was brought to this moment by a horrendous string of exceptions. Against her wishes and everything within her, Diane was convinced to leave without seeing her son. Her grief already stifled, Diane was turned away, forced to make the drive back home in the dark.

When they finally arrived back at their apartment, Diane went to the kitchen sink and began washing dishes, her mind in a daze. After a few moments, she turned to Dave. "I always worried what was going to happen when I was gone," she whispered, her face ashen. "How could this have happened?"

Diane stayed up all night waiting for police to call, but no one ever did. She sat alone in her living room, still reeling from the news of Guy's death. She couldn't bring herself to sleep, so she dug out some old photo albums and started flipping through them, trying to distract herself from the overwhelming sense of shock and disbelief. As the sky outside began to lighten, she flicked on the television and was jolted by the sight of a news report from the Santor farm. "Hamilton police are investigating the sudden death of a thirty-eight-year-old man who fell into a well last night," the reporter announced. "An autopsy is being done Monday, and his name has not been released . . . Police don't know how long the man had been in the well."

Diane's anger surged. It was an uncommon feeling for the normally calm and reserved woman. She snatched up the phone and called Choices, demanding answers. "Nobody's talking to me, and I've got to know what happened!" she shouted down the line. But all they could tell her was to call the police.

Later that morning, two detectives arrived at her door to interview her. They told her about the deplorable condition of the Santor house, and Diane's shock turned to disbelief. "Well, I was just dumbfounded," she recalled afterwards.

That afternoon, the phone rang. It was Keri. "The police told me that I wasn't supposed to talk to you, but I just had to," she sobbed. "I'm so sorry."

Diane was taken aback by the call. "Well, Keri, I think that you need to do what the police said," she replied hesitantly.

"I want to come and give you all my money," Keri pleaded. "I'll sell the house, and you can have my share. You can beat me up if you want to," she raved to the sixty-seven-year-old church-going woman.

Diane was bewildered by the offer. "Keri, if you give me all your money, is that going to bring Guy back? You need to do what the police say, and we'll go from there."

As the sun rose the next day, a swarm of reporters descended upon Choices' head office. Cameras flashed as journalists eagerly awaited any updates on the investigation. Diane's phone rang, and she answered it, expecting more bad news. It was one of the managers from Choices, informing her that they would be making a statement to the press shortly. But before they did, they wanted to inform Diane directly. Shortly after, in a sombre tone, the interim executive director addressed the gathered reporters: "We send our deepest sympathy and condolences to his family at this sad time. Choices is reviewing its third-party home-provider contracts to ensure that it is discharging its obligations as required. We are offering our full cooperation to the authorities in trying to piece together what happened."

Diane may have been getting condolences, but she certainly wasn't getting any more information. She imagined her son in the brutalist minimalism of hospital morgues where there is nothing to absorb the soundtrack of institutional life, heavy steel doors crashing shut, their latches clicking into place with spine-tingling precision. If it had been a few decades earlier, Diane might have visited Guy in a place like this, sheltered from one world while subjected to another.

When Diane finally did see her son, one can only imagine the physical and emotional anguish she must have experienced in those moments. She was still numb and would continue to be for months, her mind relocated outside her body to protect her from the full weight of the shock. Once the coroner performed an autopsy, Guy's body was cleaned up and sent to a funeral home for a private viewing before cremation took place. Diane didn't have far to travel from her apartment building to the chapel in Ancaster. Ornamented with the colours of spring, the village's normally bustling streets were reduced to background noise as Diane focused all her energy on containing her grief enough to get through this day. Impatient motorists queued at the Tim Hortons coffee shop next door, the idling vehicles an unwelcome reminder of the activity of life as she prepared to encounter death. Walking arm-in-arm with Dave into the chapel, they were met with a sea of beige, the preferred palette of such places meant to induce a sense of calm. Diane stepped lightly towards the casket, her heart sinking further with each step. Her beautiful, unique boy reduced to a biohazard enveloped by the sickly smell of chemicals and powerful disinfectant. She longed to comfort her child once more and offer reassurances that everything was going to be okay. Caressing his skin, pale and drained of most blood, she realized what lay before her now was a lifeless reminder of the animated extrovert she knew and loved more than anything else. Diane whispered her love into Guy's ear as tears streamed down her cheeks, and with one final kiss, she turned and left to begin her healing process.

As the week went on, Diane felt as though she were living in a haze. The funeral was scheduled for that Saturday. Diane was overwhelmed by the outpouring of support from the community. Guy's father, Jim, had passed away in 2004, so Diane used the funds left for Guy by his great-aunt and -uncle to cover the expenses of his funeral. These were funds that Guy could have used for his future, but that chapter had ended. Despite everything she had been through, Diane remained tearless, still caught in a stunned state of shock. The world had come crashing down on her the day she received the news of Guy's passing. The shock and disbelief that had overwhelmed her slowly gave way to an all-consuming pain, leaving her numb and hollow.

The days leading up to the funeral were a blur of activity. Diane spent countless hours gathering photos and memories of Guy to display at the service, hoping they would bring a smile to the faces of those who loved him. In a rare moment of solitude, Diane sat alone in her church, gazing at the altar. She was planning her son's funeral, a task that seemed both surreal and unbearable. Guy had been an integral part of the church community, and Diane wanted to honour his contribution and innocence. She carefully selected his favourite hymns, making sure they were the right choice to bring comfort to herself and others. During the funeral, the church was filled with mourners who had come to pay their last respects to a young man whose life had been cut short. Some funerals are treated like a celebration of life, but the tone that day was tense and mournful; stifled weeping and creaking wooden pews filled the silence between the interludes of organ music and scripture.

Those who eulogized him spoke of Guy's kindness, his compassion, and the joy he brought to the lives of those around him. Guy's stepfather, Dave, commented on the unexpectedly large turnout. "Seeing the number of people here today I know that Guy has touched many hearts in many ways." Christina, the support worker at Guy's day program, shared her insights about his humanity and the valuable life lessons he imparted to her, including the ability to find beauty in everyday, ordinary moments. "To me, you were more than just another service recipient," she began. "You taught me that you can literally seat dance to any song in the Westfield [day-program] van, and in your words, 'We always have a good time when we go out, Christina!' You taught me that basketball at the YMCA on Tuesdays and swimming on Mondays and Wednesdays never gets old. You taught me that walks at Pier 4 and feeding ducks and geese is great no matter how often you go, and kite flying is *not* for nerds."

To her credit, Keri showed up to the funeral. She sat alone amid a sea of mourners, her gaze fixed on the floor. Her heart must have felt heavy with a mixture of grief and guilt, as she silently struggled with the knowledge of her role in the tragedy that had brought them all together that day. Many in attendance knew of her involvement, but most believed it to be an unfortunate and entirely unpreventable freak accident. Despite the sympathy and condolences offered to her by the other mourners, the weight of the rumours and judgment from those around her must have been unbearable. Jennifer, the Choices support worker, approached her with a soft word of comfort, hoping to ease Keri's pain. "It's not your fault," she said, placing a gentle hand on Keri's shoulder. But Keri was not in the mood for platitudes or empty reassurances. "Just throw me down a well," she replied bitterly, before finally rising from her seat and disappearing from the church. For most, it would be the last time they ever saw her.

ooooo

As mourners gathered to peacefully memorialize Guy's life, the stark contrast to the gruesome manner of his death was impossible to ignore.

Not long ago, Guy's body lay on a cold steel table in an examination room at the hospital. His eyes were closed as if resting peacefully, but his body bore the trauma of his final moments. His bruised, jaundiced skin was drained of life, an endotracheal tube partly masking his face and a web of disconnected wires, tubes, bags, and defibrillation pads criss-crossing his blood-spattered torso as if his moment of release only just passed. It wasn't supposed to end like this. Not at age thirty-eight. Not confused and alone thrashing around in a dark underground tank of freezing water.

The forensic pathologist who performed Guy's autopsy suctioned approximately four cups of watery blood from his lungs. He had broken ribs and various abrasions, likely from trying to escape the cistern and resuscitative efforts by paramedics and doctors. Given Guy's history of what appeared to be petit mal seizures following his concussion injury in 2003 after he fell down some stairs, the pathologist did not rule out the possibility that Guy might have experienced a seizure while trapped in the cistern and therefore would have been unable to pull himself out to safety. It's unknown whether he was wearing his glasses when he went into the cistern, and if his poor vision may have played a contributing role in what happened. The pathologist indicated that there had been an injury to his neck with a force exceeding that of a punch. The bruising indicated it occurred approximately within the twelve hours prior to death. The injury would have caused pain, dizziness, raspy breathing, or coughing.

A different pathologist at the inquest agreed with most of this assessment but took a different view of the fractured cartilage on Guy's neck, arguing that it was possibly caused by resuscitative efforts to insert a catheter. He explained how forensic medical examinations cannot necessarily arrive at firm conclusions with the exactitude many would like and that it is often a process of elimination. Hypothermia will typically set in faster for someone with low BMI (body mass index) like Guy, he explained, adding that stomach contents are another unreliable indicator of how long it has been since someone ate since they could have vomited before death.

The pathologists examining Guy's body may have had different approaches, but they ultimately reached the same conclusion: his death was a result of drowning, with secondary causes of hypothermia and a fractured thyroid cartilage on the right side of his neck. It was classified as an accident, but the term seemed inadequate given the magnitude of the tragedy. An accident can be defined as an unfortunate event resulting especially from carelessness or ignorance, but whose carelessness or ignorance led to Guy's untimely death? Only a deeper dive into the investigation could sift truth from story and uncover the reality of what happened to him, beginning with the shocking details of the place he called home, a place few would consider fit for human habitation.

13.

ONE OF THE WORST

"It was absolutely disgusting," the acting sergeant testified about entering the Santor home. "It's probably one of the worst homes in my thirty plus years as a police officer." A few hours after Guy was pulled from the cistern, police led the interim executive director of Choices through the squalid house. It was the night before the last day of her contract, those hectic months filled with other pressing matters that demanded her attention. "It was a very quiet tour," the officer testified. "I think it was an eye-opener for them." Police treated the incident as a crime scene, cordoning off the property and sending in a forensic investigation team to take pictures. High-definition photographs were taken of nearly every square inch of the property and house, including highly detailed spherical panoramic shots of the grounds. Together, a viewer could literally tour through the house and property as it appeared that dark and shadowy night.

From the road, the Santor property looked like a vacant and unkempt parcel of land, the distant house walled off by mature trees that separated it from the grassy area that was dotted with wiry bushes and willows. The old cistern was located approximately two hundred feet from the road and several feet off the side of the driveway, a barely visible square black hole surrounded by clumps of grass and weeds. A tangled web of hoses and wires and two plywood covers were strewn on the ground next to the two-by-two-foot opening. Floating inside the pitch-black water of the cistern next to a blue bucket were Guy's black-and-white sneakers with

red laces and his jacket, turned inside out. Another red bucket floated next to some debris, with another few buckets sunken at the bottom. The top of the cistern to the waterline measured just over three feet with another four feet three inches of water in the approximately twelve-by-five-foot tank. The depth of the water meant Guy could have stood up, but he didn't. Maybe he was too weak from being sick all day or too disoriented and scared to realize what was happening before it was too late.

Keri said Guy left the house to retrieve the flyers from the end of the driveway, but detectives discovered the mailbox across the road was full of flyers from the previous three weeks. It was later determined by police that the flyers delivered to the mailbox were different from the flyers that were dropped off at the end of the driveway in a plastic bag. These flyers were delivered on Thursdays with the local newspaper and were normally picked up that evening or the next morning. No other flyers were found at the scene, and Stephen, one of the people who helped at the Santor home for years, testified that flyers were always picked up on Friday mornings, not Sunday evenings, and that Guy would never go alone to get them. Soaring pine, willow, and maple trees flanked the gravel driveway, and moving up the lane meant passing by the old barn, now empty and quiet, a rusted utility shed, and the seemingly abandoned camper trailer.

Shielded by the trees, approximately six hundred feet from the road, sat the Santor house, surrounded by an overgrown perennial garden, long shaggy grass, and a large fenced-in playground area off to the right. It was a uniquely shaped large building with a tan stucco and brick exterior and a roofline made up of cedar shake shingles. A massive, reclaimed-brick fireplace, rising two-and-a-half storeys above the driveway, stood tall like a central spire that anchored the rest of the house. A heavily rusted early model black Pontiac minivan languished in front of the house, packed to the roof with junk, its broken signal lights and flat tires indicating it had not moved in some time. Circling the house to the backyard area meant pushing through the outstretched branches and gangly bushes of what may have once been a well-tended garden. Untrimmed grass lapped at the windows, a broken-down trampoline a reminder of better days. Mounds of dog feces were sprinkled about the entire area like landmines.

But these exterior signs of neglect would do nothing to prepare investigators for the horrors that awaited beyond the front door. The forensic detective who snapped many of the photos also concluded the Santor home stood out in his long police career. "I found it to be one of the worst I've seen as far as feces, urine, and odour," he later testified. Stepping inside the tiled entrance, the hallway was moderately cluttered with discarded pizza boxes, bankers boxes, and a full case of beer with a few empty bottles on top. To the left was the living room. Dusty, unvacuumed, and somewhat cluttered, its carpeted floors, upholstered chairs, sofas, and coffee table still made it one of the most presentable rooms in the house. Beyond the living room was what appeared to be a music room, with a drum kit, piano, stereo, and scores of records stacked against one wall. Against another wall stood an empty terrarium and an aquarium crusted with algae and dead fish. There were two more rooms off the music room, one empty, the other with a single bed covered in balled up urine-soaked sheets and a few drops of feces on the floor. The next door was a bathroom with an accessible bath chair, the tub filled with stagnant dirty water, leaves and filth floating on the surface and a thick layer of sediment at the bottom. The unflushed toilet was filled with urine.

Doubling back to the front entrance, to the right was a large room filled with clutter, piled high with papers, binders, bottles, cardboard, plastic bags, toys, books, baskets, a hand vacuum, an old printer, an empty Budweiser beer bottle, and a shelving unit groaning under the weight of it all. More cases of beer sat against the wall. Down the hallway from the front entrance was the dining room. Like the living room, it appeared to be one of the more presentable rooms in the house, a dining set complete with buffet and hutch, and decorative pictures on the walls. The kitchen counters were cluttered with remnants of pizza boxes, take-out containers, water bottles, and beer bottles. A plate of uneaten pizza and an empty Tim Hortons soup container sat on the counter. The protective cover of the oven door was ripped off with a large towel hanging in front to shield from the heat.

The bottom part of the refrigerator was also ripped off, but it was the contents within that proved truly disturbing. Open cans of half-eaten tuna and beans, a few jars of pickles, a smoothie, an open carton of milk, a wilted head of iceberg lettuce, and various kinds of barbecue sauce, mustard, a rancid tub of coleslaw, and tomatoes. There was an open plastic tub of blue liquid and various other unknown jars, even batteries, everything caked or smeared with remnants of various red and orange condiments. The freezer was no better, containing a few containers of Chinese food, and empty boxes of Chapman's ice cream and blueberry toaster waffles. This was not a fridge that properly fed at least three adults and a young girl.

Beyond the kitchen was the mud room, a narrow hallway with built-in storage racks and cubbies stuffed full of coats, bags, boots, and shoes. Next to the mudroom was another bathroom that had dirty clothes on the floor and a toilet full of feces and urine. The laundry room held enormous piles of dirty laundry that nearly blocked access to the space with a pile of vomit- and feces-stained bedding atop other clothing around three feet high. The garage housed the oil tank, a lawn mower, a deep freezer, and more piles of clutter. The temperature inside the house was cold, and the thermostat would not activate the furnace, indicating either the gauge was broken, or the oil tank was empty.

The basement looked more like what one might find in a typical house, despite the odd clump of feces. Beyond an overturned canoe, old bricks, stacks of storage boxes, and adult diapers, there were more empty cases of Moosehead and Bohemian beer. Keri said there was running water, but that it would take a few minutes to fill a single bottle of water. Detectives found the faucets ran dry, and none of the toilets flushed. But there was likely nothing wrong with the water pump. The motor was still running, and the gauge read "zero psi" because the tank was virtually dry, intermittently sucking the final inch or two of remaining water. The lack of running water in the house left one final water source on the property: the old cistern, until recently used only for putting out bonfires and watering a strawberry garden.

After ascending the narrow staircase to the second storey, the awful state of the place also reached another level. Pockmarked pink drywall was a moonscape of unsuccessfully repainted damage, a jumble of hieroglyphics documenting the story of the home's decline. Each step higher crept towards ever stronger magnitudes of stench, a putrid bouquet of feces, urine, and vomit that hung thickly in the stale air. At the top of the landing, a pungent eye-watering and stomach-churning assault was launched on the senses. A heap of urine- and diarrhea-soaked bedding greeted them next to an overturned box of toys, a drawer ripped from its dresser, a steel bowl, and other clutter. The once light cream-colour carpeting was stained dark grey and brown with a trail of feces and dirt leading to a bedroom on the left later identified as Jennifer's bedroom. This room had hardwood flooring, but it too was caked with feces ground deep into the crevices. Toys, clothes, and bedding lay scattered on the floor and piled on the bed amid the dirt and debris with smears of feces everywhere. The bed was covered in diarrhea stains and deposits of feces lay nestled next to plush toys — teddy bears, piglets, and baby seals. Pictures of baby giraffes hung above feces stains on the walls.

The room next to Jennifer's contained a playpen, a partially dismantled crib, a desk, and a dresser. The centre of the room featured two large loose stool stains surrounded by a starscape of smaller stains sprinkled across the carpet. A few pillows lay on the floor covered in vomit and the stripped mattress was also covered in vomit and feces. A bathroom was next, featuring another pile of feces and urine-stained clothing piled around the toilet and feces smeared all over the lid and filling the bowl. The bathtub was filled with brown water, a small plastic tub and loofah resting idly in the stinking fluid. Like all the other bathtubs, the plug was still engaged, suggesting the water was preserved after each bath for multiple uses. The tiled walls of the bathtub were covered in flecks and smears of brown stains that dripped down from where they hit the wall. Next to the bathroom was a sparsely furnished recreation room, a small television and VCR with a VHS tape of *Aladdin* waiting to be replayed. Though cluttered, the room seemed miraculously spared from the worst of it all.

Across the landing was Keri's room. A steam cleaner stood near the door ironically surrounded by filth and garbage, a pathway of stains leading into the room. Clutter was strewn across the grey carpet, clothes, takeout pamphlets, plush toys, VHS tapes, and plastic bags. The corner closet was bursting at the seams with massive heaps of clothing piled at least five feet high, its door forced halfway open and stopped by a dresser littered with clutter. The ensuite bathroom was similarly cluttered, its toilet full of feces, a smashed lightbulb and shards of glass scattered around the foot of the bowl. The mattress was stripped bare, its stained pink bed skirt pulled halfway off. Atop the headboard were several bottles of Moosehead beer, a jug of water, and various books.

Ascending the final flight of stairs to the third-floor loft, they entered the domain of David and Guy. With blue walls and a vaulted ceiling punctuated by a skylight, the room was cluttered with remote control trucks, model vintage cars, collections of Hot Wheels, VHS tapes,

DVDs, and CDs. The open space had the feel of a young boy's playroom. Next to David's bed, fabric hanger cubbies acted as a makeshift dresser, and a couple boards stacked atop bricks held various knickknacks, toys, and a music collection. In a lonely corner farthest from the stairs stood Guy's bed and dresser, lovingly selected by his mother. The sense of nostalgia and longing for the innocence of childhood the space exuded contrasted sharply with the sight of Guy's bed, stripped bare and soiled with vomit.

In a house as filthy as this with no running water to even attempt to clean up or flush waste in the toilets, the old cistern — the only remaining reliable source of water on the property — must have been like a lifeline. Maybe Guy offered to fetch water to make amends. Or maybe it was his punishment for making a mess. Karen reported Guy being punished for such actions in the past, and Diane had caught Keri screaming at Guy for soiling himself before. Keri had a notoriously short fuse, and it's not hard to imagine how the situation would have upset her. The cleanup after his bout of diarrhea and vomiting would have consumed much of the limited remaining water resources and must have placed a strain on all the residents there. Maybe it was as Keri said, and Guy spontaneously decided to grab a bucket and enter the forbidden grassy area surrounding the cistern. Or maybe it wasn't his first time there by himself. Maybe he had been drawing water there for weeks or months as the residents grappled with the lack of running water in the house. Maybe it was an accident after all, but the circumstances that drew Guy to the cistern that night remained in question, and there were multiple red flags pointing in a single direction regarding Guy's death. Despite numerous potential scenarios for how he ended up in the cistern, one question persisted: Where was Keri Santor and why had she refused to undergo further questioning after Guy's death? Finding an answer to this question would be crucial to unravelling the mystery behind the fatal incident that claimed Guy's life.

14.

NO COMMENT

"Detective Tselepakis, when we broke for lunch, we had gone through the video [of the Santor premises], and you've indicated throughout the video that Keri Santor had provided you information in relation to which room belonged to which person," began Crown Attorney Shea. "You had also interviewed Keri Santor shortly after the death of Guy Mitchell?"

"I did, it was that evening," the detective answered.

"It's also my understanding that you made attempts to secure Keri Santor's attendance at this inquest?"

"Yes."

"When is the last time that you were able to contact Keri Santor?"

"It was back in August 2014, just last year, when she was reinterviewed."

"Notwithstanding the fact that you were able to contact her in August of 2014, can you just explain why it is we have not been able to secure her attendance at this inquest?"

"There were outstanding warrants for various other offences, and she would not attend anywhere," Tselepakis sighed. "I would say she was avoiding any type of police interaction. She'd been up north in different locations, so finding her was extremely difficult. That's how all our attempts turned out. And then she was gone."

"Any contact with counsel, or other avenues to find her?"

"There was a lawyer for the estate, and they tried with them. But there were so many appointments where she didn't show up and she would cancel. So, every time we had information [about her possible whereabouts] we would target our investigation towards there, but she would cancel or not show up. So, we would have to regroup and try different things. That's just not with us, it was also with her own family as well."

ooooo

A year and a half into the investigation, police still did not have the full picture about how and why Guy ended up in the cistern that night and who was ultimately responsible for the tragic outcome. There were too many loose ends and nothing to tie them all up. For instance, Guy was always losing or breaking his glasses, and everyone knew he needed them to reliably navigate the world around him. No one thought to ask whether Guy was wearing his glasses when he went into the cistern until a year and a half after his death, when a new detective was assigned to the case. Detective Pacey conducted a new round of interviews to help fill in some of the blanks.

"So Guy wore glasses," Pacey asked Christina, one of Guy's support workers at the day program. "How was his vision without his glasses?"

"Probably the same with his glasses. Most of the time they were covered in feces. Most of the time they were broken. I don't even think they were the right prescription, to be honest with you," she replied, her exasperation and disillusionment clearly audible. There was probably a time when discovering feces on Guy's glasses would have been a shocking and serious discovery, but the toxic work culture at Choices and poor communication with Keri made it routine for front-line staff to simply record the observation for supervisors, clean Guy up, and move on with the day.

"Then were there days where he would come to Westfield [day program] without his glasses?"

"More times than not," Christina shrugged. The detective probed further, wondering if Guy's mobility was affected by his glasses. "Not a lot of difference," Christina suggested. "His mom spent a lot of money getting them fixed, but more times than not, he didn't wear them."

Guy's eyeglasses were never recovered from the scene, and they didn't show up in his personal effects at either the hospital in Brantford where he was officially pronounced dead or the morgue in Hamilton where his autopsy was conducted. A year and a half later, the new detective drove to the Santor farm, but it had long been sold to new owners, and the cistern had been either removed or filled in, a large depression in the ground the only remaining evidence of the tragedy that unfolded that night. Remarkably, the flimsy plywood lid that played such an important role in Guy's death was still there, resting in the grass like a forgotten relic.

ooooo

To help tie up loose ends such as Guy's missing glasses, detectives decided it was critical to reinterview Keri. There were too many questions, and she appeared to be the only one who could provide answers. But Keri had no intention of returning for further questioning. Not long after Guy's funeral, she vanished, leaving Jennifer and David to find new homes, and abandoning dogs and cats that were eventually taken in by the SPCA, as well as a trashed house to be cleaned up and sold by her brother.

For several months, different police agencies worked together to locate Keri. They followed various leads that ultimately yielded no results. It seemed they were always just one step behind her. Keri likely knew police were after her. After arranging to pick up her mother's ashes, she sent a friend instead, spoiling potential surveillance and apprehension. Searches of social media profiles and cellphone GPS data led nowhere. Eventually, information led police to an address in Hamilton where Keri was reportedly staying with a possible boyfriend. When police informed him of Keri's multiple warrants, he directed them to Lime Ridge Mall, on the Hamilton mountain, where Keri was reportedly out shopping. Keri had called her boyfriend crying, so he agreed to pick her up. Police encircled the shopping centre and coordinated a takedown in the parking lot. As Keri walked toward the man's car, police emerged from their hiding spots and arrested her, ending months of work to locate her.

Keri was immediately transported to a local police station and ushered into an interview room, much like the one she had been in when Guy died. Wrapped in a white blanket, Keri refused to answer any questions posed to her.

"I gave a statement two years ago and I have nothing further to say," Keri said emotionlessly to a female detective when asked about her involvement in Guy's death.

The detective, solidly built with hair pulled back tightly in a bun military style, then asked, "Was the statement you gave the truth?"

"I was in shock at the time. I don't really recall," Keri responded.

To help her remember, the officer gave Keri a transcript of her previous recorded interview and asked, "Is this accurate? Is it close to how you remember things?"

Keri gave no response and maintained her silence. "No comment," she said.

The officer then informed Keri that there would be an inquest, and she would be subpoenaed to testify. The officer also advised Keri that new information had come forward and that the police investigation was ongoing. The officer gave Keri a chance to change her previous statement. "I'm giving you an opportunity to say if there is anything different than the version you gave two years ago. There may be an explanation. This is your opportunity to change or add something. Is there anything you'd like to add?"

"I have no statement to give at this time," Keri repeated as if reciting a line from her lawyer or perhaps honed from a wealth of experience being questioned by police.

The officer then informed Keri that her bail had been opposed, meaning she would not be released. Keri would be returned to the northern jurisdiction where she faced other charges, and she would remain in custody for some time. The officer tried one last time to get Keri to talk.

"The investigation will continue regardless of whether you choose to speak or not. All these pictures of the home where there was no running water, no heat, and no food will be shown at the inquest, and you'll have to answer for why these poor people who lived there lived in filth. You obviously weren't caring for them in a way you should have been and that will all come out in the inquest."

Keri sat unmoving and expressionless, her eyes fixed defiantly on the officer. "No comment."

ooooo

Police had been gathering evidence and slowly building a case, but it was up to the Crown attorney, the Canadian equivalent of the district attorney, to decide whether to proceed with charges. Unlike district attorneys who can become involved in investigations, Canadian prosecutors rely on police to present their best case to the Crown attorney's office. It is then up to the Crown attorney to decide if allegations meet a standard of proof beyond a reasonable doubt or on the balance of probabilities, and whether there is sufficient case law to support bringing the case before a judge or jury. In countries like Canada, where the rule of law is generally respected and police agencies are well-equipped to carry out detailed investigations, it can take a very long time to gather sufficient evidence to bring a case before the courts.

Police explored criminal charges against Keri. Did she fail to provide the necessities of life? Were her actions or inactions criminally negligent causing death? Both carried a minimum four-year term of imprisonment up to a maximum life sentence. After an exhaustive investigation with plenty of evidence of neglect, detectives brought the case to the Crown attorney's office to consider what charges might be laid. Unfortunately, proving charges of neglect can be extremely difficult because what constitutes neglect can be subjective and requires a high burden of proof. The failure to provide necessary care or attention can include a wide range of behaviours or omissions, so what might be considered neglect in one situation may not be in another. Proving neglect often requires establishing that the defendant had a duty to provide care, they failed to meet that duty, and the failure resulted in harm to the victim. If the neglect was a result of a lack of resources, rather than intentional or willful, it can be even more challenging to prove. When neglect occurs in a private setting, like a family home or a sprawling twenty-five-acre ranch in Jerseyville, it may not be immediately obvious to others, and the harm caused by neglect may be gradual, making it difficult to establish a clear cause-and-effect relationship. Investigations must look at the victim's medical history, living conditions, and the caregiver's history and behaviour. All in all, neglect cases can be difficult for law enforcement and prosecutors to fully investigate because they are so time-consuming and resource-intensive.

Prosecuting a case of negligence causing death of a developmentally disabled person carries an even higher order of challenges. It can be difficult to prove causation, gather evidence and documentation, analyze and understand complex medical issues, all while constrained by limited resources. To establish negligence causing death, it must be proven that the defendant's actions or omissions directly caused the death of the victim. In cases involving developmentally disabled individuals, it can be difficult to establish a clear link between the defendant's actions and the victim's death, particularly if the victim had pre-existing health conditions or other vulnerabilities. For example, Guy was unsteady on his feet and he could have easily tripped and fallen into the cistern. How do you prove that was not a possibility? Additionally, there may be limited documentation of the victim's care or the defendant's actions, making it harder to establish a clear picture of what happened, as was the case with the inconsistent and inaccurate notetaking by Guy's support worker.

One of the most important considerations in bringing criminal charges of neglect is whether a duty of care exists. During the inquest, jurors heard again and again that Guy's "mental age" was at the level of a five-year-old. This reductionist and infantilizing language, while perhaps well-intentioned, overlooked the fact that Guy was a man in his late thirties with a wealth of life experiences and an emotional aptitude that surpassed his apparent cognitive limitations. Despite this, many people simply saw Guy as a "big kid," but, critically, he lacked the legal protections afforded to children.

Had it been eleven-year-old Jennifer who fell in the cistern and died, there almost certainly would have been serious criminal charges of negligence causing death. A duty of care has long existed for children, with some of the first child protection laws passed in the late nineteenth century. These laws, based on the premise that young people are vulnerable to neglect and abuse, came about largely by sustained advocacy by parents, social workers, and other experts.

Adult protection laws vary from place to place, but in Ontario, Canada, where Guy lived, no duty of care existed for vulnerable adults unless they have been given a legal declaration of mental incompetence. In other jurisdictions, it may be possible to establish a duty of care and hold those responsible for any harm caused by their actions by identifying the nature of the relationship and relevant standards of care and evaluating the actions of the defendant. If the developmentally disabled person was in the care of another individual or organization, such as a caregiver or care facility, it may be possible to establish a duty of care based on the nature of that relationship. There may also be established standards of care that apply to the situation. Once the duty of care has been established, it's then incumbent on the prosecution to evaluate the actions of the defendant to prove they breached that duty.

ooooo

Eventually, a decision from the Crown attorney's office came down about whether it would be pursuing charges against Keri or Choices. The answer was no. Police and attorneys had looked at the case from every angle and still concluded that no one could be prosecuted in Guy's death because it was unlikely it could be proven that anyone was legally culpable. Consequently, no charges were ever brought against Keri or anyone else in the death of Guy Mitchell. As one detective explained to Diane, "[Guy] didn't die because the house was a mess. He died because he fell into a cistern." It was a disappointing outcome for the investigators and for Diane. "I thought that somebody should have been charged with something or one or two people should have lost their job," she later said.

Even the police were taken aback by the decision, with officers openly expressing their disappointment to Diane. Many who followed the case viewed Keri as the main person to blame for Guy's death and felt that it was the job of the police and courts to hold her and Choices responsible. But according to the law, what happened to Guy was not a crime. Legally Guy was an adult like any other, with all the rights and responsibilities that come with that status, and therefore responsible for his own actions. According to the law, Guy had no one to blame but himself for tolerating substandard living conditions and falling into the cistern to his death, likely attempting to retrieve water that was probably not safe for human consumption.

Diane could never have known how her instinct to protect her son nearly twenty years earlier would one day end up shielding Keri from criminal charges. Long ago, Diane had forged her bond with Karen Santor, defending Guy against an attempt by his biological father, Jim, to have him declared mentally incompetent over the issue of an inheritance cheque. After Jim died in 2004, Diane could have made another application to the court to have Guy declared mentally incompetent, but by then it didn't seem necessary. Diane trusted Karen, and there seemed to be no compelling reason at the time to go through the expensive court process to strip Guy of his rights so that they could obtain the declaration. Keri might have been his caregiver on many levels, tasked with looking after his needs and providing him a safe and secure home in accordance with her home-share contract with Choices, but breaking this civil contract did not mean her conduct was criminal. Legally, Keri was simply living with Guy and not responsible for his safety and security. Even if it could be proven Guy was explicitly sent to retrieve the water, Keri still would not have been held liable for his actions.

ooooo

The circumstances of Guy's death raised many questions that demanded answers. Was Keri a cunning and manipulative criminal who managed to evade justice, or did she simply take advantage of systemic gaps and inadequacies that never should have existed? Why did the agency responsible for Guy's care fail to intervene sooner? Why did the police, SPCA, and CAS not share information with Choices and the ministry to provide a more accurate picture of living conditions at the Santor property? Why did it seem like Guy's needs were always secondary to those of others? And why was it only a single concerned neighbour out of a whole community of people who raised red flags about the Santors in the months leading up to Guy's death? Perhaps the most pressing question of all was how someone can be given the responsibility to care for vulnerable adults and then escape accountability when things go horribly wrong.

When caregivers like Keri are tasked with ensuring the safety and well-being of those under their care yet bear no responsibility for their action or inaction, it is vulnerable adults who suffer the most. In Keri's case, she willingly accepted — in fact, almost campaigned for — the heavy responsibilities of picking up where her mother left off. That alone might have been enough to lay all the blame at her feet. After all, we exist in a culture that tends to compartmentalize traumatic events by assigning blame to a single wrongdoer while forgoing any introspection about whether blame might be shared with a deeply dysfunctional system and disconnected, non-inclusive society.

When a single person is to blame for an awful event, it is so much easier to move on without acknowledging our own complicity in allowing tragedy to happen. We must therefore turn our gaze upon ourselves — our institutions, our governments, our beliefs, and our societies — to discover the deeper causes of Guy's death and discern the changes we need to make to better protect others like him from the same fate.

15.

ALL THOSE EYES, YET NO ONE SAW

"We're here to understand what happened to Guy Mitchell. We're not here to lay blame, point fingers, or to make people feel uncomfortable, but it is an uncomfortable process," Dr. Stanborough remarked in the inquest to Jennifer, Guy's support worker, seated in the hot seat of the witness stand. "You've had a chance to think back over the years to reflect on what happened. I'm sure it has impacted on you fairly heavily. You also appreciate you're probably in one of the best positions to help us make recommendations for change."

"Right," Jennifer agreed quietly.

"One of the questions that has come up repeatedly throughout this inquest is: How is it possible that on [April 27, 2012] there was not an awareness of how bad the house was? Police, yourself, and others have remarked about when they went on the twenty-ninth they were quite shocked. There seems to be a disconnect, a tremendous amount of change in two days that defies logic or common sense."

"I've thought a lot about why I didn't smell it," Jennifer answered, momentum gathering in her voice as she darted from one thought to the next. "How did it get so bad in two days? Why didn't I know? Why didn't I see it? When I went there on Friday there was no smell, no nothing, no concerns to even suggest there was anything going on. Knowing what I know now, I should have checked upstairs. But it wasn't done at the time and now it is. I think about it a lot, and . . . I don't know why . . . I don't know why I didn't smell it. It smelled like it always did in there."

"Right, so I have thought about this as well," Dr. Stanborough exhaled. "When I used to do general practice, I used to see patients for years and then I would send them off to a specialist, and the specialist would pick up on things so quickly that I didn't see. I know family doctors would often say how they're in a good position to provide primary care because they see the patient all the time. I'm not so sure that's true. I'll tell ya why. Have you heard of the concept 'familiarity breeds complacency?' Does that term mean anything to you?"

"Yes," Jennifer replied.

"What does it mean?"

"If you see something all the time, you're less likely to pick up on things."

"Right. Your radar goes down. It's the 'same old, same old,'" Stanborough said. "In my analogy with medicine, I didn't see things that needed a fresh set of eyes because they came with a blank slate. I'm going to suggest to you that one of the problems with our system is that organizations like Choices really don't have a lot of people coming forward wanting to take these clients. It is challenging, and a tremendous amount of work and responsibility when you take on full-time, twenty-four-hour care for someone with complex disabilities. I'm sure you don't have people lining up to do that. Folks who are willing to do that are quite valuable to you. To take somebody out of a home is cutting off that resource, especially someone who has provided care for many years. So, what if the answer was that a fresh set of eyes came in?"

"That would be a good idea," Jennifer agreed.

"And where would that fresh set of eyes come from?"

ooooo

Where were we when Guy was still alive, and what responsibility must we all bear for what happened to him? The inquest into Guy's death brought to light a litany of failures and inadequacies within and between agencies and systems designed to support people like him. But what about the wider community? What role did we play in allowing such a tragedy to occur? Progressive democratic societies are supposed to be made of people with shared responsibilities towards one another and respect for equality, justice, the rule of law, and civil discourse. Whether a parliamentary democracy or republic, the freedoms we all cherish do not exist in a vacuum. We may not all share the same political beliefs or values, especially in our increasingly divided world, but, like an extended family, we all depend on one another and are bound by certain moral obligations to help others and work together to protect the rights and well-being of all citizens.

Despite the limitations projected upon Guy due to his "mental age of five," he emerges from his own life story as an exemplary democratic citizen. His actions unmistakably revealed an understanding of his obligations towards others, perhaps because these responsibilities are also intertwined with the essence of what it means to be a good person. Among Guy's many gifts was that everyone was equal in his eyes. No one could ever accuse him of discrimination or intolerance. Even fleeting encounters with strangers left them to comment on his gentlemanly conduct. He routinely prioritized the needs of others before his own, and it could be argued he sacrificed his life to be of service to the greater good. He respected the rules and always owned up to his mistakes. And perhaps most importantly, he was an active participant in his community. Whether it was working in the Hut to help provide essential resources to those in need or bringing a whole community of people in Honey Harbour together, Guy was keenly attuned to the circularity of active citizenship.

So, if Guy was an ideal member of society, how did we do in our reciprocal obligations to him? For generations, we have externalized these obligations to agencies that we task with safeguarding vulnerable members of society. If we were doing a good job, everyone who needs a place to live would have one. Our communities would be fully accessible and inclusive to all. Wrongdoers would be held accountable for undermining our sense of safety and security. Civil discourse would be civil and never exclude anyone because of their differences.

Of course, this is not an accurate picture of the world Guy lived in. But it could be. Before a cloud of scandal surrounded the late founder of L'Arche, an international faith-based organization of communities of people with intellectual disabilities, Jean Vanier introduced the world to a new model of inclusion and interdependence. Despite Vanier's inexcusable sexual misconduct and L'Arche's problematic religious undertones and questionable charitable status, L'Arche continues to show how the transformative power of inclusive and mutually beneficial relationships can be baked into the foundation of a community. Son of a former Canadian governor general, Vanier founded L'Arche in 1964 in Trosly-Breuil, northern France, after witnessing the profound disconnection and oppression of people living in large residential institutions.

Vanier turned the institutional model on its head by erasing a "them" and "us" paradigm. All members of L'Arche communities — regardless of ability — live, work, and play together, and are supported to take on multiple roles, including paid worker, volunteer, teacher, and friend. Instead of being insulated from the wider community, L'Arche programs are designed to foster social connection with the public through educational workshops, volunteer programs and exchanges, and commerce where members can sell artwork and other goods. L'Arche now supports more than one hundred and fifty communities internationally that some would argue serve as enduring models of a different approach from what currently exists in mainstream society.[40]

ooooo

The role of the public in Guy's death received little attention until the end of the inquest. It's not hard to see why. Forensically examining the details of Guy's case to determine how the system should have caught him *before* he fell is one thing. Rethinking how the system is structured is another. Even quasi-judicial hearings like coroner's inquests follow a rigorous process that does not necessarily allow for broad-ranging discussions about the treatment of a historically disadvantaged group. But in Guy's inquest, the nature of the tragedy practically invited a reexamination of how we support people to reach their full potential in a fractious, competitive society.

Guy had more support available to him than many do. Yet, with all those eyes, no one saw and knew enough to intervene before something terrible happened. Guy's death was shocking, but it shouldn't have been. There's no question Keri couldn't have done everything on her own, but even the idea that agencies like Choices are singularly responsible for what happens to their clients is flawed. Caring for vulnerable adults with diverse needs and challenges "takes a village" as the saying goes. Choices was an unquestionably flawed organization during the time leading up to Guy's death, but it was the community's trust in it and other agencies that allowed it to fail Guy so spectacularly. Placing our faith in cash-strapped agencies like Choices whose job it is to support vulnerable adults does not automatically give us the right to heap blame upon them and their subcontractors without looking at our own role as fellow members of society.

Just as Guy's support worker, Jennifer, became complacent with conditions at the Santor farm, we are all at risk of normalizing the lack of attention and resources paid to vulnerable adults unless we take the time to understand what role we play in the perpetuation of an oppressive system. In our information-rich society, where our attention is so often divided, we must look to those trusted few who help distill the deluge into something more digestible. For it is their words that can serve to reinforce or challenge our complacency about the treatment of people like Guy.

16.

THE REPORTER

Journalism can never be silent: that is its greatest virtue and its greatest fault. It must speak, and speak immediately, while the echoes of wonder, the claims of triumph and the signs of horror are still in the air.

— HENRY ANATOLE GRUNWALD,
former managing editor of *TIME* magazine

Everyone has a part to play in building a strong safety net, and it starts by paying attention. What helps us stay informed about significant events in our community? High-quality news and investigative reporting are a good start. Community journalism has historically played an important role in bringing to light the awful conditions many people with disabilities have been forced to endure. When journalism is properly valued and resourced, it has the potential to cut through the noise to help the public understand what is happening in the community and how it impacts them and their neighbours. It holds the power to spark investigations and motivate the public to care about an issue long enough to kickstart the complex process of social change.

This is exactly what happened in Guy's case. No one tried harder to attract eyeballs to the inquest than *Hamilton Spectator* reporter Susan Clairmont. As the inquest got underway, *The Spec*, as it is colloquially known, assigned the award-winning veteran journalist to the story. With her track record of reporting on crime and social justice issues in the community, she was used to sitting in courtrooms listening to awful details of crimes and tragic deaths. From day one, Clairmont's reporting grabbed the public's attention, no easy task in a heavily saturated news environment. "Perhaps the mother of Guy Mitchell can find some comfort knowing that when her childlike son was found dead at the bottom of a well, he inadvertently rescued two other vulnerable souls from the hell they lived in," read the opening line of her first front-page article.[41] For days, readers were subjected to a horrifying refrain with each headline more dreadful than the last. She scribbled the graphic details in her notebook as each witness took the stand, her stories read by thousands in disbelief that such a thing could happen in their own community. "There was no heat nor running water; toilets and bathtubs full of human waste; feces smeared on walls, floors, and furniture; the fridge a filthy mess containing nothing more than old condiments and half-empty Chinese takeout containers; beds stripped bare and smeared with vomit." Clairmont would add other shocking details and adjectives, but the tenor of each article was to thrust the awful, graphic reality of the house in the reader's face. Her provocative approach forced readers to wonder how such a place could even exist in the twentieth-first century, let alone someone like Guy dying the way he did right under our own noses.

Clairmont's reporting on Guy Mitchell's death had a significant impact beyond the courtroom in Hamilton where the inquest was taking place. Her stories were disseminated widely by the vertically integrated newspaper publishing industry, reaching readers across the country. The circumstances of Guy's death were deeply troubling to David Onley, the former lieutenant governor of Ontario and prominent advocate for disability rights. "The Mitchell case still turns my stomach," he later stated in private correspondence. With few other journalists reporting on the inquest, some wondered why there wasn't more coverage of such an important issue.[42] In fact, the Provincial Advocate for Children and Youth, an arms-length office that was later presented at the inquest as a potential model for providing oversight and advocacy to vulnerable adults, acknowledged that they only became aware of the inquest once it began thanks to Clairmont's reporting. They subsequently took it upon themselves to offer their participation.

Similarly, Donna Thomson, author of the book *The Four Walls of My Freedom*, which explores her journey as a mother and advocate for her son who lives with cerebral palsy, wrote on her popular blog, *The Caregivers' Living Room*, about her reaction to Clairmont's articles. "Guy Mitchell. Guy Mitchell. Guy Mitchell. I can't get that name out of my head. And when I think of Guy, I am afraid for my son, my mother, and my future self. I am afraid for everyone who is at risk of being vulnerable and 'cared for' by the state, behind closed doors."[43]

Clairmont did most of the heavy lifting in getting the word out about the Guy Mitchell inquest, but she wasn't entirely alone. *Toronto Star* columnist Richard Brennan conducted interviews with several elected officials regarding the inquest. His writing revealed that there was a unanimous consensus among politicians from all political affiliations that the failure to protect Guy was unacceptable and that the conditions in which he lived were deplorable. One of the politicians Brennan spoke with was Monique Taylor, a member of provincial parliament (MPP) from the New Democratic Party. According to Brennan's report, Taylor expressed shock and dismay at the conditions Guy was forced to live in, stating that it was impossible for the authorities to have missed the squalid conditions. She further expressed frustration with the lack of oversight and regulation that allowed for such conditions to exist in the first place. On the other end of the political spectrum, Bill Walker, the Progressive Conservative social services critic and MPP for the riding of Bruce — Grey — Owen Sound, was equally outraged by the situation. He expressed his condolences for the tragedy and questioned how the home managed to pass inspection and obtain certification. (An uninformed observation since family homes that participate in the host-family program are not certified like a group home is.) He also called for greater accountability and responsibility on the part of the Ministry of Community and Social Services to prevent such conditions from being allowed to persist. These interviews conducted by Brennan suggest that there was a shared sense of shock and outrage across the political spectrum over the failure to protect Guy and the unacceptable conditions in which he was found to be living. Of course, outrage is an emotion that runs hot and can flicker, then die out quickly when the next outrageous story emerges. Only time would tell whether all the attention could be sustained and whether interest in calling for greater oversight and accountability to protect vulnerable adults from such deplorable conditions would continue.[44]

Dr. Stanborough expressed his appreciation for Clairmont's role in raising awareness within the community about the issues that were brought to light during the inquest. "These inquests can never really have a full effect until the public knows what goes on behind these doors," he observed. "The fact that the public gets educated on a daily basis with detailed articles and the fact that the media is able to cover these inquests mean that the message gets out there. And these inquests are only effective if the message gets out there." Clairmont later hosted a well-attended public forum at the headquarters of the *Hamilton Spectator* to further build on action points from the inquest, a form of community service that truly exemplifies the symbiotic relationship between journalism and community building.

Clairmont's strategy of jolting her audience into focus resonated with the approach taken a generation earlier when the aim was to draw the public's attention to the appalling conditions in residential hospitals where many people who were like Guy spent their lives. Before he became America's favourite tabloid talk-show host during the late 1980s with his cartoonish smile and iconic handlebar moustache, Geraldo Rivera was an attorney and investigative journalist whose reporting made an enormous contribution to American disability history. In 1972, Rivera produced an exposé on the Willowbrook State School, a residential facility for people with intellectual disabilities located on Staten Island, New York. *Willowbrook: The Last Great Disgrace*, which aired on the ABC network's news program *20/20*, shocked viewers across the country with its graphic images of patients living in appalling conditions. His investigation revealed that the facility was overcrowded, understaffed, and unsanitary. Patients were often neglected and abused, and many were left to live in filth and squalor. The program showed patients lying naked and covered in their own excrement, while others were left to wander aimlessly in barren rooms.

The impact of Rivera's exposé was significant. It prompted widespread outrage and sparked a national conversation about the treatment of people with intellectual disabilities in residential hospitals and state-run "schools." The public was appalled at the conditions, and many began to question the ethics of institutionalizing people with disabilities in large, centralized facilities. The revelation of the Willowbrook scandal marked a significant turning point in American social history, raising awareness of the needs and rights of individuals with disabilities. The TV program triggered a wave of reforms aimed at improving conditions in residential hospitals and fostering a shift towards community-based care, a new approach that prioritized smaller, more personalized settings emphasizing independence and individualized support for people with disabilities.

If Clairmont and Rivera's reporting represents how quality journalism can create a positive impact, there are also cases where well-respected journalists get it wrong. Pierre Berton was a renowned Canadian intellectual and broadcaster. An expert in Canadian history and culture known for his ability to communicate complex ideas and issues to a wide audience through his writing and broadcasting, Berton's work was instrumental in shaping public opinion in Canada and beyond on a variety of topics. And he knew it. Berton had his finger on the pulse of the nation when, in December 1959, he travelled with his friend's son, Mark, to Orillia where he lived with more than 2,800 other residents at the Ontario Hospital School (originally, Orillia Asylum for Idiots; later, Huronia Regional Centre). Berton's curiosity soon turned to horror, and he wrote about what he witnessed there.

With evocative descriptions of neglected people and buildings, his column appeared in the *Toronto Star* on January 6, 1960, and was widely credited for cracking open public awareness of residential hospitals for people with disabilities in Canada. "The paint peels in great curling patches from the wooden ceilings and doors. Gaping holes in the worn plaster walls show the lath behind. The roofs leak. The floors are pitted with holes and patched with ply. The planks have spread and split, leaving gaps and crevices that cannot be filled," Berton wrote. He continued, describing the overcrowded conditions and inadequate facilities. "The stench here is appalling, even in winter. Many patients are so helpless they cannot be toilet trained. The floors are scrubbed as often as three times a day by an overworked staff but, since they are wooden and absorbent, no amount of cleansing will remove the odors of seventy years."

Berton ended his piece with an often cited and daring conclusion. "But Orillia's real problem is one of public neglect. It is easier to appropriate funds for spectacular public projects such as highways and airports than for living space for tiny tots with clouded minds [*sic*]. Do not blame the present Department of Health for Orillia's condition. Blame yourself. Remember this: After Hitler fell, and the horrors of the slave camps were exposed, many Germans excused themselves because they said they did not know what went on behind those walls; no one had told them. Well, you have been told about Orillia. It is, of course, no Belsen [Germany]. In many respects it is an up-to-date institution with a dedicated staff fighting an uphill battle against despairing conditions. But should fire break out in one of those ancient buildings and dozens of small bodies be found next morning in the ashes, do not say that you did not know what it was like behind those plaster walls, or underneath those peeling wooden ceilings."

Berton was later widely credited with helping kickstart the deinstitutionalization movement in Canada, but closer examination reveals this to be incorrect. Berton wasn't making an argument *against* such places; rather, he eloquently demonstrated why the government needed to allocate *more* money to improve institutions to keep up with the demand. In the same article, Berton argues parents were falling over one another to score a bed for their children, even enlisting the help of elected officials to jump the queue. He argued residents had "nowhere to go," a short-sighted conclusion that failed to account for at least a decade of grassroots efforts by parent groups, like those led by the Santors, which were struggling to fund and create services for people with developmental disabilities in the community. Berton failed to acknowledge any alternatives beyond the existing system, and perhaps most damning, within the next two decades following his "landmark" article, ten more residential hospitals were built in the province of Ontario alone, part of a trend seen across Canada.

In the aftermath of Berton's article, a game of political hot potato ensued with various politicians and administrators shifting blame, making commitments followed by inaction — an approach that would become a familiar refrain in the political playbook of disability rights. The glacial pace of social change and baked-in problems within disability policy meant the problem of what to do about the thousands of children and adults living in residential hospitals would not be so easily solved. Unfortunately, a lack of innovative thinking led policy-makers down the wrong path to spend millions of public dollars revitalizing a broken system.

Berton may have gotten it wrong when he sought to bolster the residential hospital system, but the power of journalism to wake up the public to important issues in their community was still borne out. The trusted broadcaster and writer shocked the public into paying attention to the multitude of problems with large residential hospitals for people with developmental disabilities, which ultimately energized the community-living movement and folks like Bill and Karen Santor to establish organizations like Choices. Years later, Clairmont's articles about Guy would similarly attempt to shock the public into wondering how such a thing could happen in their own backyard. Another gift from Berton was a simple answer for those future readers: "Blame yourself."

While there may be plenty of blame to go around, we must understand how the intervening years between Berton and Clairmont influenced the events that unfolded in Guy's case. Because, as the saying goes, "Those who do not read history are doomed to repeat it."

17.
THOSE BEFORE GUY

Change never happens at the pace we think it should.
It happens over years of people joining together, strategizing,
sharing, and pulling all the levers they possibly can. Gradually,
excruciatingly slowly, things start to happen, and then
suddenly, seemingly out of the blue, something will tip.

— JUDITH HEUMANN,
American disability rights activist

History has shown that tragedy can hasten change, compelling societies to confront otherwise neglected issues. But while revelations of deplorable conditions and tragic events might capture public attention, it's the accompanying winds that decide whether that news fades into obscurity or ignites a firestorm of social change. So, what catalysts were needed to drive genuine change for people like Guy?

A generation before Guy's time, individuals with intellectual disabilities in Ontario were forcibly consigned to residential hospitals and other institutions, enduring conditions no one would willingly choose. It took the tragic passing of Elijah Sanderson and the severe neglect experienced by Jean Martel to prompt a comprehensive investigation into the institutional system in Ontario. Both men lived in a residential hospital and were deemed "high functioning" enough to live in designated "approved homes" in the community, supervised by a rehabilitation officer from the hospital. This practice originated in 1927 when administrators suddenly realized that institutional containment wasn't suitable for some adults with developmental disabilities who could exist outside hospital settings. It was discovered that, instead, they could be put to work in nearby homes and farms. These community arrangements set up by hospital administrators were often informal and inadequately monitored, leaving questions about the true extent of residents' benefits from the change in environment and engagement with the broader community. Nevertheless, it was viewed as a win-win by administrators seeking to trim budgets and by local farm families in need of affordable labour.

But it was not a win for Elijah Sanderson, an Indigenous man from the Kapuskasing area in northern Ontario, who in 1971 tragically took his own life in the barn of his host after repeated denials of his requests to return to the hospital. It was subsequently revealed that he had been confined to a squalid basement room, treated akin to an indentured servant, and subjected to egregiously inadequate supervision. Elijah was not alone. The case of Jean Martel closely resembled what happened to Guy Mitchell. In 1967, Jean was placed on a farm near Ottawa, and, like Guy, was a friendly, helpful young man. He had a hearty appetite, known to empty fridges and kitchen cabinets when left unattended, perhaps a testament to his genuine hunger. When his host father passed away, the living conditions at the house deteriorated, prompting his return to the residential hospital. Reluctant to have Jean return home, his mother arranged for him to stay with another farm family in 1968 whose house was isolated at the end of a country road.

The parallels between Jean and Guy didn't stop there. The initial months with Jean's new host family appeared promising, but the situation quickly deteriorated. The family complained about his perceived lack of productivity, despite requiring him to work gruelling twelve- to fifteen-hour shifts. They felt the need to keep constant watch over him, even resorting to locking him out of the house when they were away. The hospital's rehabilitation officer, responsible for overseeing Jean's well-being and whose role was similar to Choices support worker Jennifer, was aware of the escalating issues but took no action. Jean's mother visited the farm and found no signs of mistreatment.

Over time, Jean's condition worsened as he began soiling himself and wandering off to neighbouring farms or into town. In February 1971, he was discovered wandering alone, dishevelled, and suffering from frostbite on his nose, ears, and fingertips. He was eventually hospitalized, where he received treatment for gangrene and was later returned to live with his mother. The police considered pressing charges against the rehabilitation officer and the host family for their neglect of Jean, including the failure to provide life's essentials. However, the criminal investigation branch of the police ultimately concluded that such charges "would not succeed as there are no grounds to support it." The hospital asserted that they had discharged Jean and contended that they were "no longer legally responsible for Jean Martel's future and could not be held criminally liable for any restrictions placed on them for aftercare."

Separated by forty years, the experiences of Jean Martel and Guy Mitchell raise questions about whether there has been genuine progress in the treatment of individuals with developmental disabilities and whether efforts to integrate them into society have been successful. In 1971, in response to the cases of Sanderson and Martel, Toronto lawyer Walter Williston spearheaded an investigation to examine necessary changes in the developmental services sector to prevent such neglect from recurring. This inquiry, known as the Williston Report, laid the foundation for the closure of numerous large residential hospitals, many of which had been established in the years following Berton's influential article. The report aimed to revolutionize the developmental services sector by deinstitutionalizing thousands of people with developmental disabilities and promoting community living.

Between the release of the Williston Report in 1971 and the closure of the last residential hospital in Ontario in 2010, the developmental services sector underwent substantial transformation. Dedicated efforts were made to support individuals with developmental disabilities within their communities, with funding directed toward the development of community-based programs and services, such as supportive housing, respite care, and day programs. New legislation was introduced to enhance the social inclusion of individuals with developmental disabilities, providing them with greater support for decision making and promoting their active participation in society.

But while the Williston Report laid the groundwork for deinstitutionalization and the promotion of community living, progress unfolded slowly and unevenly. Many individuals continued to encounter formidable obstacles attempting to access necessary supports, ranging from insufficient funding for community-based services to a dearth of specialized health-care resources. In some instances, a form of institutionalization persisted, as individuals were placed in smaller group homes and other arrangement were made that failed to create a genuinely inclusive and empowering environment.[45] In 2010, the Huronia Regional Centre was the last residential hospital in Ontario for individuals with developmental disabilities, finally closing its doors following a class-action lawsuit by survivors. While this action marked the official end of an era of institutionalization, its legacy endured, as many individuals and their families grappled with enduring challenges to secure adequate funding, services, and community support.

ooooo

Remembrance is powerful and can breed action to right a wrong. In the aftermath of the public discovery of what happened to Guy, caregiving advocate and author Donna Thomson wrote on her popular blog *The Caregivers' Living Room* about the need for broader accountability and change in a system that sees some wait decades for permanent housing and support services. "The sad case of Guy Mitchell is terrible, but it teaches us lessons about protecting our loved ones who are vulnerable." She went on, describing how shielding vulnerable individuals from the risk of being taken advantage of involves devising support frameworks that ensure our loved ones and their caretakers are monitored by compassionate and dependable individuals. "Agencies and governments will not love our loved ones and sometimes, tragically, they will not protect them. We need to look carefully at our loved ones and ask them questions. If we can't be there in person, we need to assign oversight responsibilities to others and then keep in close touch." Another advocate, Deanne Shoyer, wrote as much on her blog, commenting that the Disability Day of Mourning (March 1) is meant not only to mark the untimely deaths of people with disabilities, but also to attract attention to the need to change the way we treat vulnerable adults. Shoyer hoped the inquest into Guy's death, beyond holding individuals and systems accountable, would also raise the profile of others who continue to live in situations that expose them to abuse or neglect.

The challenges faced by individuals with developmental disabilities when it comes to independent living and housing can have long-term impacts on their quality of life. The lack of supported independent living options can also leave individuals with limited access to resources, such as transportation, health care, and social activities. This can contribute to feelings of isolation and dependence on others, which can negatively impact their mental health and well-being. Long wait-lists for affordable and accessible housing can result in individuals with developmental disabilities experiencing instability in their housing situation that can lead to disruptions in their support networks, making it more difficult to access services and build relationships in the community. In an era where there is increasing access to legalized assisted dying, some are choosing death over life on a seemingly endless wait-list.

Lives put on "permanent hold" was how one 2023 class-action lawsuit described the experience of many individuals and their families forced to wait years for a phone call informing them a bed has been found for an individual.[46] These challenges can have ripple effects throughout the life of an individual who may be forced to choose between housing and other essential expenses, limiting employment opportunities, education, and social connections, all of which are crucial for building a fulfilling life. Wait-lists for housing can also impact an individual's ability to access health care and other critical services, leading to long-term health and financial consequences not just on them, but also their families. To address these challenges, it is essential to advocate for policies and programs that increase the availability of affordable and accessible housing, and access to comprehensive support services, including transportation, health care, and community activities, that help individuals with developmental disabilities achieve greater independence and improve their overall quality of life.

Anne Pearson, a one-time support worker to Guy and founder of the Dundas Living Centre, a private day-program facility, observed many people living in group homes and other supported-housing environments struggle to connect with the community around them. She witnessed this disconnect first-hand. "There's five people in a group home that's not too far from where I live. But do you ever see those people? The answer is probably no because they are inside the home. Staff come and go. They probably can't come out because they are on a busy road." Anne believes this situation doesn't have to be the norm. "Institutions are what is created by people who run them, not necessarily the building," she observed, referencing the fact that people with developmental disabilities and their families have the power to create inclusive and supportive environments that promote community integration, but they quite often need others to have the political will to support their endeavours.

Since she began working in developmental services in the 1980s, Anne has noticed that many families are increasingly desperate to find suitable housing for their adult children, and when they do find a place, they are often reluctantly grateful, even if it's not what they had hoped for. "It's not where we want them to be, but there's nowhere else," she would frequently hear from exhausted parents. To bridge the gap between group homes and the community, there needs to be a shift in mindset and approach. Instead of just providing housing, facilities should focus on creating an environment that fosters social inclusion and community involvement. This could involve organizing events or activities that encourage interaction between residents and community members, or providing opportunities for residents to volunteer or work in the community.

Acknowledging our shared responsibility towards all vulnerable members of society and committing to integrating them into the social fabric of our communities are perhaps the most crucial aspects of achieving justice for Guy. Inclusion provides the best protection against abuse by empowering ordinary people to intervene or report any suspected abuse to the authorities, who must then be authorized, with powers similar to the CAS or SPCA, to investigate and press charges wherever necessary. At the inquest, Diane's lawyer, Alana Crugnale, suggested the need for more collaboration between agencies. "Agencies cannot function in a silo. While an agency may be mandated to only help animals or children, if they come into information regarding concerns about adults with developmental disabilities, there should be something in place to ensure they distribute that information to the relevant agency."

More than one hundred and fifty years ago, advocates recognized the need for child protection laws and authorities to intervene in cases of suspected abuse, including instances where evidence of neglect could lead to the removal of the child from their home. It was never questioned how such measures might compromise a child's right to choose to live in a dangerous or neglectful environment when it was evident that the situation was undoubtedly harmful to the child's safety. There should be no difference in how we approach vulnerable adults or seniors when it comes to protecting them from abuse or neglect. It is our responsibility to ensure that their rights are upheld and that they are safe and secure in their communities. Justice for Guy, then, requires us to commit to creating a more inclusive society that proactively protects all its members, regardless of their abilities or vulnerabilities. This means fostering a culture of awareness, responsibility, and action to ensure that no one is left behind and that everyone has equal opportunities to thrive. By doing so, we honour Guy's memory and ensure that no one else must experience the same neglect and fate that he suffered.

Historically, adult protection laws have empowered systems that have oppressed people with disabilities by overriding their rights and agency. However, as we saw in Guy's case, there is a need to protect vulnerable adults from harm, particularly those with developmental disabilities or limited capacity for informed decision making. To navigate this dilemma, it's essential to involve people with disabilities in the policy-making process. Policies should be developed from meaningful grassroots consultation with people with disabilities since their input and perspectives are more likely to reflect reality; they are the ones who would be most affected by any new laws. Consumer-led advocacy organizations, such as People First of Canada, Council of Canadians with Disabilities, American Association of People with Disabilities, or Disability Rights UK, should be given a leading voice in the policy-making process. These organizations, and others like them, should be well-resourced to guide policy-makers and educate the disability community about their right to live free from abuse or neglect. It's essential to strike a balance between protecting vulnerable adults and respecting their autonomy and agency. By involving people with disabilities in policy development and ensuring they have a seat at the table, we can create laws that strike this balance and hold agencies and caregivers accountable when they fail to protect vulnerable adults from harm.

One way to improve their protection is to establish a strong adult protective services system that would include an independent public advocacy office working in tandem with adult protective services workers. During the inquest into Guy's death, the jury heard that having a Public Advocate for Vulnerable Adults modelled after the Public Advocate for Children and Youth would be a desirable outcome. The Public Advocate for Children and Youth was responsible for ensuring that the rights of children and youth were respected by decision-makers and service providers. This was accomplished through a variety of means, including investigations, reports, individual support and advocacy, advising the government and organizations, and public education initiatives. The Public Advocate for Vulnerable Adults would have a similar mandate, but would be focused on protecting the rights of vulnerable adults, including seniors, adults with developmental disabilities, and others who may be at risk of abuse or neglect.

By having an independent officer who is responsible for ensuring that the voices of vulnerable adults are heard, and their rights are respected by decision-makers and service providers, unnecessary deaths like Guy's can be prevented. Having an adult protective services system on the ground can also add another layer of defence against the abuse and neglect of vulnerable adults. Adult protective services workers can help identify cases of abuse or neglect and provide support and intervention to prevent further harm. They can work with other service providers and the public advocate to ensure that vulnerable adults are receiving the care they need and that their rights are being respected.

At the inquest, counsel representing the Ministry of Community and Social Services acknowledged the potential value of creating an independent advocacy office for vulnerable adults, but indicated there was little appetite for a new layer of oversight such as an improved complaint process. "It is the ministry's position that there are other ways to achieve that goal." Counsel also signalled the ministry's commitment to consulting with disability advocacy organizations, such as People First of Canada, to structure and implement the inquest's recommendations. However, any ongoing consultative or decision-making role for advocacy organizations has been carefully sidestepped. As of this writing, there continues to be no independent advocacy office, and consultation with disability advocacy organizations continues in an ad hoc fashion.

In Canada, each province and territory has its own system of social services, including services for vulnerable adults. In 2015, the decision to fold the mandate of Ontario's Public Advocate for Children and Youth into the Office of the Ombudsman left a gap in the landscape of children and youth advocacy in Ontario and raised concerns about the future of child and youth rights in that province. The decision effectively scuttled the idea of a specialized advocacy office for vulnerable adults. This decision highlights the challenges in establishing a robust and effective system for protecting the rights of vulnerable adults.

While some provinces, such as Ontario and British Columbia, provide funding for advocacy services for vulnerable adults, the systems and structures for protecting the rights of vulnerable adults vary widely across the country. In Ontario, for example, the Office of the Public Guardian and Trustee is responsible for protecting the legal and financial interests of vulnerable adults who are incapable of managing their own affairs. However, this system requires a legal declaration of mental incompetence, which is not always practical or affordable for many vulnerable adults or their families. In British Columbia, by contrast, the Office of the Ombudsperson investigates complaints from vulnerable adults who have been mistreated by government agencies or officials. In Quebec, an entirely different system exists where the Commission des droits de la personne et des droits de la jeunesse (Human Rights and Youth Rights Commission) is responsible for protecting the rights of vulnerable adults, as well as children and youth. Other provinces and territories may have different structures and systems. Across Canada, there is no specialized advocacy office with a focus solely on safeguarding certain adults from abuse or neglect. This gap underscores the need for a more comprehensive and coordinated approach to protecting the rights of vulnerable adults across the country. Such an approach could include the establishment of a specialized advocacy office for vulnerable adults, as well as increased funding for advocacy services and greater collaboration among government agencies, service providers, and advocacy organizations.

The situation is somewhat different in the United States. The Administration for Community Living (ACL) is a federal agency that aims to promote and protect the rights of older adults and people with disabilities. The ACL provides funding to state and local agencies that offer a range of services and supports to vulnerable adults, including legal advocacy, protection from abuse and neglect, and assistance with accessing health care, housing, and other essential services. In addition to the ACL's efforts, many states in the United States have established their own adult protective services (APS) agencies that investigate and respond to reports of abuse, neglect, and exploitation of vulnerable adults. APS agencies work to safeguard the safety and well-being of vulnerable adults and can provide advocacy and support to help them navigate complex systems and access needed services. However, APS agencies are not without their limitations. As Guy's story highlighted, it can be difficult to balance competing interests and ensure individuals aren't unnecessarily stripped of their rights when there is a conflict between protecting a vulnerable adult from harm and respecting their autonomy and agency. Furthermore, APS agencies tend to be underfunded and understaffed, limiting their ability to adequately respond to and prevent abuse and neglect of vulnerable adults.

In recent years, some US states have taken steps to address these issues. For example, in 2018, the state of California established the Long-Term Care Ombudsman, which is responsible for advocating for the rights and safety of residents of long-term care facilities, including vulnerable adults. This office aims to provide a more independent and effective means of advocacy and support for vulnerable adults who may have limited or non-existent family support or circle of care. While the ACL and APS agencies provide important support and protection for vulnerable adults in the United States, there is still room for improvement in terms of balancing the need for protection with the need to respect individual autonomy and agency, as well as increasing funding and support for these agencies.

In the United Kingdom, the government has a range of services and supports for vulnerable adults. The Department of Health and Social Care is responsible for overseeing and implementing policies related to adult social care, including the protection of vulnerable adults. Under the Care Act (2014), local authorities are required to establish adult safeguarding boards and designate safeguarding adults' leads to ensure that vulnerable adults are protected from abuse, neglect, and exploitation. These boards and leads work with a range of agencies and organizations to develop strategies and plans to safeguard vulnerable adults. The Department of Health and Social Care provides a range of services and supports to protect the rights of vulnerable adults. However, there are also several independent advocacy organizations that work to promote and safeguard the rights of vulnerable adults. One such organization is the Advocacy Alliance, which provides independent advocacy services for adults with learning disabilities, mental health issues, and other vulnerabilities. Age UK is another advocacy organization that provides support and advice to older adults to help them maintain their dignity and independence. Other advocacy organizations, such as the British Institute of Human Rights and Disability Rights UK, focus on promoting and protecting the human rights of people with disabilities. These organizations advocate for policies and practices that uphold the rights of vulnerable adults and hold governments accountable for upholding their obligations.

ooooo

While many countries have regulations and licensing requirements in place to ensure the safety and well-being of individuals living at home, with a host family, or in other alternative-care settings, there have been many cases in which individuals with developmental disabilities have died or suffered severe neglect in the care of others. The causes of these deaths have varied, but they often involve neglect, abuse, or other forms of mistreatment. In some cases, caregivers may lack the necessary training or resources to provide adequate care for individuals with complex medical or behavioural needs. In other cases, the host or foster family may intentionally harm the individual or neglect their basic needs, leading to serious health complications or even death.

There remains a need for more action to safeguard the rights of vulnerable adults across the globe. Policy-makers need not reinvent the wheel. By listening closely to the needs and aspirations of service recipients and their families, and crafting policy from the bottom up, we may better avoid perpetuating or recreating systemic echo chambers that fall short of expectations. In the past, governments have played a more active role in supporting advocacy organizations and even creating engines of advocacy within government. Why did they do this? Typically, public pressure played a key role. But the past few decades have trended towards smaller government and a more hands-off approach to social issues, which directly impacts advocacy organizations through base-funding cuts and a reduction in essential support services for vulnerable adults. The unfortunate irony is that chronic underfunding for advocacy ultimately harms everyone when overlooked opportunities for systemic improvement result in increased costs for policy research and development, not to mention the needless erosion of public trust and accountability.

"It is often said that societies are judged on how they treat the most vulnerable of their members," wrote the Ontario Ombudsman in a 2016 report. Citing the Guy Mitchell inquest directly, the report called for a comprehensive and collaborative developmental services system that can meet the needs of individuals and families in crisis. Despite some progress made after the Mitchell inquest, the Ombudsman wrote, significant additional improvements were needed to assist those in crisis. Unfortunately, none of the sixty recommendations in the Ombudsman's report considered the potential role of a specialized advocacy office or imagined a different role responsible for promoting and upholding the rights of adults with developmental disabilities. While case managers or adult protective services workers can advocate for their clients to some extent, not everyone has access to these professionals when they need them.

When people like Guy are granted rights but denied the means to fully exercise them, everybody loses. No modern society would admit to actively creating systems that foster neglect and abuse, but the sins of omission are equally unacceptable. Governments must prioritize the creation of a responsive and effective advocacy system that ensures the safety and protection of the most vulnerable members of society. Advocacy organizations and government agencies must collaborate to identify and address gaps in the system. This includes providing better support for individuals and families in crisis, as well as implementing preventative measures to ensure that neglect and abuse do not occur in the first place.

ooooo

The death of Guy Mitchell was ruled an accident. "An unfortunate event resulting from carelessness, unawareness, ignorance, or a combination of causes," as the *Merriam-Webster* dictionary puts it. But was it really? Whose carelessness or ignorance are we talking about? "Unaware" is about the last thing anyone should have been allowed to claim as justification for what happened with such a wealth of information indicating a dangerous decline in the quality of support being provided to three vulnerable individuals. Had that information not been locked up in various echo chambers of "support" and "protection," which never fully clicked together into something more comprehensive, Guy's story could have followed a different course.

To create a society free of these sorts of "accidents," we must actively work towards building stronger connections with those who are most at risk of falling victim to our collective blind spots. This requires a proactive approach that prioritizes the needs of vulnerable individuals and ensures that their voices are heard and their rights are protected. By creating a more connected and inclusive society, we can reduce the risk of neglect and abuse, and we can create a culture of empathy and understanding by taking the time to listen to those who are marginalized or ignored to better understand their needs. Working together we can create solutions that benefit everyone.

18.

BE LIKE SUSAN

All of us, at some time or other, need help. Whether we're giving or receiving help, each one of us has something valuable to bring to this world. That's one of the things that connects us as neighbours — in our own way, each one of us is a giver and a receiver.

— FRED ROGERS,
children's television host

Of all the people to testify at the inquest, arguably the most important was the neighbour, Susan. Her struggle to intervene at the Santor farm exposed the seams of our social fabric and provided a snapshot of the disconnection of vulnerable adults from the community. A representative of the broader public, Susan did everything that might be expected of someone not personally connected to any of the arrangements at the Santor farm. She kept a watchful eye and informed the relevant agencies of what she saw and even went above and beyond by trespassing — against police and SPCA orders — when she witnessed the neglect of helpless animals and suspected the neglect of the residents. Driven by a strong sense of moral obligation, she tearfully expressed her guilt at not doing more to safeguard the welfare of Guy and the other residents.

As the only member of the public to say or do anything about the deteriorating situation, what more could be asked of Susan? She trusted the authorities were doing their job to protect the vulnerable residents from harm, and it would be unreasonable to expect someone in her position to do more. But her efforts to grapple with the system that supported Guy conveyed the powerlessness of ordinary citizens to do much beyond contacting agencies and trusting them to follow through. Sometimes she got feedback about what transpired, more often she had no idea what happened after her reaching out. Her involvement ended there, and she was forced to have faith that her concerns were being taken seriously and that the people surrounding Guy would spring into action.

People like Guy should have a reliable support system in place to empower and protect them. But what happens when this support system falters? Several factors can influence the level of support a person receives, ranging from ineffective caregivers to agencies facing crises. Sometimes, these issues converge to create a perfect storm, with the individual being supported caught in the middle. In the aftermath, Choices managers and public administrators confidently asserted what happened to Guy will never happen again. But it does happen again. And again. And again. It's probably happening right now as you read this. A few incremental changes to the way things are normally done will not fix these problems. Guy did not sacrifice his life for the sake of a few new rules; he did not die in order to become a sad case study taught at workshops. We already have far too many of those and we don't need any more.

Susan's struggle to get someone to intervene at the Santor farm speaks to the critical importance of widening our definition of support. Friendship, companionship, or casual acquaintanceship can be an antidote to abuse and neglect. Social and caregiving circles can be built not just of the people who get paid to support someone but of family, friends, neighbours, and the dozens of acquaintances who might interact with that person on a regular basis: the neighbour next door, the barista at the coffee shop, the cashier at the checkout, the teller at the bank, the lifeguard at the rec centre. It's a vision of social cohesion that can be replicated in any rural environment or large city neighbourhood so long as vulnerable people are treated as full, active participants in the community. Seeing someone regularly, on a weekly or monthly basis, doesn't necessarily mean you truly know them, but it does increase the likelihood of someone noticing changes in their appearance or habits or noting when they're not around. Truly inclusive communities genuinely pay attention when a person with a disability is missing, rather than considering their absence as a defining aspect of living with a disability.

Rural living has its own advantages and challenges for vulnerable individuals. While living in a rural area can offer a peaceful environment free from the urban hustle and bustle, it can also contribute to social isolation, which can have adverse effects on an individual's mental and emotional well-being. It can mean group-home staff or other paid caregivers are among the few people with whom an individual interacts each day. Before approving the placement of a group home or supported living unit in a rural setting, it's imperative to conduct a comprehensive evaluation. This assessment should consider the specific needs of the individuals and whether they would genuinely benefit from a rural environment, as well as any safety concerns that might arise due to the relative remoteness of the location.

Throughout Guy's story, jurors heard how appearances didn't always match up with reality. How even someone like Guy, who initially appeared to have a solid support system in place, can still experience neglect and mistreatment. Despite his mother's efforts to stay involved in his life, Diane wasn't always privy to all the information around Guy's care arrangements or the decisions made for and with him. On the surface, Guy enjoyed his job in the Hut and had a close-knit group of friends at the bowling league. He had a loving mother and pseudo-adopted family in the Santors. But it took a closer examination of his circumstances to reveal that Guy's support system wasn't exactly ideal. His job was unpaid and was arbitrarily taken away when "his turn" was over. He had limited opportunities for social interaction outside of prescheduled structured activities with planned supervision due to safety concerns. Living at the Santor farm in Jerseyville also presented challenges for Guy to fully integrate into the local community. Had the Santors made more of an effort to connect with their community, chances are there might have been more people familiar enough with Guy and the others to notice when things started to go off the rails.

One Choices manager who testified at the inquest explained that supporting someone with an intellectual disability involves helping them work towards independence in the community. Independence might be how we have allowed capitalism to organize people into economic units of production and consumption, but it doesn't provide a strong foundation for a connected society. *Inter*dependence, on the other hand, promotes cooperation, mutual support, and shared resources, which ultimately benefits everyone by fostering greater stability, economic growth, and social cohesion. For someone like Guy, it means ensuring individuals have people besides family and paid caregivers in their lives, so they can build meaningful relationships and connections with the wider community. This could mean helping them join community groups or classes, attending religious services, or regularly visiting local establishments such as coffee shops or corner stores. By supporting and empowering vulnerable individuals to build connections and relationships within their community, we can all participate in building a more inclusive society where everyone has the potential to thrive within a safe environment.

On the witness stand, Choices manager Sarah posed a rhetorical question: "How do you know if someone is safe and has a strong presence in their community? [They] can walk to the corner store or the coffee shop without needing their support worker, because the regulars there know them well from seeing them every day." Neither the ability to walk nor the absence of a support worker should be a prerequisite for supported independent living, but her point is otherwise clear. Active participation in community life, including involvement in organized activities, group memberships, event attendance, and just being a familiar face, fosters a safer environment for individuals with disabilities since a well-known presence in the community acts as an additional layer of protection and support. This underscores the significance of building connections and relationships within the community, emphasizing the pivotal role ordinary individuals can play in supporting those with developmental disabilities.

ooooo

The community living movement emerged in response to the negligent treatment of people with disabilities, with the overarching aim of offering them the opportunity to lead independent lives and realize their full potential. Prior to this movement, many individuals with developmental disabilities spent their entire lives in institutional settings, devoid of essential aspects such as privacy, independence, agency, and dignity. The promise of community living presented an escape from this predicament, facilitating integration into the broader community where active participation in society, gainful employment, and the development of relationships with individuals from diverse backgrounds became feasible.

Community living places paramount importance on full inclusion, participation, and streamlined access to resources and support services, enabling individuals to live in and enrich their communities. This approach also entails challenging stereotypes and discriminatory attitudes that frequently hinder people with disabilities from transcending societal margins. Achieving this goal necessitates continual advocacy and concerted efforts to construct a more equitable and inclusive society. But the success of this endeavour cannot be simply outsourced to service agencies and disability activists. We all share a responsibility to ensure that our communities are inclusive and equitable for everyone. To accomplish this, we must recognize the moral obligations and social contract that exists between individuals and society.

19.

JUSTICE FOR GUY

How many other Guy Mitchells are out there, lingering in unsafe or inappropriate housing arrangements because their support systems failed them? Guy's story serves as a strong warning about the potential consequences of disregarding those who require help by trusting "the system" to take full responsibility over vulnerable adults. History is already full of examples of this deferential approach, and it has never ended well.

Justice for Guy needn't be retributive when it can be restorative. The motto of the coroner, "We speak for the dead to protect the living" is a poignant reminder that tragedy can be transformed into positive change. It prompts us to reflect on the unfortunate circumstances of one person and use their experience to prevent others from suffering a similar fate. It is a call to action that urges us to learn from past tragedies, identify the gaps in our support systems, and take steps to build bridges so that we may safeguard the lives of others. Mere words of sympathy are insufficient to honour the memory of those who lost their lives; concrete steps towards change are required. We must take active measures to prevent others from suffering the same fate. We must commit ourselves to doing everything in our power to protect a human life. Ultimately, justice for Guy involves giving a voice to those who have been silenced and bolstering supports to avoid any more tragic fatalities.

The story about what happened to Guy is incomplete because it lacks at least one key perspective: his own. A man of few words, Guy still possessed the ability to communicate his thoughts and feelings. He was curious and sociable and had a remarkable memory, always eager to learn more about the world around him. Guy's habit of asking others about their plans or activities was not just small talk; it reflected his genuine concern for their well-being. He consistently demonstrated his kind-hearted nature; his warmth and excitement in forming new bonds or participating in activities that made him happy. Guy was not immune to powerful emotions. He knew the pain of sadness, loss, and depression.

So, what would Guy have said about his situation and the aftermath? He thought he was surrounded by people who cared about him and looked out for his best interests, which is why he chose to stay in a place long after he probably should have left. If there was any overriding characteristic that defined Guy's personality, it was his sense of compassion and desire to be of service to others. Perhaps he would have been gratified to know that he continued to help others long after his unfortunate death, that sweeping changes at Choices might have saved some of his peers from neglect or abuse. As someone who always tried to follow the rules, maybe he would have been disappointed no one was ever really held accountable for what happened to him. We can only imagine his reaction to the fact that several of the key recommendations from the inquest were not implemented, including the introduction of an advocacy office for vulnerable people and an enhanced role for adult protective services workers.

After Guy's death, a Facebook group called "Justice for Guy" was created, where his friends gathered virtually to share their memories and grief. A commemorative book was created in his honour by one of the Santor siblings that resembled a register book at a funeral, capturing expressions of love and gratitude of those who knew him. Guy's iconic high-fives, benevolent acts, boundless enthusiasm, humour, and infectious cheer were all memorialized in these repositories of recollections. They also served as a platform for Guy's acquaintances to share their sorrow and commemorate his existence, guaranteeing that his legacy would endure at least in the affections of those who cherished him. A few of the comments stood out as a demonstration of his impact on others.

> Guy wasn't just my best friend, he was my brother. Me and that man used to always race down the driveway when we were asked to grab the mail and paper. We used to bounce that trampoline until we couldn't bounce anymore! I remember teaching him to play cards and Pokemon on my Gameboy. He taught me how to laugh, play, and smile again like a normal kid should have. I love Guy and always will. I'm not lying when I say just posting this has me tearing up. I've lost a lot of people in my short twenty-two years, but when we lost Guy a part of me passed with him. Guy was the most amazing friend or brother anyone could ask for! I'm blessed to have shared those eight years with him. One more high-five buddy! Miss ya tons man.

> I worked with Guy for eighteen years. If you took the time to understand Guy, he needed five minutes to process what you ask, then instantly he did what you wanted . . . He knew when you're on vacation, where you were going, and with whom. He counted the days. In August, he said, "Black Friday is coming. Did you get the same hotel? Who else is going?" When all else failed, who did he call on, Ang. "Get Ang, she knows!" This is a man I treasured and respected and feel such a sadness it has consumed me. It's time I tell everyone what he meant to me.

I grew up with Guy and loved him like a brother. I moved away from home in 2000 and I remember every time I came back to visit he would come running to the door as fast as he could, greet me and give me the biggest high-five. He rocked the high-five like no other. I remember him coming to the cottage with us in the summer and loving the beach. I'll never forget the stacks of papers he always had and how hard he worked scribbling away on them. I'll always wonder what he was writing about. I will also never forget this shirt that his mother bought him for his birthday one year back in the 90s. It was this blue T-shirt with a "cool" duck driving a red convertible and written underneath it said, "What a Guy!" That one got serious groans from my parents, but he loved it. He was such a sweet soul and I miss him dearly every day.

I remember Guy as such a quiet, gentle soul who was always wanting to lend a hand — to help someone with random tasks or definitely to high-five as he walked past.

Guy taught me compassion, patience, and how to truly be present in the moment. He helped to make who I am today, and I will always be thankful.

Guy was my cousin. Sadly, he passed away only a couple of weeks after my son was born. He never did get to meet him. My husband and I chose not to find out if we were having a boy or girl at the time. We wanted a surprise. Guy was so sure we were going to have a boy though. His rationale was that because my brother and sister-in-law already had a girl, we must obviously be having a boy.

Guy was my nephew. I know how much Guy loved his paperwork, his briefcase, his pens, and all his other office material. He also could not wait to have a ride if anyone in the family had a new vehicle. He was not in the house very

> long when he would have to go back out and have another ride in the new vehicle. He just could not wait. He holds a special place in all his family's hearts.

Guy's life contained a value that could only be realized with the fullness of time, time that was stolen from him and his family. Irreplaceable years of personal growth and time spent with his loving mother and friends vanished when he disappeared into the cistern. Who knows what might have awaited him after the Santor home was sold off and he was resettled with a new host family. It could be that his best years were ahead of him, providing comfort to his mother in her old age and forging new acquaintances and friendships with people attracted to his happy-go-lucky outlook in an age of increasing uncertainty.

In a different world where policy-makers, agencies, advocates, and the public work together more closely, things might have turned out differently for Guy. Maybe his story would have had a happy ending:

Guy Mitchell had been living with the Santor family for years, but concerns have been raised about his well-being. A neighbour suspects Guy and other residents at the home are not being properly cared for. Guy is on the roster of an independent advocate who checks in with him periodically to ensure he has the support he needs to access services. They work for the advocacy office responsible for receiving and investigating complaints from community members and other agencies about potentially vulnerable individuals.

The advocate conducts an unscheduled meeting to see how Guy is doing in his natural environment on a typical day at the day program. Based on the complaint and other information gathered through a robust information sharing system, the advocate decides to make an unannounced visit to the Santor family home to assess the situation. As soon as the advocate arrives, they notice the lawn is overgrown, and the exterior of the house is in disrepair. Entering the home, they discover the interior in a squalid state. There is no heat, no running water, and the fridge is empty. The home provider, normally ready with a list of excuses and deflections, has nowhere to hide because the unscheduled visit has revealed that Guy is not adequately supported.

The advocate knows they have to act quickly to safeguard Guy. A supported decision-making agreement along with a complete and accurate report on the home and paid caregiver are drawn up, enabling the advocate to help Guy decide if he should move. Guy has been well trained in recognizing the signs of neglect and abuse, and is able to communicate his needs and wishes to the advocate with the help of another support worker present.

The advocate immediately contacts several agencies and organizations to find another home where he could be properly supported by trained and vetted home providers, which would allow him to thrive. Thankfully, the advocate is well-known in the community, and everyone knows the number for the office, which is treated the same as contacting the Children's Aid Society or Society for the Prevention of Cruelty to Animals with information of neglect or abuse. After a short search, the advocate finds a new home for him. It is warm, welcoming, and has a friendly and caring family who lives in a close-knit neighbourhood where everybody looks out for one another. Guy is ecstatic to be there, and he quickly settles into his new routine. The advocate will continue to check in on Guy, ensuring that he is happy and well-cared for.

Back at the office to type up the report, the advocate writes that the unannounced home visit had been a turning point for Guy. It led to the discovery of inappropriate living arrangements and safeguarded the lives of two other individuals who lived in the home. It resulted in the caregiver being prohibited from supporting other vulnerable individuals while she is facing charges of criminal negligence, the result of an updated Criminal Code that includes a revised definition of the duty of care.

Most importantly, the investigation has reminded Guy and his mother that they are not alone in their dealings with the service agency they rely on so much. The advocate's unwavering commitment to protecting Guy's rights and well-being has demonstrated the importance of having a trusted third party that vulnerable individuals, their families, and concerned community members can turn to for support. It also allows the cash-strapped service agency that supports Guy, with its limited but dedicated staff, to focus on core delivery of services. Tonight Guy is sleeping in a new bed with clean sheets, his safety and happiness a comfort to all those who love and look out for him.

20.

AT THE CLOSE

On the final day of the inquest, a subtle shift in weather breathed new life into the weary souls who gathered day after day at the old courthouse in their Sunday best to bear witness to the proceedings. Behind large sunglasses, Diane addressed reporters on the lawn across the street, the normally soft-spoken woman forced to raise her voice above the din of roaring buses and pedestrians making the morning commute. She expressed her hope that something good would come out of the inquest and that what happened to her son should never be allowed to happen again.

Inside, Dr. Stanborough prepared to deliver his final remarks. It had been a career-defining inquest for him. Just a few short months later, he was unceremoniously fired, some would say for his overtly critical and outspoken conduct during the Mitchell inquest and other reported allegations. "They love inquests that just go through the motions, that are totally superficial — oral flatulence," he explained to *CBC News* about his government overseers.[47] Addressing jurors for the final time, he confirmed this had not been a mere formality and expected tangible results to emerge from the inquest. "Who is Guy's voice? I would suggest to you ladies and gentlemen of the jury, that this inquest is Guy's voice, and more specifically, you are Guy's voice to the people of this province," he proclaimed. "It is my sincere hope that the Office of the Chief Coroner will never again do an inquest into a death similar to Guy Mitchell's, that this is the last time we meet and do an inquest into any death of a vulnerable adult."

Dr. Stanborough acknowledged that evidence and testimony presented at the inquest primarily pointed towards the need for establishing an advocate for vulnerable adults and an investigative agency tasked with addressing concerns and conducting comprehensive investigations. He conceded that some might hesitate to pursue these options for several reasons, including concerns of intrusive "Big Brother" surveillance and additional workload. Implementing these recommendations also entailed a commitment of resources in a system already operating at maximum capacity. But despite these valid concerns, he stressed the necessity of striking a balance to ensure access to trusted third-party protection of vulnerable individuals and thorough investigative procedures since the paramount priority should always remain the well-being and safety of vulnerable individuals.

ooooo

The courtroom was abuzz with anticipation as the coroner read out the verdict from the jury, a series of non-binding recommendations that would leave the courtroom and hopefully produce needed changes to various systems. After deliberating for five hours, the jury reached its verdict. The case involved ninety exhibits and twenty-five witnesses spread out over more than two weeks of testimony, with the jury proving to be exceptionally intelligent, asking many tough and astute questions throughout the process.

The verdict was accompanied by sixteen recommendations directed at preventing similar deaths from happening in the future. After reading out the recommendations, the coroner, a man of imposing stature, rose slowly from his seat, his eyes fixed on the audience. "Officer, would you please give the proclamation to close this inquest."

"Oyez, oyez, oyez! This inquest is closed, and the jury discharged. God save the Queen!" With those words, the courtroom erupted into a flurry of activity. Lawyers scurried to gather their belongings, spectators began filtering out of the room, and journalists scribbled frantically in their notepads.

As the courtroom began to empty, Diane remained seated, her eyes fixed ahead, lost in thought. She came here seeking justice for her son, but now that the inquest was over, she felt a sense of emptiness. She hoped the verdict would bring her some sense of closure, but instead, she felt lost, unsure of how she was supposed to process it all. She spent months, years even, preparing for this moment, poring over evidence, trying to piece together what really happened to her son that night. But now, as she sat in the near empty courtroom, she tried to resist the idea that her efforts had been in vain. The verdict left her with more questions than answers, and she couldn't shake the feeling that justice had not been served. Finally rising to her feet, she gathered her things and made her way back through the gilded hallways and out of the downtown building. Diane breathed in the fresh air and made her way to the parking lot. She thought about Guy, about all the things he would never get to experience, the things she would never get to share with him.

Diane sat in her car, her hands tightly gripping the steering wheel as she sighed, pulling out onto the busy road. It had been a difficult and emotional day, and now she needed to visit her son. As she drove towards the cemetery, Diane's mind drifted back to the day she buried her son's remains. It had been a sunny day, much like today, but the air had been heavy with grief. Now, the cemetery was peaceful as the sound of gravel crunching under her tires echoed through the quiet. Parched grass rustled underfoot as she made her way towards the granite headstone where his name was etched. As she stood in front of the grave, Diane couldn't help but feel a sense of comfort. Although her own spirit was unsettled, Diane found comfort in knowing her son was at peace. She sat down on the grass beside the headstone and began to talk to him, sharing the news of the inquest with him.

She felt hopeful about the future, that justice would finally be served and that she could find closure. The cool feeling of the granite headstone against her back was soothing, and Diane felt a sense of calm wash over her. She knew that life would never be the same without Guy, but she was determined to keep his memory alive and to honour him in everything she did. As the sun began to set, Diane reluctantly got up from the grass and made her way back to her car. She knew that she would visit her son's grave again soon, but for now, it was time to leave and begin the healing process. And so, with a heavy heart, she drove away, knowing that the memory of her son's tragic ending would always haunt her, a reminder of the injustice that had been done. Diane now realized the closure she sought might never come, but she owed it to her son to never stop trying to find justice in a world filled with so many other Guy Mitchells.

NOTES

1. "Coroner's Inquests," Government of Ontario, November 5, 2021, online.
2. Jim McGillivray, "Profile — Dr. Jack Stanborough '79: Speaking for the Dead to Protect the Living," *The Andrean* 57, no. 2 (2013): 43, online.
3. McGillivray, "Profile — Dr. Jack Stanborough '79," 43.
4. Molly Hayes, "Cistern Victim Won Medal as Special Olympian Snowshoer," *The Hamilton Spectator*, May 4, 2012.
5. Hayes, "Cistern Victim Won Medal as Special Olympian Snowshoer."
6. Susan Clairmont, "To Tell or Not to Tell," *Hamilton Spectator*, February 4, 2012, online.
7. Diane Paton, personal communication, December 21, 2021.
8. Diane Paton, December 21, 2021.
9. Ruth Colker, "Blaming Mothers: A Disability Perspective," *BUL Rev.*, 95 (2015): 1205.
10. Colker, "Blaming Mothers," 1205.
11. "Types of Hearing Tests for Babies and Children," Stanford Medicine: Children's Health, accessed November 23, 2022, online.
12. Stacey A. Bélanger and Joannie Caron, "Evaluation of the Child with Global Developmental Delay and Intellectual Disability," *Paediatrics & Child Health* 23, no. 6 (2018): 403–410.

13. M. Seltzer et al., "Adolescents and Adults with Autism: A Study of Family Caregiving," *Report #4: Recommended Resources from Families of Adolescents and Adults with an Autism Spectrum Disorder*, (2022); "The Unfortunate Reality of Divorce in Couples with a Child with Special Needs," My Child at CerebralPalsy.org, accessed November 24, 2022, online.
14. Flamborough Archives & Heritage Society, "Glenwood School — S.S. #8," Facebook, November 19, 2019, 11:30 a.m., online.
15. Diane Paton, personal communication, December 21, 2021.
16. Diane Paton, personal communication, March 26, 2022.
17. Diane Paton, March 26, 2022.
18. Alan Rayburn, *Place Names of Ontario* (University of Toronto Press, 1997).
19. Diane Paton, personal communication, January 5, 2022.
20. Diane Paton, personal communication, December 21, 2021.
21. North Wentworth Association for the Mentally Retarded, Familyhome Provider Home Study, Reference Request, Mary Almonte, May 1992.
22. North Wentworth Association for the Mentally Retarded, Familyhome Provider Home Study, Bill and Karen Santor, October 3, 1992.
23. North Wentworth Association for the Mentally Retarded, October 3, 1992.
24. North Wentworth Association for the Mentally Retarded, October 3, 1992.
25. Diane Paton, personal communication, January 5, 2022.
26. Susan Clairmont, "A Happy Soul," *Hamilton Spectator*, August 8, 2015, p. A1.
27. Anne Pearson, personal communication, January 11, 2022.
28. Anne Pearson, January 11, 2022.
29. Anne Pearson, January 11, 2022.
30. Diane Paton, personal communication, January 5, 2022.
31. Anne Pearson, personal communication, January 11, 2022.
32. Anne Pearson, January 11, 2022.
33. Krista, Smith, "Music teacher, volunteer was a 'fantastic guy,'" *Ancaster News*, April 28, 1999, p. 15.

34. "Heat Wave Blankets Ontario, Quebec," *CBC News*, July 6, 2010, online.
35. City of Hamilton, Bylaw No. 10-118 Yard Maintenance Bylaw, Item 9 Planning and Economic Development Committee, May 26, 2010.
36. Choices Familyhome Program Annual Review, Bill & Karen Santor, February 10, 1998.
37. Choices Familyhome Program Annual Review, February 10, 1998.
38. Ministry of Community and Social Services, Familyhome Guidelines, 2004, p. 4.
39. Keri Santor, interview by Hamilton Police Service, April 30, 2012.
40. Madeline Burghardt, "Brokenness / Transformation: Reflections on Academic Critiques of L'Arche," *Disability Studies Quarterly*, March 8, 2016, online.
41. Susan Clairmont, "Searching for Answers in Tragic Death at Group Home — Facility Had No Water or Heat, Feces Smeared on Walls and Floors, Proceeding Hears," *The Hamilton Spectator*, July 7, 2015, p. A1.
42. Louise Kinross, "Why Is Guy Mitchell's Death Receiving So Little Coverage? *Bloom Blog*, Holland Bloorview — Kids Rehabilitation Hospital, July 21, 2015, online.
43. Donna Thomson, "A Tragic Death, a Cautionary Tale and Lessons about Protecting Our Loved Ones." *The Caregivers' Living Room* (blog), July 24, 2015, online.
44. Richard J. Brennan, "Hamilton Police Sickened by 'Shocking' Conditions Where Developmentally Delayed Man Lived, Inquest Told, *Toronto Star*, July 14, 2015, online.
45. Megan Linton, creator, *Invisible Institutions*, podcast, episode 4, "Lifetimes in Long-Term Care," April 6, 2022, online.
46. Jessica Smith Cross, "Developmental Disabilities Lawsuit Scores a Win Over Ford Government's Negligence Shield Law," *Cambridgetoday.ca*, online.
47. Adam Carter, "Former Hamilton Coroner Slams Ministry, Says It Wants Inquests That 'Don't Rock the Boat,'" *CBC News*, September 5, 2017, online.

MANAV SAINI

Dustin Galer is an award-winning writer, biographer, and historian known for his writing on disability history and labor. He has his doctorate in history from the University of Toronto and is the author of *Beryl: The Making of a Disability Activist* and *Working Towards Equity: Disability Rights Activism and Employment in Late Twentieth-Century Canada*. He lives in Hamilton, ON.

Entertainment. Writing. Culture.

ECW is a proudly independent, Canadian-owned book publisher. We know great writing can improve people's lives, and we're passionate about sharing original, exciting, and insightful writing across genres.

Thanks for reading along!

We want our books not just to sustain our imaginations, but to help construct a healthier, more just world, and so we've become a certified B Corporation, meaning we meet a high standard of social and environmental responsibility — and we're going to keep aiming higher. We believe books can drive change, but the way we make them can too.

Being a B Corp means that the act of publishing this book should be a force for good — for the planet, for our communities, and for the people who worked to make this book. For example, everyone who worked on this book was paid at least a living wage. You can learn more at the Ontario Living Wage Network.

This book is also available as an eBOUND Digital Certification (EDC) ebook. ECW Press's ebooks are screen reader friendly and are built to meet the needs of those who are unable to read standard print due to blindness, low vision, dyslexia, or a physical disability.

This book is printed on FSC®-certified paper. It contains recycled materials, and other controlled sources, is processed chlorine free, and is manufactured using biogas energy.

ECW's office is situated on land that was the traditional territory of many nations including the Wendat, the Anishinaabeg, Haudenosaunee, Chippewa, Métis, and current treaty holders the Mississaugas of the Credit. In the 1880s, the land was developed as part of a growing community around St. Matthew's Anglican and other churches. Starting in the 1950s, our neighbourhood was transformed by immigrants fleeing the Vietnam War and Chinese Canadians dispossessed by the building of Nathan Phillips Square and the subsequent rise in real estate value in other Chinatowns. We are grateful to those who cared for the land before us and are proud to be working amidst this mix of cultures.

ecwpress.com